What readers are saying a

An incredible story of a family of eight innocent children growing up with deep suffering and tragedy but who find new life and freedom through Jesus Christ. An inspirational call to love society's castoffs.

—**John Pellowe**
CEO, Canadian Centre for Christian Charities

Judy takes you on a romp through her life, sharing poignant and humorous stories of her family's journey. At each step she reflects on the grace of God and how He was always there, no matter the challenge. The reader will be encouraged that the one thing you can always count on is that God will never leave you or forsake you.

—**Mark Hughes**
Pastor, Church of the Rock Winnipeg

By the Grace God Go We is a compelling read. Judy Richichi masterfully draws the reader into her and her siblings' true life story, which is heart-wrenching yet powerfully optimistic. Bonds of family and a grounded, centred belief in God permeate her story and make it irresistible. I could not put this book down and recommend it as a must-read for everyone.

—**Brenda Probetts**
Retired Educator, St. Ignatius School

I met the author in September 2017 when asked by a group of seven presidents of Winnipeg-based corporations to arrange a tour of Siloam Mission, to which we all were long-time donors.

The mission connected me with Judy Richichi, and after speaking with her for a half-hour I was convinced that she was "the real deal." This is the term our group of presidents uses to give a person instant credibility, authenticity, sincerity, and competence when explaining their qualifications to people we're about to meet.

The seven of us spent three hours touring Siloam Mission with Judy and then committed substantial donations to its Make Room capital campaign, which was later followed up with the largest donation the mission ever received.

Judy is indeed the real deal, and her book is a must-read to understand what it takes to be an aspirational and inspirational survivor of not only homelessness but also abject poverty, hunger, assault, humiliation, and fear.

The grace of God is omnipresent in the lives of Judy and her seven siblings. It is the essence of their survival to become successful, solid citizens, and good parents who show kindness, consideration, and assistance to those who need it most.

It is my honour and privilege to endorse this book and encourage all to read it. Its title, *By the Grace of God Go We*, demonstrates the presence of God in all our lives and inspires us to be loving, caring, empathetic, and compassionate of others. For what goes around, comes around.

—**Gary T. Steiman**
Philanthropist, FCPA ,FCA

A riveting collection of true stories of how eight children from an "ordinary" family endured poverty, abuse, bullying, a toxic marriage, divorce, and a parent with schizophrenia. It will make you laugh, cry, and feel enraged as their stories of adversity, perseverance, survival, and faith unfold.

An astonishingly honest, raw, and personal account of what life was like growing up under unimaginable circumstances and how each sibling triumphs over adversity by the grace of God and accepts Jesus Christ as their Lord and Saviour. It will enlighten you and remind you that good prevails over evil, and that the Lord is at work in the good times and the bad, never forsaking us. It will touch the heart and soul of everyone who reads it.

—**Janet Mcleod**
Principal, The Mcleod Development Group

I was in the room the very first time Judy Richichi shared the story of her embattled childhood. Several hundred conference attendees sat with their mouths half-open and expressions of mixed horror and delight. The room erupted in a long ovation for this captivating communicator. While the delegates exchanged glances that expressed the impact of what they had just heard, I was looking for Judy's husband—and he was easy to spot, for Joe glowed with pride.

Judy vividly recounts her childhood of poverty and abuse in this, her first book. Though graphic at times, she uses imagery from her siblings' accounts to open the reader's eyes to what life is like for many young people in homes affected by poverty and addiction. More importantly, she shows how God is with each of them in His grace, every step of the way, and how by His grace can redeem any situation to be used for His purposes.

—**Tim Coles**
National Director, Youth for Christ Canada

BY THE GRACE OF GOD GO WE

BY THE GRACE OF GOD GO WE

A FAMILY'S FAITH JOURNEY OUT OF POVERTY

JUDY RICHICHI

BY THE GRACE OF GOD GO WE
Copyright © 2021 by Judy Richichi

Scriptures taken from the Holy Bible, New International Version®, NIV®. Copyright © 1973, 1978, 1984, 2011 by Biblica, Inc.™ Used by permission of Zondervan. All rights reserved worldwide. www.zondervan.com The "NIV" and "New International Version" are trademarks registered in the United States Patent and Trademark Office by Biblica, Inc.™ Scripture marked KJV taken from the Holy Bible, King James Version, which is in the public domain.

Names have been changed to protect the privacy of the people involved in this story.

ISBN: 978-1-4866-2104-0
eBook ISBN: 978-1-4866-2105-7

Word Alive Press
119 De Baets Street Winnipeg, MB R2J 3R9
www.wordalivepress.ca

WORD ALIVE
—P R E S S—

Cataloguing in Publication information can be obtained from Library and Archives Canada.

HONOUR AND DEDICATION

FIRST, MY SIBLINGS AND I HOPE THIS BOOK HONOURS OUR MOTHER, ANTOINETTE (Toni) Adams. She struggled with mental health issues but did everything she could to ensure we kids succeeded in life. She spent time on the street and in and out of homeless shelters because of her mental health challenges and inability to care for herself, but her dedication to the Lord through all our hardships, and her constant prayers, inspired us all to follow Christ, which helped us to succeed. This was the best gift she could have given us and we thank her for it! Her final wish and prayer was that all of us would be saved and love the Lord. By the end of this book, you will learn that her prayer came true.

This book is also dedicated to our brother, Daniel Anthony Needham. Danny was born on October 14, 1958 and passed away April 6, 2015. He was our oldest brother, the firstborn child to Antoinette Adams and Oliver Steve Needham Jr., and he was instrumental in helping us all find the Lord.

This book is dedicated to all the people in our lives who stepped in to help us on our journey, the ones who chose to be good neighbours. Many of these folks don't even know who they are, but we do—and God does. That's all that matters.

Finally, this book is dedicated to our Lord and Saviour Jesus Christ. Without Him, we are nothing. Through Him, all things are possible. He is the super to our natural and the extra to our ordinary. Thank You, Lord, for everything. We love You.

CONTENTS

ACKNOWLEDGEMENTS

I WOULD LIKE TO ACKNOWLEDGE THE FOLLOWING PEOPLE IN HELPING ME create this book.

First and foremost, I thank all my siblings who played an instrumental role in allowing this to unfold into the book it has become. Danny, David, Connie, Cindy, Doug, and Duane, thank you for sharing your stories with me so I could capture them. Your collaboration is what makes this story relevant and interesting as we all navigate our lives and give glory to God. I pray it makes the impact we hope for.

To Brenda Probetts, who helped me edit the story in order to submit it to the publisher. It is a large manuscript and her positive encouragement and help gave me the confidence to complete this project. Editing is a lot of work and she completed it with love and ease. I also thank the publisher's editor, Evan, who helped give the book polish and clarity.

To my stepmom, Merrilee, for having the courage to bring us four younger children to Canada and give us a new life. Your influence made our house a home and gave us a chance to succeed.

To my parents-in-law Raffaele and Angelina Richichi (may they rest in peace) and Maria and Agostino Richichi for showing me and my siblings what true love and family is all about, and to the extended family for always being there to celebrate the holidays, milestones, weddings, funerals, and babies in our lives. Familia!

To my Youth for Christ family, St. Ignatius family, and Church of the Rock family for showing me true friendship and faith in mankind. Your leadership and friendship helps me to grow closer to Christ every day.

To Janet Mcleod, Floyd Perras, and the staff I had the privilege of working with at Siloam Mission, including all its philanthropic partners who support the ministry, especially Garth Manness and the Make Room capital campaign board, and Gary and Gwen Steiman and members of the World Presidents Organization, who continue to make an impact in our community and around the world. I also thank Gail Morberg and Bonnie and John Buhler who contributed to the largest gifts made to the campaign and gave the vision credibility. Together we made great change in our community, and your ongoing encouragement and support was an inspiration to me in writing this book.

To John Pellowe and Tim Coles for inspiring me to share my testimony, and for giving me the confidence to continue to share it to make an impact for the kingdom.

To the participants of Siloam Mission and Youth for Christ for reminding me of my roots every day and keeping me humble and compassionate as I continue to try and help change people's perception of the plight people experiencing poverty and homelessness endure each day. May I cry and weep daily and never think it's okay to live at risk or on the street. Your stories of change inspire me and my siblings to continue to advocate for change in our communities.

I would like to thank my children—Raffaele (Mary), David (Christa), Michael, and Angelina (Shane)—and my husband Joe of forty years, who have stood by my side through all this. I am so proud of all your achievements and all that you have become. You each continue to make an impact in all that you do and I am excited to be a part of your journey. Thank you for allowing me to share what is also a part of your story. It's not an easy story to tell, but I believe we all need to use our testimonies to make an impact in this world. When we overcome adversity, it is our duty to share our stories to help others. None of us can do it alone and as I have taught you, sharing is caring. We all need to pull together and be the change we want to see in this world. Together we are stronger. Your love for me makes me stronger every day.

Finally, I would like to thank my Lord and Saviour, Jesus Christ, from whom all good things come. I have no idea how I accomplished this, but I know You were with me every step of the way. You are my strength and my song.

INTRODUCTION

NOBODY DREAMS OF BEING HOMELESS. EVERY ONE OF US WAS BORN A CHILD, A precious baby, who depends on those around us to survive. Every one of us had dreams, desires, hopes, and wishes when growing up.

But none of us dreamt of being homeless.

Homelessness can happen to anybody. We are one job loss, one divorce, one family death, one mental health issue or addiction, or one calamity such as a fire, hurricane, or flood away from becoming homeless.

Each one of these traumatic events can have an adverse effect on our mental, physical, financial, and spiritual health. The real question is whether we have supports and coping mechanisms to deal with them.

Do you have a network of people who will surround you in your time of need? Many of us have family and friends to see us through.

But what if you have no one?

There are approximately 37.3 million people who call Canada home. According to a 2016 report on the state of homelessness in Canada, at least 235,000 Canadians experience homelessness in a given year.[1] The actual number is potentially much higher, given that many people who are unhoused live with friends or relatives and don't come into contact with emergency shelters. Data from an Ipsos Reid poll in March 2013 suggests that as many as 1.3 million Canadians have experienced homelessness or extremely insecure housing at some point during the past five years.[2]

---

[1] Stephen Gaetz, Erin Dej, Tim Richter, and Melanie Redman, *The State of Homelessness in Canada 2016* (Toronto, ON: Canadian Observatory on Homelessness Press).

[2] Tanya Gulliver-Garcia, "Ask the Hub: Which City in Canada Has the Most Homeless People Per Capita and Why?" *Homeless Hub*. January 10, 2014 (https://www.homelesshub.ca/blog/ask-hub-which-city-canada-has-most-homeless-people-capita-and-why).

Broken down, the number of Canadians who experience homelessness on any given night in Canada is estimated to be minimally 30,000 individuals,[3] although this is only a rough estimate. Nonetheless, it's the best estimate of homelessness developed in Canada to date.

Compared to what other countries are experiencing, these numbers are solvable. We *can* eliminate homelessness in our country.

There are other countries around the world with millions of people experiencing poverty and homelessness. We, as Canadians and Americans, go to these countries on mission trips to try to take care of them. It is the noble and right thing to do. But people aren't coming to Canada or the U.S. to help us solve our problems, because they think we don't have these problems.

We live in the land of the rich, and we are better off than ninety percent of the people in this world. But the reality is that we need to take care of our own country, too, because if we don't, our issues will just get larger and larger.

This doesn't mean we shouldn't help those other countries, though. We can do both, and we should, but let's remember to take care of the people in our own communities.

I believe that if we build strength around our weakest members, they will become stronger and eventually make a difference. As a country, we can eliminate poverty and homelessness once and for all, and once we do we can be a beacon of hope for people all around the world. We can then be better ambassadors to help solve homeless issues elsewhere.

But it starts with us. It starts with us being good neighbours to each other and caring for the people next door and around us, in our communities and in our neighbourhoods. The choice is ours. The solution is very simple. It's universal, and it's biblical as well.

We just need to love our neighbour.

When God looks down to earth from heaven, what do you think He sees? I can tell you what I think He sees: dark clouds of bitterness, anger, resentment, mistrust, and slander, all covered by a gigantic smog of unforgiveness.

He sees how the unforgiveness of our past historical offences prevents us from attaining our global future and all that He has planned for us.

He sees what He created as the Garden of Eden, destroyed by war zones.

He sees war and people killing each other.

He sees strife.

He sees famine.

---

[3] Ibid.

He sees people who are rich, living in mansions, next to people who are homeless, trying to survive while living on the streets or in tents, exposed to the elements.

He sees division.

He sees people living in fear next to their neighbours because they are different from them.

He sees labels put on people He never intended them to have, like LGBTQ, immigrant, homeless, mentally unstable, prostitute, African American, black, white, Italian, Jew, German, Indian, Muslim, Chinese, Japanese, South American, Asian… the list goes on. None of that truly defines who we are.

First and foremost we are *all* God's children. We are *all* precious in His sight and He wants us *all* to be with Him in heaven one day.

What defines who we are is character, what we believe in and what we are willing to do to make a difference in our world.

As we read in James 2:14–17, faith without action is dead:

What good is it, my brothers and sisters, if someone claims to have faith but has no deeds? Can such faith save them? Suppose a brother or a sister is without clothes and daily food. If one of you says to them, "Go in peace; keep warm and well fed," but does nothing about their physical needs, what good is it? In the same way, faith by itself, if it is not accompanied by action, is dead.

There really are only two commandments Jesus gave us:

Jesus replied: "'Love the Lord your God with all your heart and with all your soul and with all your mind.' This is the first and greatest commandment. And the second is like it: 'Love your neighbor as yourself.' All the Law and the Prophets hang on these two commandments." (Matthew 22:37–40)

Who is our neighbour? Absolutely everybody! It is the LGBTQ, it is the immigrant, it is the homeless, it is the mentally unstable, it is the prostitute, it is the African American, it is the black, it is the white, it is the Italian, it is the Muslim, it is the Jew, it is the German, it is the Indian, it is the Chinese, it is the Japanese, it is the South American, it is the Asian. It is all of those, and many others.

If we truly love our neighbour, we help them in their time of greatest need. We do not judge them. Judgment is up to God, not us. We are not afraid of our neighbours, and we certainly don't persecute them.

Most importantly, we forgive them. How many times, you ask?

Then Peter came to Jesus and asked, "Lord, how many times shall I forgive my brother or sister who sins against me? Up to seven times?"
   Jesus answered, "I tell you, not seven times, but seventy-seven times. (Matthew 18:21–22)

This doesn't mean we change our beliefs to be like everyone else, nor does everyone else have to choose to believe in what we believe.

The Bible tells us, *"Judge not, that ye be not judged"* (Matthew 7:1, KJV). The only person who has the right to judge is God Almighty. We are all sinners saved by His grace. We are only called to love, to serve one another, and to be His hands and feet.

It's time for all of us to stand up and be who He has called us to be. It's time for us to love our neighbour and care for the poor, the sick, the widows, the lost, and the broken. It is time for us to put our faith into action and be the hands and feet of Christ.

The only way to make our world great again is to love our neighbours and love each other as God has asked us to do: unconditionally and without judgment, to ensure that our brother and sister on either side of us is able to achieve their best. Because when we all achieve our best, we all succeed. Then we can let God do the rest.

Will you make the commitment to love your neighbour? Loving your neighbour will remove the smog of unforgiveness; dissipate the dark clouds of bitterness, anger, resentment, mistrust, and slander; release the past so we can concentrate on our future; relieve famine and strife; house and feed people experiencing poverty and homelessness; unite the nations and end war; remove the impact of fear and labels; and allow the presence and grace of God to flood the earth with His warmth so we can live in community in this beautiful place we call home.

The following story will share how my family had a good start in life but then experienced sudden trauma, the impact of which eventually led to homelessness. It was a dark period, one we never thought we would overcome, but our faith in God and His grace brought us through our strife to achieve above and beyond our expectations. Faith in God removes the mountains. Grace keeps the mountains from moving you.

But by the grace of God go we.

Through a praying mother, *we learned that we can do all things through Christ who strengthens us* (Philippians 4:13).

Eventually, each member of our family developed a love for and relationship with Jesus. When we look back and reflect on our lives, we are able to see that He was with us every step of the way, helping us through our difficulties. He did this through our neighbours and many people who made a difference in our lives. Although we may not have seen it at the time, His grace was sufficient for us.

You would not look at the Needham children today and assume we experienced homelessness and trauma. We are all successful in our communities, giving back to those in need. I share my story, and excerpts from my siblings, to break the stigma and draw attention to the hundreds of thousands of people in North America today who are suffering the same fate of poverty and homelessness.

We as individuals and as a community have a choice: to ignore poverty and homelessness and pretend it doesn't exist or to become a part of the solution and make change, make a difference, so that we can eliminate it. If we ignore it, it will only grow larger, like a cancerous tumour. If we become a part of the solution by loving our neighbour, we can find a cure and actually reverse it, even eliminate it.

I hope and pray that after reading our story you will make the commitment to love your neighbour and be a part of the solution to bring about change in our world!

BY THE GRACE OF GOD GO WE

THE STORY YOU ARE ABOUT TO READ IS FILLED WITH GRACE. IT'S THE STORY OF eight children who each experienced trauma and brokenness at young ages and yet through the grace of God survived and came through unscathed.

Grace is a gift from God that allows us to overcome extreme circumstances. Grace means being able to look back on our lives and laugh at the situations we found ourselves in because we know that the story has a happy ending.

Despite all that we went through, none of us became bitter, angry, or resentful. God's grace allowed us to forgive everything we experienced and every person who wronged us. Through God's grace, we are now blessed with the fruits of the Spirit: love, peace, joy, and happiness. We now walk in God's grace, filled with the Holy Spirit, and look to be a blessing to others by giving back in any way we can. We walk in appreciation of the many people who helped us along the way and now we look to help others in the same way. We are all happy, successful, and blessed to be a blessing.

Grace is having the ability to look back on your life and hardships and see that you were never alone, that God was with you the whole time. Grace is knowing that as you take each step, pass beyond it, and look back, you can see the loving grace of God carrying you through every situation, allowing you not only to survive but to overcome as He shapes and moulds you into the person you are to become, for Him and for His glory. You come to realize that every step has made you better equipped to manage the next challenge that comes your way, and you realize that when the next challenge comes you will be able to foresee God's grace, knowing that He is in every situation.

So you can walk into the future unafraid and empowered, knowing that He is not only going to get you through the battles that come your way but make you stronger and better because of it. With God, everything is for your good. God is going to improve and increase your situation over and over again, because that's the God we serve and the grace He provides to us.

Grace lives in every moment and every situation. We know that God is with us every step we take, for it's all about knowing that our Father in heaven loves us unconditionally and forgives us for our sins. There is nothing we can do to separate us from that love. Grace is knowing that even through hardship, we are so blessed!

Grace is knowing that after everything we went through we are still a tightknit family that loves each other. When we had the privilege of reuniting with our mother and father, we discovered with them a bond that will never be broken because of God's grace and love for us.

Grace is knowing that we are blessed to have so many children and grandchildren who will now go on as our offspring, loving and serving God and making an impact in their world for generations to come. We are so proud of them and excited for them, because they truly are our legacy.

Grace is knowing that each of us have found our purpose by loving and serving God, who gave us grace by loving us unconditionally despite our poor beginnings. Grace is about Jesus dying on the cross so our sins could be forgiven. Grace is in knowing you only have to believe in Him to receive all of this and more. What an incredible blessing!

PREFACE

MY MARRIED NAME IS JUDY RICHICHI. I HAVE BEEN WITH MY HUSBAND FOR MORE than forty years and we've been married for more than thirty-five. We have four beautiful children and my life can only be described as a Cinderella story.

I've been serving in ministry for fifteen years. I started in ministry as an accountant, moved on to become the Director of Development, then Director of Finance and Development, and finally became the Director of Major Gifts and Corporate Relations at Siloam Mission, a homeless shelter in the city of Winnipeg.

In a word, I claimed my title to be Dr. WIT (Whatever It Takes) to help ministry succeed. At Siloam Mission we helped people experiencing homelessness, struggling with addictions, and suffering mental health issues—the lost, the broken, and those who needed hope, love, and community. We provided our services with dignity, love, and respect, remembering that each and every person coming through our door was a person who needed to be valued and loved. We created a one-stop shop for people in need, providing food, clothing, shelter, and physical, spiritual, and mental healthcare to help them transition off the streets and into their own homes.

Most importantly, we offered community. This ministry helped people experiencing homelessness to understand that it can happen to anyone, and when it does people need supports to help them through it.

Currently, I am the Director of Development at Youth for Christ Winnipeg, which is one of the largest YFC chapters in Canada. We serve youth between the ages of twelve and eighteen in our community and offer programs and services free of charge to those who need it. The goal is to see the hope and potential in every youth and help them live fully in Christ. As I see it, we stop the bleed into homelessness, because if we can help youth make better choices during their most difficult years and stay on track, they'll have a good chance of succeeding. Many of our programs serve at-risk youth with the hope of preventing them from making decisions that will get them into gangs, drugs, addictions, prostitution, or homelessness.

It is an absolute privilege to be working with youth and preventing homelessness and brokenness from overcoming our young people. I love my job and am inspired and encouraged to go to work every day knowing that we as a staff and caring community truly are making a difference.

But I have to admit that this type of ministry was the last place I wanted to work. Working with people who are marginalized, broken, and in need was not what I aspired to do. I dreamt of a corner office in a skyscraper with a view of the city, basking in my success as an accomplished professional. That's what I was groomed for—not serving the poor. I wanted nothing to do with that! This sector was where you volunteered, not where you held a career.

Why did I think that, you ask? Because I was born into a family of eight children who have gone through all the issues and challenges people experiencing homelessness and at-risk youth face. And when you've been through it, the last place you want to work is back in the middle of it. No. You want to be on a fast track to success, living the dream life.

Emotionally, it is extremely difficult to go back. Internally, it makes you weep. Being a part of it brings back all the buried memories. My education had gotten me off the streets and I wanted to work as far away from it as possible.

But God had another plan… let me tell you from the beginning.

1.

IN THE BEGINNING

Grace in numbers; thank God for large families.

"DANNY, SUSIE, DAVID, CONNIE, CINDY, DOUGIE, JUDY, DUANE!" MY DAD WOULD shout at the top of his lungs from the front door of our home at 11143 Stoneham Road in Parma Heights, Cleveland, Ohio. "Time for suppperrrrr!"

My dad always bellowed and screamed. That was how he got our attention and kept it.

We were the Needhams. There were eight of us children, each born one year apart, and we were called home every night by my bellowing dad. On the weekends, our task was to get out of the house and stay out all day, until supper was ready. That allowed my mom to clean the house and catch up on the laundry. To avoid angry outbursts and potential spankings, we stayed away.

It was a bit different during the week. When Dad came home at 5:00 p.m., we'd all be lined up waiting for his imminent return from work. My mom would greet him with a martini. He would check our hands to make sure they were clean, and then we would all sit down very quietly to eat supper.

To make sure there were no dawdlers at the dinner table, the first one who finished got seconds. So as soon as we said grace, the race was on. There was never enough for all of us to have seconds, so we learned to eat as quickly as possible.[4] The big kids usually won the race, but my dad sometimes took pity on us little kids by picking out the thinnest one and letting them have seconds.

My oldest brother, Daniel Anthony, always managed to get seconds because he was the superstar athlete. He got everything he wanted whenever he wanted

---

[4] This became a detriment when we got older. When the younger four kids were teenagers, eating quickly at the table was an annoyance for my now-older father, and it would make him so angry that he would scream at us to slow down. But it was too late. We had been trained to eat that way.

and never had to do chores and that was just the way it was. He was the favoured child, the firstborn. We even created a song about him, which we sang as we did our chores: "We work all day, we don't have time to play, we do this, we do that, hurry up you little brats, except for Danny, he sits on his big fanny, na na na na nananananana…"

Danny was the only one with a bike—a brand-new bike with all the bells and whistles. He got all his clothes new whereas the rest of us had hand-me-downs. Danny was the golden child and we called him Mr. Perfect. It wasn't fair. He got to play all the organized sports: wrestling, track and field, baseball, football, and basketball. He even played in the band. The rest of us only got to watch.

Being the oldest had its privileges, but it also had its responsibilities. Danny had to do all the shopping for the family at a local grocery store called Fazio's. My dad would give him a couple hundred dollars and away he would go with his best friend, Sam, who lived down the street. Danny grabbed the groceries and tossed them to Sam, who put them in the cart. It helped them with their football game, and it was a way to have fun while dispensing with a rotten chore.

They also made a point of trying all the free samples. Sometimes it was their lunch.

The store clerk felt sorry for us, because she knew how many kids our family had, and although there was usually food on the table in those days it was never in abundance. There was just enough. Snacks and seconds weren't an option and you learned to eat everything offered.

We were very lanky kids. Hot dogs and bologna were our staples, and I understand why: one pound of hot dogs could feed us all. Danny must have been fixated on hot dogs when he was little—either that or he went to bed hungry—because, according to my aunt, he used to sneak out of his crib and go to the fridge every night looking for food. Every morning he could be found with a package of hot dogs in his hands, half of it eaten.

Danny also had to babysit when he was old enough, and we were a pretty rambunctious group. But he was the strongest, and we were afraid of him. He spanked us younger ones if we got out of line, and that was usually how the evening ended. When we got older and had Danny over for supper, we were always afraid that we wouldn't have enough food. No matter how much you cooked, it just barely seemed to be enough for him. He loved his food.

His need for food never left him. Later in life, when we had family gatherings, the amount we prepared depended on whether Danny was coming. If Danny was going to be there, you tripled everything. The infamous line became "So what's for supper? You know Danny is coming, don't ya?" He also appreciated the cooks. Every time he ate something that had been prepared for him, he proclaimed, "Man, this is good, isn't it? This is the best I've ever tasted. It's so good, I'm going for seconds." As if he didn't always go for seconds!

Later in life, he often visited us in Canada. Every time, he got stopped at the border. He had a criminal record from his younger years, but we didn't think that was the reason the border guards wanted to check him; it was the tuna fish sandwiches he carried in his luggage in case he got hungry. And it wasn't just sandwiches… it was cans of soup, ravioli, pasta. He was always afraid of going hungry, so he'd come with a suitcase full of food.

Danny also loved to play practical jokes. He was always making everyone laugh. When we were young and my parents got a babysitter, he would gather us all together and say, "Okay, when the babysitter gets here, this is what we're going to do." Then he would hatch a plan that would absolutely terrorize the sitter, and they would never come back. Most of it was in good fun, but when eight kids turn against you… well, it probably wasn't fun to be the sitter.

He would play jokes on people all the time, lighting firecrackers in the middle of conversations, shouting out animal calls while walking in the woods, anything to get a laugh. To this day, the sound of a crow—caw! caw!—always makes me think of Danny.

Next is my oldest sister, Susie, whose name has been changed and who, for the purpose of this book, prefers to remain private.

David DeWayne was child number three. David was stocky, shorter and tougher in appearance than Danny. David did everything he could to live up to his older siblings, but he never seemed to think he succeeded. He was always angry, too, probably because my dad was so rough and abusive. He kept that anger bottled up inside, but every once in a while it came out. He was also highly driven and determined.

For some reason, there was a bone of contention between David and my dad, and it was noticeable whenever they were in the same room together. My dad beat my mom and the children, and David didn't like it. It made him angry. He was the only one who would challenge my dad and threaten him during one of his bouts.

Dad's toughness caused the older boys to train their little brothers to fight. As Dave recalls:

The one thing my dad taught us was to be tough. So Dan and I would get together with our friends and their little brothers and have them fight Doug and Duane to toughen them up.

That's one of the reasons Doug grew up to be so tough. Doug was always the smaller guy. He kept getting beaten up over and over again, sometimes really bad, until finally he overcame it all and was able to beat anybody up.

There was one kid he fought all the time that he always lost to—until one day Doug was finally able to beat him up. Then the kid left Doug alone.

Connie Marie, blond-haired and blue-eyed, was the fourth child—and she was the smart one. She did well at school and could do everyone's homework if she wanted, even her older siblings'.

Although somewhat quiet, Connie did everything asked of her and was obedient. It was easier to just do what needed to be done than talk about it, delay the inevitable, and get in trouble when it didn't get done on time. So she did what needed to be done and kept the peace.

Being child number four made it easier to become invisible. You don't get in as much trouble if you stay under the radar. The only time I remember her getting into trouble was when she rode her bike on the curbs one day, being a daredevil. She crashed and cracked open a cut just above her eye and had to go to the hospital to get stitches. She was lucky she didn't lose her eye. But according to Dad, she shouldn't have been riding on the curb in the first place, so she got in trouble. Going to the hospital was expensive, and above all we were supposed to avoid having to go there.

Cindy Lou was child number five. She had short brown hair and big blue eyes, and right after she was born my mom had a nervous breakdown. As children, we didn't realize what was going on. Perhaps this is when my dad first noticed that she had mental health issues, or maybe he had always known.

For the first six months of Cindy's life, our mom was in a mental institution, and so she was influenced by my Uncle Billy. My dad, of course, had to work full-time to take care of all the children, so my uncle took care of the kids during this time. From what we remember, he was a good caregiver.

When my mom finally did come home, Cindy was six months old and didn't know her. This estrangement early in life made it difficult for Cindy and my mom to bond. Suddenly Uncle Billy was gone and this new person was in her life.

My mom, in her illness, resented Cindy and blamed her for her mental health issues. On top of that, my mom was heavily medicated and stayed on that medication for quite a while. Cindy became the scapegoat for everything and the child my mom picked on. As Cindy recalls:

Dad said I was a very good child. I always did what was asked of me. But Mom resented me. He said he used to have to follow Mom around the house because of her mental state. Being heavily medicated, she used to just drop me randomly. Dad said he was catching me all the time. She would say, "Here you go, Cindy," and then drop me in mid-air, and dad would run around her trying to catch me. He said I was lucky to be alive.

With my mom's mental health issues, she could be Dr. Jekyll or Mr. Hyde. We never knew who we were going to get, but Cindy always seemed to get Mr. Hyde. If something was wrong or didn't get done, it was always Cindy's fault. This made Cindy very quiet and introverted. She rarely talked, just stared.

She was shy and the only outlet she had was singing. Cindy would sing all day and sit in the rocking chairs, singing to herself as she rolled back and forth. I sat with her some days and we'd sing all day together. It was our one source of joy, and it allowed us to practice for the performances we were sure to be asked to perform come evening. To this day, Cindy and I love to sing together.

Douglas Edward was child number six. Doug had a buzzcut, green eyes, and a terrific belly laugh. He was Mr. Mischievous—and if there was a dare to be attempted, Doug would attempt it. He had no fear and a crazy sense of humour. He would try anything once.

Doug got into everything along with our youngest brother, Duane Patrick. They were always together. Nothing was safe from these two bandits, and the first years of their lives were spent in and out of hospitals because they drank everything they found, whether it was cleaning spray or motor oil. If it was in a bottle, they figured it must be for human consumption, and would end up needing to get their stomachs pumped. I'm sure the nurses thought we had nothing to drink but cleaners. Back in those days, I'm not sure there were any safety rules like there are today about storing dangerous products.

Doug also loved to live on the edge. Duane struggled with the "tr" sound, which always came out like an "f," and Doug took great joy in getting Duane to yell "Truck!" at the top of his lungs to see what kind of reaction he could get from the neighbours and our dad. Then he'd quickly say it wasn't his fault because Duane was the one who had said it. He was always getting the rest of us in trouble and managed to look squeaky clean in the end. We were stupid enough to follow his lead. He was the funny daredevil, the older brother we wanted to impress.

I am child number seven, Judy Lynn. I was very quiet growing up and felt somewhat overwhelmed at times by my whole family. I would watch people, or hide in the neighbours' weeping willow so no one could see me. I tried not to draw attention to myself, and nothing good ever came of it. I was also a thumb-sucker. I'm not sure why, but that was what I did when I felt afraid, unsure, or insecure. I think I even had a blanket I liked to carry around.

My most vivid childhood memory was taking swimming lessons at the local pool. My mom made all of us take them. One day when I was five years old and just a beginner swimmer, my friend went into the big pool.[5] She was much a better swimmer than I was and was showing off. Well, she challenged me to jump in, too. I knew I couldn't swim, but she told me I could do it. The water was five feet deep and I was only three feet, three inches tall.

"Look, you just jump in and grab the ledge, like this," she said. I watched as she did it with ease.

The logical side of me thought it looked pretty easy, so I decided to take the plunge. Unfortunately, I jumped too far out and wasn't able to reach back for the ledge. Instantly I went down. I touched the bottom and pushed myself up out for a moment, but after taking a quick breath I panicked. I tried to doggie-paddle, but all I did was splash around. I was losing the battle.

My friend stood outside the pool, laughing at me. "Oh, you are too funny. C'mon, Judy, reach for the ledge."

But I couldn't and I was drinking in more water than I could handle. I desperately looked to the lifeguard, who was busy doing something else. I started going under.

I'm sure I swallowed a whole ocean of water before a big hand suddenly reached out and pulled me closer to the side of the pool so I could grab the ledge. Finally, someone had seen me. It turned out to be my friend's mom, who proceeded to pump all the water out of my little lungs.

I was weak and puking up water, but it felt so good to be out of the pool.

---

[5] Everyone wanted to swim in the big pool because at the end of the season the people who took care of the park released a whole bunch of goldfish into the pool and allowed all the kids to jump in and catch them. It was a blast and everyone went home happy afterward. They put some in the little pool, too, but there were always way more in the big pool.

"Are you okay?" the woman asked.

"Yes, I'm fine."

I sat there, terrified, and really wanted my mom. When the woman asked if I needed a ride home, I bravely declined, even when she asked me a second time.

Eventually I stood up, my legs feeling like jelly. I was shaking from head to toe, but I slowly walked home. It was the longest walk of my life. I was cold, lonely, frightened, and tired—and yet I chose not tell anyone what had happened for fear that I'd get the belt for jumping into the pool in the first place. Besides, my siblings would have just made fun of me. So it was my secret.

I've been careful around water ever since, and I never did get the chance to swim in the big pool to catch those goldfish. One, I was too afraid, and two, we moved before I got the chance.

I think that was a defining moment for me. It taught me how to persevere on my own, to be brave and not let my emotions rule me. This was also the first time I experienced God's grace. He saved my life and gave me another chance. I remember thinking, *Cats have nine lives. I hope that applies to humans!*

Finally, my brother Duane Patrick is the youngest. He was so small and cute, with blond hair and blue eyes. He was the baby, and everyone adored him. He was everyone's favourite and the rest of us carried him on our hips wherever we went. I don't think he ever needed to walk on his own, having so many people offering to hold him.

Duane's only downfall was his inability to hold his urine. I think we were just so busy that he would forget to go to the bathroom. He constantly peed his pants, to the point that he soon had the nickname "Duane Patrick Pee-Pants." Whenever we called him that, he'd run to the rocking chair and bury his head and cry. I always felt sorry for him and would try to console him.

We were a large family and he was a follower, going wherever the crowd was. Because he was so young and cute, he could blend in with any of us kids or our group of friends.

Managing eight kids under the age of nine couldn't have been easy, so my parents' method of keeping us out of trouble was to keep us working. My dad was of German descent and was OCD—although we didn't know this when we were young. Everything had to be spotless all the time. If the house wasn't spotless when he came home from work at 5:00 p.m., we all got a whooping, and my mom kept lists every day of our misbehaviours.

We took turns doing the dishes after dinner, with the younger kids standing on stools to do it. Once the chore was complete, Dad would come by and inspect every detail. If he wasn't satisfied we would have to rewash them. He got so frustrated, but some of us kids were only three years old. Nothing was ever good enough for him.

Grandma once told me that we all deserved a pension by the age of five from how hard our dad worked us. If there wasn't a chore to be done, my dad would create new ones just to keep us busy, from yardwork to dusting to washing the floors on our hands and knees. We worked hard! Cooking dinner for eight was no small chore, and all the girls pitched in.

After the dishes, we would all have to perform something, kind of like the Von Trapp family from *The Sound of Music*. The girls usually sang while the boys showed off their athletic feats, like push-ups or sit-ups. The best was when they stood on their heads. We had regular contests to see who could do the most sit-ups or who could stand on their head the longest. When company came over, it was a bit of a freak show. My dad would just say, "Hey, boys, go stand on your head, or give me a hundred push-ups… " You never said no or you'd get the belt.

Doug remembers that our dad used to make the boys do push-ups for money:

I remember Dad used to make us do push-ups and sit-ups and stand on our heads. His friends would come over and he would say, "I bet you ten bucks my kid can do a hundred push-ups." And then he'd make us do them and take everyone's money. I was doing a hundred push-ups by the time I was in first grade. Duane was in Kindergarten. He would give us a couple of bucks in front of them, like he was a good dad. Then as soon as they left he would take the money from us.

Have I mentioned my dad's army background? That could explain the regime he put us through.

In the evening, there would be our just-before-bedtime treat. Out would come the lists my mom had kept all day, and the belt. We'd all line up for our daily spanking. I'm not sure what I could have done at three and four years old to deserve it, but it must have been bad because many times we went to bed with welts on our butts, or on our arms and legs if my dad missed, which he often did.

The worst time was when we decided to outfox my dad by putting on all the underwear in our drawers. It was the "big plan" and we all did it—we had to; it was all or nothing. When it was our turn for the belt, we each knew we had to scream as loud as we could and cry uncontrollably or he might notice that something was wrong.

We all got through it with little pain or welts… until it was little Duane's turn. We were listening in from our rooms, giggling, and knew that if we could just get through Duane's spanking we would have gotten away without pain for one night. As we listened, we heard the usual *bam, bam, bam, bam, bam*—he always started with five smacks—and Duane cried. But then he got up and yelled, as he was leaving the room, "Ha, ha! That didn't hurt!"

My dad got angry. "Hey, get back here."

Duane went back and he did it again, five successive smacks.

Again Duane screamed during the spanks, but then he got off our dad's lap and laughed as he headed out the door. "Ha, ha! That didn't hurt!"

Now my dad was really angry. "Get back here!" he bellowed at the top of his lungs.

When Duane went back, my dad pulled down his pants and discovered the multiple layers of underwear. One, two, three, four, five, six, seven, eight, nine, ten… every time he removed a layer, he spanked him again and again and again until he got to the bare bottom and then five more spanks.

We were all in our rooms, cringing. Poor Duane.

"All you other kids, get back in here right now!" He was pissed and there wasn't enough time for us to take off our underwear. We were caught with our pants on, and we all got spanked for every pair of underwear we wore, plus five more on the bare bottom.

After that we never got spanked over our pants again, always on the bare bottom. Lesson learned. Don't try to outfox the fox.

Needless to say, my little brother Duane got a few more spanks from all of us when he came to bed with us that night. We had been so close to getting away with it.

Doug remembers one other incident:

I remember the time in Ohio, Duane decided he was going to hide Dad's belt. He hid all of them.

So that day Dad comes home and says to us, "Okay, everyone stand up. It's time for you all to get a whipping." He says to Duane, "Duane, go upstairs and get my belt."

Duane goes upstairs and comes back and says, "Sorry Dad, there are no belts." So Dad goes up to get them and comes back empty-handed. He has like five or six belts, and he can't find any of them.

He comes down smoking a cigarette with this mean, slanted-eyed look on his face. You can see him calculating what is happening.

"You think you guys are going to pull one over on me?" he asks. He took the lamp cord, grabbed the lamp, and pulled the lamp away from the cord. The lamp went flying across the room and he whipped our butts with that lamp cord.

I remember going downstairs after. He whipped us so hard that we had these big red, black, and blue marks on our bum cheeks, but I remember also seeing blood dripping. You can't see your own butt, but we saw Dan's and Dave's, and they were just leaking blood. That was the worst he ever beat us. We never, ever hid the belts after that.

Even through the beatings, growing up in Ohio was pretty cool. We were a large family and everyone knew who we were. We always had lots of people to play games with, even if it was just our own family.

Our favourite game was Kick the Can. We played the game in the "big circle," which most people would now call a cul-de-sac. They weren't as common back then. We would play for hours, both there and at a large nearby park that we went to often.

We attended St. John Bosco Catholic School, which seemed far away from home. Catholic school was very strict and we had to wear uniforms at all times. It was run by nuns who'd never had kids but had big rulers which they'd use if you didn't listen. That was the way it was back then. The nuns would take the ruler and whack your hands if you talked out of turn or didn't pay attention.

We had a hard time keeping babysitters because we were such a large family. Can you imagine how hard it must have been to babysit eight kids? As Dave remembers:

We used to stick butter knives in the trim of the door that went downstairs, leaving part of the knife sticking into the door so you couldn't get out. We had one babysitter—I don't remember her name, we only had her one time—who went downstairs and we put butter knives in the door. So she was locked in the basement and couldn't get out. My parents came home and she was crying… and of course we got our asses kicked again. We did have our fun. There was only one babysitter who could babysit us and that was Christine. She wasn't afraid, and she did a good job.

Our parents owned a black Volkswagen Beetle. We rarely went anywhere together, but somehow we managed to get all of us kids in when we went on daytrips to special places. I remember going to Cedar Point and the zoo. When we drove, the four big kids sat on the bottom in the back and the four little kids sat on their laps. In those days, seatbelts weren't mandatory so we could get away with it. We would stop at lights and people would point at us and laugh. There were ten of us, so I guess it was funny. My parents would just look at each other and laugh back. My mom had a high-pitched melodic laugh that was so infectious. She was petite, blond, and very beautiful. When she was happy, her smile could light up a room.

The rule when going out was that each of us younger kids were paired up with an older child. So Duane would go with Dan, Doug with Dave, Connie with Cindy, and me with Susie. It's one of the reasons these particular duos stayed close over time.

When I was five, we went on our first family road trip to Florida so we could go to Disneyworld. We rented an RV, and we thought this was the coolest thing we had ever seen. It had a table and bunkbeds and a small kitchen.

The day we were leaving, Duane stepped on a piece of glass and sliced his foot. We had to rush him to the emergency room, delaying our trip by half a day. Everyone was so mad that no one played with Duane all the way to Florida. He played by himself with a ball. When we drove downhill, the ball went down the hall in the RV; when we drove uphill, the ball came back to him. But none of us would help him. He had delayed our trip, and we were mad.

We stopped at hotels along the way and half of us would stay in the RV while the other slept in the hotel. It was an awesome trip, from what I can remember, and our first plunge in the ocean was so much fun! We were supposed to just get out of the RV to look at the ocean, but it was impossible to control all eight kids under the age of fourteen. It only took one leader daring us to go into the water for the rest to follow.

The daredevils were David and Doug. They led, we followed. Talk about sand in your shoes! Now multiply that by eight, and as you can imagine we were a mess. But it was a blast! The weather was, of course, awesome and it was fun to be able to play outside all day in the middle of winter.

I think the nice weather enticed my parents to think about moving. I cannot imagine being cooped up with eight kids in the house in the middle of winter. Sure, we could go sledding and play in the snow, but can you imagine cleaning all our winter boots and clothes? Florida had all the makings of a much easier life, and my parents discussed moving there over and over.

Our family was especially popular because Danny was a great athlete. He played football really well and broke records in track and field. He was one of the fastest runners his age. He used to run around the block and have my dad time him. He would try repeatedly to beat his time and get faster and faster.

Just as my parents finally decided to move the family to Florida, Dan was offered a full scholarship to play football for Padua Franciscan High School. He was that good and his best friend, Sam, offered to let Danny stay with them while the rest of us moved away. But my parents said no; it was too far away from Florida.

It turned out that the move to Florida had nothing to do with the weather, the palm trees, or the beaches. Apparently my dad had been having an affair with his secretary and my mom had given him an ultimatum: move away or get a divorce. My dad loved the ladies and was a known womanizer.

So it was time to leave. Florida was the land of real estate and if my parents both got real estate licenses, they could work, work at their marriage, and care for us kids.

At least that was the plan.

For our last week in Ohio, the whole neighbourhood spoiled us. We were taken out for ice cream, chocolate bars, and candy. We were a large family and everyone was going to miss us. The older kids didn't want to leave because they had so many friends.

My godparents, who were Italian, lived down the street from us and were very close friends of my parents. They invited me over to give me a very special going-away gift: a wood-beaded rosary, blessed by the pope. They had just come back from a trip from the Vatican and they wanted me to have it. Perhaps they foresaw what was to come, because my dad was very physical towards us, and I think they knew about my parents' stormy relationship.

Although my parents had a passionate relationship, they argued constantly. My dad was a very difficult man to live with. He was a perfectionist and verbally abusive to the ones he loved. In those days, the man of the house got served, and I'm sure life was very difficult for my mom, especially having so many kids and no help.

My dad's anger could cause the strongest man to cringe, and many times when my parents fought in the bedroom you could hear them throwing things against the wall. I used to run to my room and cover my ears to block it out.

So I think my godparents giving me the rosary was their way of not stating the obvious. What they did say was, "You're moving two thousand miles away and we won't be there to help. So here's a rosary to pray with when you need help. God will always be there for you in your time of need. We love you. Good luck in Florida."

If they only knew how important that gift would turn out to be.

Dave recalls a final incident that happened right before we moved:

Right before we moved, the kitchen caught on fire. Our house was already sold and we were all ready to move. We had a toaster that didn't come up on its own, so the person making the toast had to do it manually.

One day, somebody put the toast down but forgot to pull it up when it was done. And of course it didn't come up. The toast caught on fire.

The toaster was underneath the cabinets, so it burnt the cabinets above it. Because the house was sold under contract, we had to get the insurance company to fix it before we left. It wasn't terrible, but it was a big deal at the time.

I can't imagine how frustrating it was as parents having that many children trying to deal with all of these kid accidents and mischievous moments. We never knew who burnt the toast.

Connie remembers the toast incident as well:

I was making toast and watching it because I knew I had to pop it up manually. Then Mom called me from a neighbour's house and told me they had some clothes that might fit me. That was a big deal because we never got new clothes and I was excited! I was the second girl and all I ever wore was my older sister's hand-me-downs, and of course my Catholic school's uniform.

So I ran out of the house, totally forgetting about the toaster.

I remember coming home and I felt so bad. Of course I didn't own up to it. The fear of punishment kept me silent. I didn't even tell any of my siblings. When we were growing up, we all stuck together and nobody narc'ed on anyone. My dad used to tell us, "You can fight like cats and dogs in this house, but when you go out there," and he pointed outside, "you stick together."

Unfortunately for him, we stuck together against him too. The problem was if he couldn't find out who did something, we would all get in trouble, which meant the belt. So when this happened, we would pressure the guilty one to confess.

We had just recently gone through this with Dave. He had carved a G in the kitchen drawer with a knife, and I remember everyone ganging up on him to tell.

So I stayed silent and unfortunately they blamed Duane. I don't remember him getting into too much trouble, because he was so young, but I always felt bad about it.

Dad had a type-A personality and never should have had kids, but he ended up having eight. He always said that Mom didn't believe in the pill, and he didn't believe in abstinence. We're all grateful she didn't believe in abortion either. But my dad had to work three jobs just to support us. The responsibility definitely wasn't easy. Most people couldn't do it today.

On our last day in Ohio, we drove around the block twice. Every neighbour stood outside their house and waved to us. Many were crying, and so were we. We knew we were going to miss this very special place where we had so many friends.

My dad honked his horn, we all waved, and before we knew it we were on our way to opportunity, never to return. Florida was the Promised Land, the land of great weather, sunshine, beaches, and palm trees… the place where my family was going to make its fortune in real estate.

Or was it?

2.

FLORIDA, THE SUNSHINE STATE

Grace comes in the form of sunshine.

I REMEMBER OUR FIRST HOUSE ON IVANHOE STREET IN PORT CHARLOTTE. I would have been seven years old and going into Grade Two. My first impression of Florida was that everyone was old. All the neighbours on our street were old and the only place we saw kids was at school.

As a family of eight, we were quite the new neighbours for these people, especially since most of them were retired. My brothers and I[6] would play around in the yard, but there really wasn't much to do. The schools were too far away and we had to take a bus to get there. There also weren't any parks close by. Every neighbour seemed to have a birdbath, so we would chase the birds while the neighbours scolded us.

Dave has a memory about what it was like when we arrived in Florida:

What I remember about Ivanhoe was that there were literally no kids. In Ohio, we were eight houses from the park. We came from a neighbourhood where we could get a baseball team together in a matter of minutes.

And then we moved to Florida. The neighbouring street to ours was about three-quarters of a mile long and you could walk down and not see anybody. There were old people and they stayed inside their houses because of the heat.

There was one kid who lived about a quarter-mile away, but he was the only one. His parents were a little older and they might have been

---

[6] I always hung out with Doug and Duane because I was right between them, age-wise. I was also a tomboy.

his grandparents. The only thing we could do was go fishing. We didn't catch a lot, but we did catch fish and frogs. And one time I caught a water moccasin. That's all I remember about that house.

One day, out of complete boredom, Doug, Duane, and I decided to use my brother's shark fishing pole to try to catch a seagull. The neighbours had a birdfeeder, and from watching the birds there we knew they liked bread. So we took the pole and cast it into the neighbour's yard with a piece of bread on the line and waited.

We waited and waited until, lo and behold, a seagull came. Seagulls can sense bread anywhere, because they're scavengers with noses like hawks; tourists always come to the beaches in Florida and think it's cool to feed the birds, whereas the natives hate to have the gulls around since there can be hundreds at a time, pooping everywhere.

Well, before we knew it my brother Doug[7] hooked a great big seagull. It took off, trying to fly away, but Doug held onto that pole like there was no tomorrow. The bird flapped its powerful wings and started pulling, and still Doug held on tight.

Now, Doug was only eight, and not overly big or strong, so you can just imagine the way this looked to a bystander: this little boy with a great big rod with a seagull hooked at the end, the gull screaming at the top of its lungs. Doug ended up flat on his bum trying to hold the bird.

The neighbour next door must have heard all the commotion because before we knew it he came running out of his house, fists pumping in the air.

"What are you doing to my precious birds?" he yelled.

I have to say that we hadn't really thought about the pain we were causing the bird, nor did we truly understand why old people liked to watch them. We were just young kids, bored and trying to find something to do.

Much to our chagrin, the neighbour came over, boxed Doug's ears, and with a pair of scissors proceeded to cut the line. We were devastated. He then scolded us about how rotten we were.

But then, seeing our remorse, he sat down and explained how precious animals were and how we shouldn't hurt them but enjoy them. He told us that gulls are God's creatures and we should respect them. By the time he was finished talking, we had a better understanding of old people and why they watch birds and have birdbaths in their yards.

---

[7] Of course it was Doug. It was always his idea to do things that ended up getting us in trouble.

We discovered that the neighbour's name was Bill. He offered us each a cookie if we'd leave the birds alone—flower-shaped shortbread cookies with lemon flavouring, coated in sugar. So good. We didn't have many treats at our house, and after seeing how much we enjoyed the cookies Bill promised if we didn't bother the birds we could come by his house for cookies anytime—and we did, for many years afterwards. We didn't take advantage of his hospitality, but it remained our secret, and our treat. We even went back years later after moving away, just to say hi and get a cookie. It was our first lesson in respect, and our first experience with seniors.

In school, we had our challenges. Fitting into the culture was the first one.

Danny, a ninth grader, and David, in seventh grade, both attended Port Charlotte Junior High. One day David was outside at recess, sitting at the base of a tree talking to a ninth grader named Paul who seemed to think he could kick Danny's butt. David assured Paul that his brother could kick the crap out of him.

David struck a nerve and Paul decided to kick David in the head with his boots.

I remember being home sick with chicken pox at the time, along with all our other siblings. David came home super upset and angry, explaining that Paul had gotten some new boots and decided to show them off by kicking him in the head a couple of times. David's head was full of lumps and he had a black eye.

My mom, having been warned by the assistant principal that David had been in a fight, decided to go to the school to settle the matter. Danny, who was just about over the chicken pox himself, asked if he could go with her under the pretence of needing to talk to the coach about some sports-related matter. My mom agreed but warned Danny to stay out of it.

Danny told her not to worry. Famous last words.

What my mom didn't know was that Danny had assured David that he knew exactly where to find Paul.

When they got to the school, while David and my mom went to the principal's office, Danny said he was going down to the gym to talk to the coach. He actually went to find Paul and teach him a lesson.

Dave and my mom hadn't been talking to the principal very long before the coach interrupted them to tell the principal there had been another fight, and this time a boy had been hurt pretty badly.

We found out the next day that Paul had gotten beaten up so bad that he almost lost his eye. The parents wanted to sue us.

Danny was very remorseful, as he'd just wanted to teach him a lesson. Everyone in the school was tired of Paul's bullying.

Since we had no money, the case never went to court and Paul never bothered David again. Eventually they became great friends, in fact.

One thing was for sure: we were all very loyal and stood up for each other. People soon discovered that you didn't mess with the Needhams. There were just too many of us. We didn't intentionally look for trouble, nor were we mean; it just seemed that with so many of us, someone was always involved in something.

When we moved to Florida, Danny got into track and field, wrestling, and football. He broke every record in Charlotte County and even a few for all of southwest Florida. He was incredible. By the time he finished Grade Ten, everyone knew who we were. We went from being the family who was picked on because we were new to the family who was to be respected because Dan Needham helped win football games. He was a running back,[8] and as he started lifting weights he became a powerhouse. He truly was unstoppable.

In our area, Friday night was high school football night. Everyone went to the games. It was *the* thing to do. The stadium was always packed! The fans even followed the team as they played up and down the coast in places like Naples, Sarasota, and Fort Myers. Football was the most popular sport in town and the Needhams were good athletes. Suddenly, we were in.

---

[8] His jersey number was 32.

3.

THIS IS NOT PUPPY LOVE

Grace is feeling loved.

GRADES TWO AND THREE WERE GOOD YEARS FOR ME, AND IT SEEMED THAT Florida was an okay place to live. My brothers were all popular, which helped the rest of us to fit in. We started making friends—usually the siblings of other players on the football team—and things were starting to look up.

Doug, Duane, and I remember that when we walked to school, we had to pass a lot of dogs to get there. As Duane explains:

> I remember we used to walk to Neil Armstrong Elementary School, and we were afraid of the big dogs we had to walk by. They used to bark a lot and scare us, but later we had compassion for them. They were on chains.
>
> We never had any pets, and we felt sorry for the dogs on the chains. We decided to try to be friends with the dogs by offering them our lunch. Coming from an abusive family, we never felt loved, so we befriended the dogs first with our lunch and then with chocolate milk powder. They would lick our palms.
>
> I just loved visiting them. We loved those dogs and they started loving us. We realized they just needed some loving.
>
> One of the first hugs I ever got was from the beige pitbull. I remember hugging the dog, and he hugged me back. I remember grabbing the dog and all of a sudden the dog started wagging its tail. He was so excited to see me. I remember thinking, *This dog is actually hugging me and actually loves me.* I was surprised he wasn't biting me. The memory is so vivid because we never got any of that kind of attention at home.

We lived on Ivanhoe Street at the time and we would walk to school down Beacon Drive along the ditch. Doug, Duane, and I used the ditch as a shortcut to school because when we walked along the street the kids from school made fun of us.

At first we thought the dogs were enemies, but they turned out to be better than the kids, and they eventually became our friends. After a while we couldn't wait to see those dogs. It was the only positive, unconditional love we knew.

We soon moved from Ivanhoe to Olean Boulevard into a house that had been custom-designed for a family of eight, as the previous owners had had a family the same size. It was super cool with built-in bunkbeds in two of the bedrooms, a wraparound counter with ten barstools in the kitchen, four built-in couches in the kitchen alcove, a water fountain that always had cold water, and a swimming pool!

The backyard on Olean sloped into a ditch that had a lot of dry grass in it since the days were so hot and sunny. One day, my brothers and I accidentally lit the grass on fire, and it spread rapidly. Unfortunately we didn't own a hose so we had to borrow one from the neighbours to put it out. Thank God they had one!

We were lucky we didn't start any houses on fire. Just plain lucky… by the grace of God.

The back yard was scorched black, though, and before my parents got home we had to cover the whole yard in dry hay we had found along the ditch further down the road. The neighbours knew how tough my dad was and how mad he would be, so they all helped us cover it up.

Although life looked good on the outside, for the most part, our family still had some major issues. Our parents fought constantly and screamed incessantly at each other. They were having financial problems.

Cindy and I spent a lot of time in the rocking chair in our living room. The rest of the family didn't use the living room much, so we would rock and sing all day long. It was far enough away from the main room where everyone gathered that we couldn't hear what was going on in the kitchen. If we sang loud enough, the sound of yelling would go away, which made us feel better. Singing was joyful, and it served as a defence mechanism from all the anger and pain that surrounded us. It was a way for us to escape our reality and pretend that the arguing didn't exist. We lived in fear, and it was no fun. Singing was fun. To this day, Cindy and I love to sing together—in the car, at the lake, at church, anywhere.

My dad was still very physical with my mom and us kids, especially Susie. She always seemed to be in trouble and seemed to get hit the most. He would beat her so bad that the younger kids would run next door to call the cops. He would beat her until she was bleeding, screaming, crying, and in so much pain that it horrified us.

He tried to justify it by saying she was rebellious, but there was no justification for that kind of abuse. There just wasn't.

We called the cops many times from Ivanhoe and Olean until Susie finally just ran away at the age of fifteen. We didn't know where she went, but I knew in my heart that she was happy, safe, and in no more pain.

Many young people who are on the street today have been abused, and sadly the streets somehow seem safer to them. This is a real problem and we need to address it by getting to know them and providing opportunities for change in their lives. We can make a difference.

We never stayed long in any house. With eight kids, we just couldn't take good care of the homes we rented and we weren't consistent in paying rent. My parents weren't doing very well financially; real estate was lucrative as long as the houses were selling, but if not there was big trouble since income is based on commission. My parents needed to manage their money well, with the long stretches between sales. The housing markets boomed during tourist season, which was generally mid-October to mid-April. Then things slowed right down.

I cannot imagine living this way with eight kids. It would be very hard to budget, and they were always needing to borrow money. It caused a lot of arguments and took its toll on their marriage.

4.

COME SAIL AWAY

Grace comes from a frightened father.

FROM OLEAN WE MOVED TO SMALL STREET. THIS HOUSE DIDN'T HAVE A POOL, but it had the next best thing—a canal! It was a nice house with a lanai and a yard that swept down to a dock on the water. We didn't have a boat like other people on the canal, but we did love to swim in there. The neighbours thought we were crazy because the canal led to the ocean and there was no guarantee we weren't swimming with stingrays, manta rays, jellyfish, and sharks.

We knew there were blue crabs, though, because my brothers and I used to catch them and steam them for dinner. We would crawl along the seawall with a line and hook. The crabs hid under the barnacles, but sometimes, if you looked hard enough, you could see their claws sticking out. Doug would slip the hook in the crook of the claw and yank the crabs onto the seawall. Then Duane and I would bucket them. This is probably why to this day we love seafood so much!

It was in this house that our parents' marriage really got rocky. I think Susie running away played into it, along with all the verbal and physical abuse. My mom had had enough. Although they were still together, they were estranged for sure.

The food supply started to get scarce, so we were grateful for the crab.

One day, Duane, Doug, and I decided that we would run away, too. I was nine, Duane was eight, and Doug was ten. We decided to make a raft, like Tom Sawyer, and collect milk jugs to place between planks of wood. Doug, always the creative and adventurous one, would try anything.

By the time we were finished, the raft was pretty ingenious—not to mention quite large, so all three of us could easily fit on it. It had a large pole in the middle for a potential sail and something to hang on to.

We dreamed as we worked. If we could just sail down the canal and out into the ocean, maybe life would be better somewhere else. We were highly motivated, doing anything we could to get away. It was better than being at home listening to all the fighting and screaming.

I will never forget the launch. Duane wasn't a strong swimmer, and neither was I. The raft was a little tipsy with all three of us on it, so we decided it would be better if just two people went. At the last minute, I had flashbacks of my near-drowning in Ohio and chickened out. So the two of them took off.

Down the canal they went, and I thought, *Holy smokes. This is really working. They're going to get away!* I followed them along the seawall, down the canal, and watched as they kept paddling towards the ocean. I talked to them as they went, and we all thought it was the greatest thing ever.

As they came to the final curve that would take them out to sea, I had a sudden fear that I would never see them again. I panicked and I could see they were frightened, too. Doug was a never-say-die sort of kid, so he wouldn't back down or quit, but Duane was scared because he couldn't swim.

I ran back home as fast as I could. Thank God that Dad was home. Once I'd told him what had happened, we took off along the seawall. I think he was secretly impressed not only with how far we had gotten but with our beautiful workmanship.

By the time we got to where the boys were, they were close to the open sea. I could tell my dad was afraid, too, especially since he couldn't swim either! With all the patience he could muster, he called out to the boys to bring the raft in.

Reckless Doug, I could see, was tempted to keep going. He was free—free from our dad, free from abuse, free from everything. But then Dad started yelling in that autocratic voice we knew so well: "Doug, you get back in here right now or I'm going to spank the living daylights out of you."

I could see Doug was having second thoughts, weighing the options. Would he make it? If he didn't, what would happen? He'd get the crap beat out of him. Maybe it would be less of a beating if he just gave up.

Dad, meanwhile, was scared to death. There was really nothing he could do other than yell. So yell he did, until Doug finally took the paddle and came ashore. Needless to say, once they got on dry land there was even more yelling, and lots of spanking. We were all grounded and told never to do that again.

Despite all the punishment, though, we received the admiration of our siblings. Not only were they impressed by the raft itself, they were in awe that we'd had the guts to try and sail away. We went from being little kids to big kids that day.

Everyone agreed the raft was brilliantly made, and then my siblings all took great joy in tearing it apart so we could never sail away again. Try as we might, we could never rebuild a raft like that one… and believe me, we tried.

5.

A BUG'S LIFE

Grace is having a good sense of humour.

LET'S TALK COCKROACHES. WHEN WE LIVED IN OHIO, WE NEVER, EVER SAW A cockroach. The climate was much too cold for them to survive. However, in Florida the weather was perfect—hot and humid. The palmetto trees outside the front yard were a nesting place for cockroaches.

Damp, moist areas in a home cause cockroaches to gather and build nests, and most people in Florida spent a fortune on pest control to ensure cockroaches don't invade their home. Being poor, this wasn't an option for us. With eight children and our different changes of clothing, you can imagine what our laundry looked like at the end of the day, after we played outside and did our thing. Laundry needed to be a priority every day.

But that was impossible. Needless to say, the clothes piled up in the laundry room, which was located in an outdoor part of the house attached to the home but part of the carport. On many occasions the clothes wouldn't get washed and would pile up and become a wonderful place for cockroaches to hide.

One evening, Danny pretended he had a surprise for Cindy and me. He brought us into the carport and proceeded to explain that he had a special surprise for us. The lights were off as he pulled us into the room.

Now, my sister and I were very gullible, and once inside he closed the door and held it tightly shut. Then he turned on the light and to our horror we saw hundreds of cockroaches squirming and running all over the floor. We had never seen so many cockroaches!

My sister and I screamed at the top of our lungs and jumped up and down on our tiptoes, trying not to touch any cockroaches. Dan thought this was the funniest sight in the world.

Cockroaches have always terrified me, and this experience continued to haunt me and Cindy in our nightmares. From that day onward, she and I were always on the lookout for cockroaches. We checked the beds, the perimeter of the bedroom, and drawers as we opened them. They were nasty and we wanted no surprises.

But life goes on and our days revolved around going to school and coming home. Danny was still the football star and we looked forward to Friday night games. That was our social life. His car became one of the main attractions, and something to look forward to. Since he was the oldest, he used to have to watch my brothers and would drive them around in his new car.

Duane tells the story of what happened one day while they were driving:

I remember getting into an accident in Danny's car while going about sixty to seventy miles per hour on the highway. We didn't have our seatbelts on. As a matter of fact, we never wore them. On this day, though, while driving Danny looked over and said, "I don't know why, but boys, you better put your seatbelts on." It was the only time my brother asked me to wear a seatbelt.

No sooner did we put them on when he had to slam on the brakes. We rolled and flipped the car. The passenger side where we were sitting was smashed all the way in until we were almost in Dan's lap. Luckily we didn't get injured and made it out alive.

We would not have lived if we hadn't had our seatbelts on. This was a divine appearance by God and His angels. God's grace and spirit warned Danny to get the belts on and we were saved.

We had no idea what was going on, but I remember climbing out of the window, saying, "Man, that was fun! Can we do that again?"

That smashed car became a focal point at all the football games. Because the entire passenger side was bashed in and it wasn't drivable, Danny decided to spray paint the name of the opposing team on the side of the car. At every home game when you went into the stands, you'd see that smashed-up car with the name of whatever team we were playing. This became a great place for hometown fans to take pictures.

6.

DON'T TALK TO STRANGERS

Grace is given in discernment.

MY BROTHERS AND I LOVED TO CHASE BUTTERFLIES AND CATCH BUGS AND snakes. We also caught swallowtails in the park. These are the most beautiful of all the butterflies, and they were everywhere. They aren't seen anymore because buildings and cities have taken over, and the car exhaust has probably killed them off. But in those days there were a lot, and we had so much fun chasing them with nets. It kept us outside and out of everyone's hair.

Eventually we wandered farther and farther from home. When you have little parental supervision, the zone in which you feel safe expands. We found our way to the local strip mall, located on Highway 41. It was down the street a ways and then down a path. My brothers and I would hang out at the mall and look for bottles and loose change.

Two pivotal things happened during these wanderings. The first was meeting a man named Bill. He was an old man who used to sit outside the grocery store and say hi to the kids shopping with their moms. Every once in a while Bill would give a kid a quarter to buy a soft drink from the machine. My favourite was orange and grape soda, and we always felt lucky when Bill gave us a quarter. We'd ask Mom if it was okay, but everyone knew Bill. He was just a harmless old man.

One day, Doug and I went to the mall and saw Bill sitting right where he always did outside the grocery store. This time we had walked there and weren't with our mom, who thought we had gone to the park. Bill offered us a quarter to buy a drink, and we took it. Things seemed cool as we hung out with Bill.

Then Bill said, "I would give you a dollar, but I don't have it here. It's at my house. If you want to come to my house with me, I can get it for you."

My brother and I looked at each other.

"Where is your house?" Doug asked.

"It's not far. Just behind the store."

I felt uneasy, because we were already farther from home than we were supposed to be. If my mom had known we were hanging out at the mall, she would be very angry.

Doug looked at me. "Come on, Jude, it's not far. Just behind the store. We're already here. It's only a little further."

Remember, Doug was the daredevil, and he was irresistible when he was trying to convince you to do something.

"Well, if you aren't going, I am," Doug said after a while.

But that would leave me by myself, and our number one rule was to stick together, so I finally gave in.

We followed Bill to his home, which was right behind the store like he'd said... well, a few houses in. He had all sorts of ornamental statues around his home. It was old and a bit dilapidated, with stuff everywhere.

The next thing I knew, Bill had the dollar and called us over to come inside.

"Not you," he said to Doug. "You wait outside."

When I went in, there was barely a place to sit down. I felt uncomfortable with my brother outside, but I was mesmerized by the mess and didn't know what to do. In this context, he was the adult and I figured I should be able to trust him, right? He was Bill, the guy who was always nice to kids at the store, who gave us treats. Everyone knew him...

So I walked over and he gave me the dollar. But the next thing I knew, he grabbed me and got me on his lap and kissed me and touched me between the legs. I had never been so revolted in my life: old man breath, old man stubble, old man kissing me on my mouth... he had to be seventy, and I was eight. I started pushing away, but he held on tight.

I pushed and pushed and eventually got out of his arms. I ran out the door.

My brother was outside down the walk, but I just ran past him and yelled, "Come on!" He came up fast behind me and we ran all the way home.

I was terrified, angry, disgusted, and wanted to throw up. I decided I would never go there again.

When my brother asked what had happened, I screamed at him that I had been right and that we shouldn't have gone there. I told him what Bill had done and Doug just looked at me, first with chagrin and then with his goofy grin.

"Well, at least you still got the dollar," he said.

He always had a sense of humour, and I think that's what got us through all the things that happened to us.

When I think of my own kids at this age, they weren't even allowed to leave the yard, never mind go down to the mall. I always knew where they were. But my parents never knew where we were. It's a lesson for parents to always protect their children and know where they are. They are precious and vulnerable. Not everyone is a friend.

I always hung out with my brothers because the girls teased me, made fun of me, and bullied me. Probably because I was such a tomboy. I didn't have the pretty clothes and fancy hair ties and barrettes. I didn't have a mom who did my hair and helped me dress. I was on my own.

But one day a girl invited me over to her house, and I was excited to go because I had no friends. We were giggling and sharing secrets on her bed, as eight-year-old girls do, when suddenly she started petting me and trying to go into places no one had ever tried to go before except Bill.

First it was Bill, and now it was this girl... what the heck was going on?

I had no idea what was happening, since this behaviour had never been explained to me. But I knew instinctively that it was wrong. I immediately told this girl I had to go home and left.

Because of these experiences, I continued to have no friends. I had no one I could trust. I just felt like me and my whole family were freaks, the big poor family of eight.

Unfortunately, these strange sexual encounters were only a foreshadowing of what was to come.

It was at the home on Small Street where the family started to fall apart. My dad and mom were fighting more and more and the older kids were starting to get into drugs to escape the violence.

As my brother Dave recalls:

There was no infrastructure for kids and absolutely nothing to do in Florida. Drugs were kind of an escape. They were easy to obtain. We used to listen to music, too. We started listening to Black Sabbath, Iron Maiden, and music that probably wasn't the best for kids at that time. I was really heavy into drugs on Small Street, from the ages of fourteen until about nineteen. With no parental supervision, it was easy to find trouble.

When I was fourteen, I remember my friend Johnny once dropping me off at the house, but I started walking the wrong way. We had been partying hard, so I was pretty hammered. He saw me walk away from my house, but he thought I would figure it out.

Small Street went around and down by the water, and the next morning I woke up in a station wagon. I thought it was ours, and I remember thinking, *What the heck am I doing in the car?* So I went to the door of the house, but the door was locked. Our door was never locked.

I was still kind of half out of it, thinking, *Wait a minute. This isn't our house.* Then I looked over at the car and realized, *That's not our car.*

I started walking and didn't know where I was. I suddenly realized I was only a block from our house. When I got home, I didn't have my wallet so then I had to go back to the car looking for the wallet. But it turned out my friends had my wallet.

I share this story because my life gets a little hazy after that. I don't remember seeing my dad that much on Small Street. I think he was there at first, but at that point Mom and Dad were starting to live apart. My friends were Johnny and Pete, and Johnny's brother Robert. All we did was look for drugs.

I snorted heroin one time. I did cocaine, LSD, acid, mushrooms, uppers, downers, and meth. I always had a standard that I would shoot nothing in the arm. I think that was God protecting me. I was just partying to forget and have fun. It was an escape.

The fighting between my mom and dad soon escalated to the point where my parents were evicted from Small Street, and we moved to Dolphin Avenue. Their attention was on their marriage and not on us kids. The lack of family structure saw us all go our own ways and get into things we shouldn't have. David was doing serious drugs and hitchhiking across the state on his own at fifteen. My brothers and I hung out at malls, vulnerable prey to people with bad motives. Our family was unravelling fast and there was nothing we could do stop what was to come.

7.

THE BEGINNING AND END OF INNOCENCE

Grace comes from the love of a brother.

ONE DAY DURING THE SUMMER WHEN I WAS IN GRADE THREE, MY MOM CALLED all of us kids together to tell us that my dad had left. Actually she'd kicked him out, which was a very brave thing to do. He was more than happy to leave behind all his responsibilities. The two of them just couldn't keep going together and they were tired of fighting and not getting along. They felt the move would be better for everyone.

Now, as tough as my dad was, I was his favourite child and Daddy's little girl; I didn't get in trouble nearly as much as my siblings. Regardless of how mean he could be, losing him was devastating. No matter how old you become, your mother is your mother and your father is your father. They're all you have and you love them unconditionally.

I immediately burst into tears that day. I was very, very sad.

I will never forget David's response when he saw me crying. He picked me up, put me on his knee, hugged me tightly, and said, "Don't worry, Judy. I'll take care of you. Everything will be okay. I won't let anything bad happen to you."

Looking back, it didn't matter to me if my brother could take care of me or not. What mattered was that he wanted to, and in that moment I felt so much love for him. I named my second son after Dave, because at a time when my world was falling apart he gave me hope and big brotherly love. That was so special, so important.

With Dad gone, we did okay at first, but we were even poorer now. We only had two bedrooms in the house on Dolphin Avenue. Cindy, Doug, Duane, and I slept in the same room, in the same double bed. I'm not even sure if we had sheets, to be quite honest. The challenge was to fall asleep, and stay asleep, which was hard with all the elbows and knees hitting and kicking you. Many times we fought, and someone would always end up on the floor.

But at least we got a bedroom. The older kids slept in the living room on the couch and on the floor.

We had a brown rabbit name Thumper. A neighbour had given us the rabbit and the cage, which Mom couldn't say no to since we were going through such a hard time without Dad.

Thumper became a source of joy to us. We had an empty treed lot next door to us and we used to let Thumper out there to play hide and seek in the woods with him. We always found him and brought him home. It would be funny when we found him, because rabbits are really good at camouflaging themselves in their environment. And of course they are really quiet. We were surprised he kept coming back. It helped pass the summer in this new home.

We had great neighbours, or so we thought, who used to take turns looking after us. Their oldest boy from the family behind us became friends with Duane. We were grateful for it because Duane was so little. We thought this older boy was being really sensitive to our situation by making Duane his little buddy and watching out for him.

Unfortunately, something more sinister was happening which was very traumatic and painful for my brother to even share until years and years later:

I remember hanging out with Jimmy and reading *Playboy* magazines— okay, we looked at lots and lots of *Playboys*. I was seven years old, and he was seventeen. Many times he watched me while Mom was out and there was no one home.

He was a black belt in karate and all of his buddies had black belts. I thought he was really cool. He always took me for motorcycle rides.

The only thing I can remember is reading *Playboys* and watching *Playboys* and looking at pictures with him and going for rides on his motorcycle.

Then one time we came back to his house after a ride, and we were dirty. He said, "Hey, we're too dirty, let's take a shower. Do you want to take a shower?"

"Okay, sure," I said, thinking nothing of it. My oldest brother was around seventeen and I would have had a shower with him. We always took baths together. Giving eight kids a bath one at a time would have been an all-day chore, so we would all buddy up to make it go faster and conserve hot water.

Jimmy turned on the shower, filled the bathtub up with water, and then said to me, "Hey, why don't you suck my dick?" And he started jacking off.

At first I didn't think there was anything wrong because I had a relationship with him as a friend.

"I just want to take a shower," I told him.

"No. You suck my dick and I'll suck yours."

As I sat there, he reached down and started putting his lips on my dick. I pushed him away and asked, "What are you doing?" I was confused. I didn't know what he was trying to do.

"Well, just suck my dick," he said.

Then he grabbed me. I had really long hair because we couldn't afford haircuts, and he pulled me by my hair and pushed me down. I was close to his groin and he pulled me close and I suddenly took a whiff. It was the most disgusting smell I had ever smelled and I knew it just wasn't right.

Knowing it wasn't right was God's grace and protection.

Suddenly, something came out of me. It was an anger, fear, and an energy. I remember punching him as hard as I could. I then grabbed my clothes and ran out of the bathroom. His dad and sister were just sitting there as I ran out of the house.

I never went back, but I can still smell his scent to this day. It still brings up the same gut-wrenching feelings.

I was so innocent at that age, and I was just beginning to trust the adults in my life. My dad was gone, my mom was just plain weary, and so my siblings were the only people in my life.

But I knew this story was one I could never share with anyone, even though I didn't understand why. I know now that it's because I felt confused, ashamed, guilty, disgusted, and embarrassed. I thought that what had happened was somehow my fault.

I was afraid to ever be alone with Jimmy again, which is why I never went back.

I didn't realize until much later in life that Jimmy was gay. This stuff wasn't exposed like it is today in the media. Quite frankly, I had no idea that any of this behaviour existed, and according to my faith this was all wrong.

When I came back to Florida years later, I wanted to find him and confront him. I found out he had moved from Port Charlotte and a part of me thought he should be dead. But when I found the Lord, I knew I had to forgive him and let it go. That's what God's grace does— it forgives and lets go and gives you the strength to get through the difficult times you face. I pray to God Jimmy isn't preying on other young innocent children.

8.

GOD HAS A PLAN

Grace comes from a vision shared and the power of prayer.

Let us then approach God's throne of grace with confidence, so that we may receive mercy and find grace to help us in our time of need. (Hebrews 4:16)

Out of the depths I cry to you, Lord; Lord, hear my voice. Let your ears be attentive to my cry for mercy. (Psalm 130:1–2)

A FEW MONTHS AFTER MY DAD LEFT, I REMEMBER COMING UPON MY MOM crying uncontrollably. When you're a child and see your parents crying, it's devastating. They're the ones who are supposed to take care of you, so they shouldn't cry, right? I asked her what was wrong and she looked at me bravely through her tears and said, "Don't worry, Judy. Everything is going to be okay. God has a plan. Everything is going to be just fine. God has a special plan for each one of you children. Everything is going to be okay."

Looking back, two Bible verses come to mind to support my mom's theory, but at the time I didn't know them:

For I know the plans I have for you… plans to prosper you and not to harm you, plans to give you hope and a future. (Jeremiah 29:11)

And we know that in all things God works for the good of those who love him, who have been called according to his purpose. (Romans 8:28)

Shortly after that, the four youngest siblings, including me, went into our first foster home. It was the worst day of my life. My mom needed to get a grip on her life and we required too much attention. The older kids were fairly independent, though, and were told to take care of themselves.

As my sister Connie explains:

All I remember is hearing that Dad left. Of course, I remember Mom always yelling at him to get out and leave. So I guess he finally did.

The first time my brothers and sisters went into foster homes, I was in the ninth grade. I have no idea why me and my brother Dave weren't in care, but my mom told us to find a place to stay.

Luckily my friend's mom offered to let me stay with them until my mom got back on her feet. It was a blessing. We were starting to get into drugs then, but nothing heavy, and her mom never caught us.

Because of the good work ethic my dad beat into us, I helped her mom around the house and she always praised me for it. I did feel bad, though, because she would tell her daughter she should help around the house like me and compared our efforts. I was just grateful to have a good place to stay and be a help instead of a bother.

As Dave recalls:

I went to live with Johnny and his parents when Dad left. He wasn't the best influence. Johnny really liked his drugs. When I realized he liked his drugs more than people, I wasn't that interested in hanging out with Johnny anymore.

He had a solid family, so I don't know why he was so heavily into the drugs. I slept in the garage. It was actually nice because it was part of the home. I think I had a mat on the floor or a cot to sleep on. I don't remember.

I was going to high school when I lived there, halfway through Grade Ten. I had three months left of school, which seemed like an eternity in kid years.

The teachers told me I wasn't getting a proper education because I was missing too much school. If you missed more than seven days, you wouldn't get your credits. I had all A's and B's, except for an F in biology because I didn't like the teacher.

The teacher told me that if I came to school every day and didn't miss any classes, I would be able to get my credits. I thought, *Are you kidding me?* I couldn't even fathom showing up to school the next day, never mind for the next three months. I didn't have any clothes, papers, or books.

When you're that age and hardly have any clothes, you have no stability. You're living with your buddy in his garage and hitchhiking to school because it's so far away, trying to go to school every day for three months… It seemed way too impossible, so I dropped out.

Cindy went to stay with a family whose dad was a cop. Doug went to another home that was already fostering another boy, and my little brother Duane went somewhere in Punta Gorda. It was too hard to keep us together.

I ended up in a home with parents and two children—a boy and a girl close to my age. I think the mother was the secretary at my mom's workplace. Taking me in was very generous of her and her family.

I spent my entire Grade Four year in this home, as well as part of Grade Five, with people I didn't know. Every night I clung to the rosary beads I'd gotten from my godparents, praying that God would get us back to our mother. I knew one prayer, the Lord's Prayer:

Our Father who art in heaven, hallowed be thy name. Thy kingdom come, thy will be done on earth as it is in heaven. Give us this day our daily bread and forgive us our trespasses as we forgive those who trespass against us. And lead us not into temptation but deliver us from evil. Amen.[9]

That was what I prayed over and over again. I would cry myself to sleep, but it was more than crying; it was weeping, the kind of deep, mournful weeping that sucks the life right out of you.

I didn't understand why this had to happen. I was scared. I was lonely. I felt abandoned. It felt like nobody loved me or cared for me. On many levels, it felt as though my situation was my fault.

I prayed for forgiveness through the Lord's Prayer over and over, really trying to understand the words and what they conveyed. Believe it or not, I could feel that God was listening. In my heart, I knew He would take care of us. But

---

[9] This is how I memorized it. The full text of the Lord's Prayer can be found in Matthew 6.

sometimes it was hard to believe that He was real. It was hard not to feel the pain and sorrow.[10]

Prayer is so powerful and it literally moves mountains. I encourage people to learn to pray. Praying effectively is easy. You just talk to God. It certainly saved our family.

Everyone at school knew my situation and I found it hard to make friends. All my clothes were hand-me-downs and I remember trying to look older and cooler than I was just because I didn't want to be bullied. I also thought that if I could look older and prettier, maybe I would get some attention like the other girls.

I had a crush on a boy named Jeff, but I knew I would never be able to have him as a boyfriend because I was from the other side of the tracks. People who knew us before the separation started to treat us differently once they found out we were in foster homes. They stopped hanging out with us. And if they did, it was out of pity, which was worse.

I felt like an alien. Everything that was happening to me was so strange. Other people's lives were so normal while mine had completely fallen apart.

It was a very lonely year being away from all my brothers and sisters. I had no friends and didn't bond well with my foster family. Although the foster mom made the best goulash ever and tried hard to coax me out of my shell by making my favourite foods. But most of the time I just cried. There is no greater trauma than a child being separated from their family. It doesn't matter whether you have good parents or bad, your family members are the only ones you have. As a child you love them and care for them. They're yours.

Looking back, I know that God was listening. He was putting His plans in place to save me. Prayer is powerful and I've seen it answered over and over in my life.

Faith is a muscle you have to use in order for it to grow and become stronger, and my baby faith and God's grace were what got me through this difficult time. As the Bible says, *"Rejoice always, pray without ceasing, give thanks in all circumstances; for this is the will of God in Christ Jesus for you"* (1 Thessalonians 5:16–18). I'd mastered the part about praying without ceasing, and as God continues to answer my prayers I've learned to rejoice and be thankful in every situation.

---

[10] As I'm writing this, the church I attend is completing a forty-day prayer study on this very passage and on how to pray. I can honestly say that I think I nailed it at the age of eight. It was an incredible study. The worship team at Church of the Rock is incredible, led by Derick Zeilstra, and Pastor Mark Hughes is a gifted speaker who speaks with relevance on today's issues with practical biblical applications. It's a charismatic interdenominational evangelical church. You can watch the services on Facebook and online at www.churchoftherock.com.

I learned that hardship allows us to lean on God, learn the heart of God, and through prayer press into the power of God and the Holy Spirit in our lives. It allows us to stir up the Holy Spirit to move on our behalf in ways we cannot fathom. We often don't see the results of prayer until long after the fact. We need to build up our faith, pray incessantly, and just believe and trust in Him.

But at the time, I was just scared, sad and lonely.

My sister Cindy recalls her first foster home:

The place where I stayed treated me very well. They were always very nice and made sure I was well taken care of. I used to hang out with my friends, and sometimes we smoked a little pot. I'm pretty sure the dad knew since he was a cop, but he never said anything and treated me very nicely. He just wanted to make sure I was safe.

My brother Doug, who was eleven, got it worse than all of us. His family was very abusive. There was at the time another foster boy with him named Johnny, and he had to sleep on the floor. They beat Johnny regularly, yelled at him, and kicked him. Johnny wasn't fed properly and locked in his room where he was forced to sleep on the floor.

Doug was new there, so they were nice to him at first and treated him okay. When he saw what was happening to the other boy, though, he was shocked and scared. He didn't know what to do. Lucky for us, Doug was a fighter and knew it was wrong. As Doug shared with me:

I went into the Romano foster home. There was another kid, Johnny, who was in there because his mom was a drug addict and a prostitute. He used to have to watch his mom have sex while they were in hotel rooms.

The foster couple was very abusive to Johnny. He was in there full-time and they kept promising him they were going to adopt him. They kept saying, "If you want to be adopted you have to do this, and if you want to be adopted you have to do that."

Mrs. Romano would come into our room in the middle of the night all pissed off and start kicking him in the ribs. He would be all curled up on the floor. They used to beat him up real bad, and he slept on a mat.

The biological daughter used to do mean things to Johnny like put shaving cream in his hand and rub it into his face. She would force him to do it in front of her friends, thinking it was funny. For him, it was humiliating.

One day I was on the phone talking about papers. Mr. Romano heard me, and he knew I was talking about marijuana. He came in, grabbed me, and started saying that they were going to start to beat me if I didn't watch it. This was after five months dealing with them, but they were starting to push me and slap me a bit too much. Not like Johnny, but it was enough.

I got real scared and called my brother Dan. He came over immediately, knocked on the door, and said, "Where's my brother Doug?"

"Who are you?" asked the father.

"I'm his older brother, and I need to talk to him."

"You can't talk to him."

But I was in the other room and heard him, so I walked in to where they were talking and said, "Hey Dan, what's going on?"

Dan looked at me. "Come on, Doug, let's go. Get your stuff. We're getting out of here!"

"You can't take him out of here," Mr. Romano said.

But Dan was really built and strong. He pushed open the door and said, "Yeah, yeah. You're coming with me, buddy. Come on. Go grab your stuff."

So I grabbed my stuff.

The old man said, "You're not taking him anywhere."

But Dan just looked at him and said, "Are you going to stop me?"

Mr. Romano started laughing. "Yes, I am."

I was kind of afraid because I didn't know what this guy was going to do. All the while, Danny kept telling me to go grab my stuff.

Suddenly Romano grabbed me, and Danny pushed him really hard and he fell down.

Now it was Dan's turn to start laughing. "Come on, buddy, lets go."

Dan took care of me for a day or two and then he took me to family services. We told them about the abuse and I got moved to a different home where I got to be with Duane.

Looking back, we can see God's grace in giving Doug the power to tell someone what was going on. So many incidents of child abuse go unreported, back then and now. Kids are afraid to speak out against adults.

For us, abuse was all we knew. We never reported our dad's abuse to a level that did anything to spare us, but somehow Doug had the courage to speak out on behalf of the other little boy in care. That took tremendous courage.

Johnny never did tell family services that he was being abused. He really just wanted to be loved and adopted. But eventually he got tired of being humiliated by his foster sister, and in his pain and frustration from abuse he decided to light the daughter's car on fire. This took place only a few years after Doug left. The police caught him and he ended up in jail, which is quite a common fate for many abused and neglected children.

Sadly, jail was probably a better place for him.

9.

BULLY OR BE BULLIED

Grace gives the ability to reflect, rise up, and make a difference.

DOUG AND DUANE STILL DIDN'T HAVE IT EASY. DOUG'S LIFE CAN BE MARKED AND measured by all the fights he got into and going into different foster homes meant different schools. As he shares:

> When we were on Dolphin Avenue, I had really long hair and was always getting in fights at school because everyone made fun of it. I was also getting in fights to protect other kids who were getting picked on. Since I knew what being picked on felt like, I used to defend others. People were always bigger than me, but I didn't care. I didn't like to be picked on and didn't like watching other people get picked on.
>
> When I moved to the Romanos, I went from going to Meadow Park School to Peace River School. New school, new fights. Everyone wants to pick on you because you're the new kid on the block.
>
> Then I moved over to Duane's foster home and we were in Punta Gorda. This was redneck territory and nobody liked long hair.
>
> While going to school there, we lived in a trailer park. I met a guy from down the street. He was a pretty big guy in the same grade as me. His name was Leo and he smoked pot, so we would smoke together but had to hide it.
>
> On the first day of school, Duane and I were on our way to school when a sixth grader came up to Duane, pushed him, and said something about his long hair. I jumped on top of the guy, grabbed his head, and beat the crap out of him. This was on our way to school!

So this guy and his buddies, who were rednecks, started following me around at recess. They were trying to get me away from the teachers and staff who were walking around, but I was really fast. I could outrun them and always keep my distance.

Finally, the one guy got me alone. We were one on one, and I beat him up.

The bullies were getting frustrated because they really wanted to beat me up. So they talked to Leo, not knowing that he was my friend and said, "Leo, you get on the same bus as the new guy, Doug. He keeps dodging us at recess. We'll give you twenty bucks if you beat Doug up."

So my friend Leo said to me on the bus later, "Yeah, they want to give me twenty bucks to beat you up."

"That's crazy!" I said. I thought about it some more and then said, "Hey, how about this? I'll go to school with a band aid on my face tomorrow and make it look like you beat me up, and we'll split the money."

"Yeah, let's do that!"

And we did, and we split the twenty bucks. I was done with those guys.

Doug was always the smallest guy, and unfortunately that made him easy to pick on. What people didn't realize, though, was that he came from a broken home. This was very uncommon in the 70s. Inside he was angry and hurt, so any provocation would bring out the pain and anger, which could be all-consuming. He never backed down and the uncontrollable anger helped him to win fights and survive.

It's really hard to describe the depth of pain that's felt when parents abandon their children, or when parents separate and the family falls apart. The pain was so bad that it became a pit of rage. It helped me to understand my dad a bit more, because he had also been abandoned at an early age by his dad, after watching his dad abuse his mom. We were caught in a vicious cycle.

I think we all had that rage within us until we developed a personal relationship with Christ and were graced with the fruits of the Spirit. Praise God for the gifts of love, peace, joy, and happiness. That's the freedom in knowing Christ.

Although Duane's foster home was better than Doug's and wasn't abusive, Duane also experienced pain, although it was pain of a deeper, more personal kind. He was the youngest, so my mom had decided that the rabbits we owned would go with him. That way, he wouldn't be so lonely and have an easier time adjusting. He explains:

Stumper and Thumper were our only pets, but both got eaten by raccoons. That's what I was told anyway. I was devastated because they were all I had. I had no parents, no brothers, and no sisters... just my rabbits, who were now dead.

To console me, my foster mom used to French kiss me. I was only nine years old. That seemed really weird to me.

Then Doug came to the foster home after about five months because his family had been abusing him and abused another child really bad. I was glad to have my brother with me after everything that had happened.

The foster parents were planning a trip to Disneyworld. We were very excited. Most of the time when I was away from my family, I was sad, but going to Disneyworld was something every kid looked forward to doing.

But when it was finally time to go, they left me and Doug behind. We stayed home with Grandma. We even overheard them talking about it. We hid behind the corner in the kitchen while they discussed it in the living room: "Now that we've taken Duane and Doug in, we can make more money, and we can go to Disneyworld."

We were devastated, sad, and so disappointed. People are cruel.

For the most part, we've all recovered from our past and don't think about it. But sometimes when you allow yourself to feel how you felt long, long ago as a child, you remember the abandonment, the desolation, the pain, the anguish.

While new memories replace it, I still remember the raw emotion of being a child left by my parents and then left by my new foster parents. It's a devastating experience I will never forget. You hide the pain, but when you're told that you are a part of a new family and then they don't take you on vacation with them, it's devastating. So, so hurtful.

Foster parents aren't supposed to allow you to get attached to them, but that's the one thing you need most as a kid. You need a hug. You need to be loved. You need to feel that you are special. That's what makes it real and that's what makes you part of the family, when you're treated the same as the other kids.

Yet they left us and it hurt. And they did it several times.

As my brother shared this story with me, he wept like a child. He is a successful businessman today, but the pain came back raw, unexpectedly. He felt bewildered and betrayed.

Interviewing my siblings and getting their perspective for this book has made me feel so sad for all of us and what we lost as children. For the most part, we haven't had to share our memories. We've buried them in the past, never digging too deep. But for this book they opened up many of their memories and emotions and I could tell it was very hard on them.

It also made me sad for all the kids in care today. Our nation's children are still hurting.

Now, it's important to note that fostering children is a very noble undertaking, and I want to thank all the parents and families who choose to foster kids, those who take their role seriously, who do a good job, and who really care! Most families are dedicated to caring for the children in their care and provide safe and loving environments. They fill an important role in keeping families together and filling the gaps in a child's life when their parents cannot be there for them.

So on behalf of all children in care, I thank you. When we're going through the experience, our pain is too raw for us to understand what a great service you're providing. We may not seem grateful, because we're focused on our own pain, but please know that we do end up appreciating all that you do. Once we mature and get our lives in order, we learn to understand.

But if my brothers could end up in not-so-good homes, how many other people are being hurt in the system right now, today? How many other kids are in foster care and being neglected or abused by their foster families? How many of these families are in it for the money, using the money that's intended to care for the kids to make other purchases? It's a bigger situation than most people realize.

It's hard to keep foster families accountable, since the assumption is that the kids are being cared for. With social media, one would think this kind of abuse would be revealed, but it isn't. When you're in care, you sometimes feel lucky just to have any place to live. And like Johnny, you don't want to rock the boat because it's all you have. Kids are afraid to speak out against adults. There's a power imbalance that makes them especially vulnerable.

When I look at healthy children today, who are ten to twelve years old like we were, they are so innocent. Growing up, I never felt innocent, young, or carefree. When you're surviving through care, trauma, and poverty, you can't dream and you quickly lose your innocence. You can't be a kid. You can't look to the future or get excited about what's going to happen next.

I don't know how kids feel today, but I remember constantly being hurt and violated. We couldn't speak out. There was no one to share it with. We felt that no adult is safe.

I pray for kids today because I can't imagine what's happening. There are more than eleven thousand children in foster care in Manitoba today, and more than twenty-three thousand in Florida. Take a look across Canada, the United States, and around the world. There are a lot of uncaring people out there, and that's what makes me sad. We need to fight for our children and the youth. We need to do everything we can to help them succeed: fight the evil, fight the negativity, and fight the bad things that are going on. That's why we are sharing our stories. Because if not us, then who?

There are some amazing organizations today helping kids in care. Safe Families helps these struggling families by partnering with them, by placing kids in Christian homes, and by helping families retain custody of their children during the placement. Families can come from any background and be referred by a school, hospital, church, pregnancy centre, homeless shelter, child welfare agency, or neighbour—or they can contact Safe Families themselves when in a time of crisis. Volunteers serve without compensation and are motivated by the compassion and grace they first received from Jesus Christ. I wish this organization had been around when we were going through our crisis.

I would like to see our youth speak out so they can be advocates and be the change in the world. I would like to see our kids become lights for future generations. They need to be bold and strong in the Lord and in everything they do. We need our children to take the torch.

So if you're reading this book, this message is for you and your children: be the change you want to see in this world.

These feelings resonate strongly with each of us siblings as we share our stories. Even though we're fine now, we mourn for those who right now have no voice and aren't okay, for those who are suffering in silence, surviving but not thriving; they're just existing.

Doug also remembers the racial discrimination that was happening in the 1970s:

We moved with those foster parents from the trailer park to a different part of town, right next to a black neighbourhood. I had never lived close to black people before. In Port Charlotte there had been some black people, but not a lot. Here there were a lot, in downtown Punta Gorda by Cooper Street.

There was a community swimming pool that only cost thirty-five cents for the whole family to use, so Duane and I decided to go to the pool with our foster sister. We walked over there, and before we left we tied up the dog, a great big German shepherd named Candy, who was very protective of us.

We went to the pool and there was not one white person there. The medium-sized pool was packed with at least a hundred kids. It had one diving board.

We noticed there were a lot of black people, but we didn't really care. We were just kids and we wanted to go swimming. It was Florida and ninety degrees outside!

When I jumped in the pool, all of a sudden we noticed that it got completely quiet. Everybody was staring at us. When you have a hundred people staring at you, it's pretty obvious.

Then one of the people came up to us and said, "What are you honkies doing here?"

Duane and I started thinking, *Uh-oh, maybe we need to get out of here.* So we quickly got our things and started walking home.

On the way home, five guys came by on their bikes and started spitting on us, calling us a bunch of honkies. As we got a little further down the road, we started yelling back at them.

This was the 70s, and there was a lot of racism. But as a kid, you're not really racist. You don't think anything of it.

When I yelled at them, suddenly they turned their bikes around and started chasing us. We took off running and got to our house while they flew after us. Candy was sitting in the front yard and I ran up and unleashed her.

"Go! Go get them, Candy!"

You never saw people run so fast. It was funny. They started running across the field in front of the house, which was all full of sand spurs, screaming at the top of their lungs, "Hold him back! Hold him back!"

Needless to say, they never bothered us again. But we also never went back to the pool. Lesson learned.

Racial prejudice was a large part of the culture. Even though the city had de-segregated in the late 1960s, it took people a long time to change their behaviour. Things don't change over night. I remember being encouraged to drink out of different water fountains by kids my age and not go into the washrooms together with black kids.

The sad reality is that we enjoyed hanging out with the black kids, even more than the white kids. They were so much fun. Their music was really cool, too. Many of them didn't have a lot of stuff, like us, so we had a lot in common. We had secret black friends we used to hang out with. Luckily for us, though, we could get along with the black kids and the white kids.

Prejudice towards black people still exists now, but in a different way. Today it's geared toward both their culture and their socioeconomic situation. If someone is equal in economic status, they are accepted. The prejudice is more towards those experiencing poverty and homelessness, those who use social programs, and since black, Hispanic, and Indigenous people are overly represented in this sector, prejudice still exists towards them.

What we need to do is learn to understand why they are overly represented and be a part of the solution for change. We shouldn't be prejudiced against any culture, ethnicity, or people who are different. We're all the same in God's eyes. We are His people. We need to learn to love each other for what we have in common and learn to accept and respect our differences. We need to know and teach our children that it's okay to be different. That would eliminate a lot of bullying and hatred.

We also need to find ways to lift people out of poverty and help them succeed.

10.

REUNITED

Grace comes through doctors, teachers, and neighbours.

BY THE GRACE OF GOD, MY MOTHER WAS ABLE TO GET US CHILDREN BACK AFTER about a year and a half, and eventually we all started living together at a home on Calvin Lane. My mom still sold real estate, but the income was very sporadic. In those days, Port Charlotte wasn't the hotspot it is today. A doctor friend of her charged only $20 a month for us to live there, and he would have offered it for free but my mother had too much pride.

Anyway, it was a dream come true. Anybody can afford $20 a month. Living in this home seemed like a great deal.

I was finishing Grade Five and doing very well. I was also a very good student and worked hard, especially at math, which was my favourite subject.

There was a sixth-grade math teacher, Mr. Gantnor, who would post math problems around his room, little stumpers, some of which were really tough and made you think. For each question you got right, you won a gumdrop. Then there were the super-stumpers, usually posted once per week, which were really hard. The first student who correctly answered a super-stumper won a teddy bear or some other sort of stuffed animal.

Since I was in Grade Five, I wasn't allowed to participate. But one day Mr. Gantnor noticed my inclination for math and I started hanging out in his class after school, bugging him all the time. I would stay after school late and do the contests just for fun, since I had nothing better to do with my time.

So Mr. Gantnor decided to let me start participating in the contests, and I'm proud to say that I won almost every math problem he posted, winning everything from gumdrops to dolls. It was a fun challenge and it kept me away from worrying about all the other things that were going on in my life.

Grade Five was probably my happiest year of school. For that one year, I felt like I belonged and that I had some friends—and that I was smart. I even performed in the school plays. I usually got lead roles and had to memorize a lot of lines, but I was motivated.

Even though rent was cheap, our family was still poor and most of the time we didn't have food to go home to. Thank God for the school's free lunch program. We got hot meals delivered to the classroom, and if your family was on welfare (which we were) your lunches were free. The key was to show up for school, since that might be the only meal we got all day. I loved the mashed potatoes with ground beef and gravy. That was my all-time favourite, with corn, salad, a roll, and chocolate milk.

Thank God for people who care and give to food hampers at their churches and local food pantries. Periodically we would get home from school and find a food hamper on our table. We relied heavily on people to provide these in order to get by. Every time a hamper came, it felt like Christmas.

In those days, you didn't have to lock your doors, especially when you lived out in the boondocks, which is why we'd get home to discover the table loaded with groceries. It was unbelievable from a child's perspective to get home and find our favourite cereals, bread, pasta, macaroni and cheese, and milk in the fridge.

It's such a struggle not to have food. The hunger pit in your belly never goes away, and you feel dizzy and weak all over. Then when food comes, it's such a special feeling. Your stomach sings, and you feel warm and happy.

At Christmastime, the hampers came with presents, too. That was how I got a real Barbie, my first and only doll.

The hampers were always anonymous. People didn't want us to know that they knew we were struggling. My mom was a very proud woman and didn't like to have to be on the receiving end of these gifts. She didn't want people to know our business. She was also a prayer warrior and believed in going to church as much as possible, so I'm pretty sure it was her friends at the Catholic church who gave us the hampers.

Again you can see the power of the Holy Spirit working in the people in our community. Because of their care for us, and by the grace of God, we were able to eat.

As a child, it was a huge encouragement to know that someone, somewhere, cared. As we were going through the worst times in our lives, God planted angels to provide encouragement and hope in our time of need.

Today many of us buy canned goods and non-perishables for food hampers. We do it without a second thought: add it to our groceries and toss it in the bin. I want to encourage you to try to envision the children in the home that's on the receiving end of that gift. Really care about the choice when you purchase something. Really care about the child who will eventually feel your loving touch.[11]

Say a prayer that these children's circumstance don't overcome them and that they'll have the ability to lean into God who can give them strength and courage. This is so important. The people we're feeding are real people with real issues, issues we may never understand. Our gift lets them know that we care.

---

[11] My favourite cereal was Captain Crunch, so while I try to choose healthy foods for the families I purchase for, I always throw in a box of Captain Crunch as a treat for the children.

11.

SPIRALLING INTO DESPAIR

Grace comes through encouragement.

ALTHOUGH MY MOM HAD US BACK TOGETHER, SHE WAS STARTING TO SUFFER from severe depression. As kids, we weren't aware of what was going on. We were too young to understand. The depression would make her unable to get out of bed in the mornings. She stopped selling homes and started selling cosmetics, but this couldn't support eight children. I can't imagine what it was like to try keeping us all together on so little income.

Based on where we lived, we should have gone to Neil Armstrong Elementary. Unfortunately, the principal there didn't like our family and had banned us. The next closest school was Meadow Park, where we loved the teachers and felt good. It was a long walk, though—five kilometres, about an hour each way. But the teachers were awesome and Mr. Gantnor taught me math. I managed to maintain straight A's and helped Duane with his homework, doing my best to care for my little brother.

Unfortunately, because of that long walk and the struggle of living in a home with very little food, we didn't always make it to school. Sometimes we were just too tired. So we would hide in the house. Mom would think we'd gone to school but we were sleeping in the closet or under the bed. We ended up missing more than eighty days of school that year, but I still managed to do very well and get straight A's.

We had no electricity at this house, so I remember doing my homework under the streetlight out on the sidewalk after dark. The work would come out a bit bumpy but mostly legible. At least we tried.

Mr. Gantnor would catch us sometimes as we were walking to school and pick us up. He knew how far we had to go, but there really wasn't anything else he could do about it, just help as best he could.

Teachers are so important and have such an impact on their students. When they gave us encouragement and told us we were good at something, it planted seeds of confidence and hope. Being told that I was good at math led me to eventually take up accounting. Teachers also inspire us to stay in the game and never give up.

So thank you to all the schoolteachers and educators out there. You'll never know how many people you've impacted. Because of your persistence, we succeed!

12.

BEING POOR HAS ITS PRIVILEGES

Grace comes from understanding the plight of the poor and becoming an advocate.

I REMEMBER HAVING ONE PAIR OF PINK BELLBOTTOMS. I HAD A T-SHIRT AND A brown bathing suit that acted as an undergarment for both a bra and panties. I wore them every day wherever I needed to go, whether it was school or around the neighbourhood. Pink corduroy pants, a T-shirt, and that was all I had. I had no shoes. We tried to get flipflops, because the streets were so hot. Flipflops were cheap, but they also broke easily. It was a good day if we had a pair of shoes to wear.

You can just imagine how I might have looked: not showering regularly, wearing the same clothes, walking in bare feet on tarred pavement, through the dirt… I can't imagine what other people must have seen or thought, but I'm sure they saw someone fairly dirty, smelly, and unkempt. I didn't smile much, either.

Old people used to walk around me and look at me strangely, in fear that I might steal from them. They'd hug their purses tighter to their chest and mark a path around me when passing on the street. I remember thinking, *Wow, I'm just a kid and you're afraid of me? You actually think I'm going to hurt you, steal from you?* I was the one who was terrified! We were just trying to survive and get by in life.

It was one of the most humiliating experiences of my life. It also created a chip on my shoulder, because you get hurt when others judge you by your appearance or circumstance. It has made me much more sympathetic to people experiencing poverty or homelessness.

At the time, I was just in a fog, going through life wondering what was next. As Duane shared with me:

The worst experience was coming home to no electricity and no running water for months at a time. Even though it might have only been a year and a half or two years, it felt like your whole life. When you're seven, a year is more than ten percent of your life, especially when you don't remember from one to three years old.

It was very hard and depressing, especially when you're going to other people's houses, and they're eating and have electricity and clothes. Even if they weren't rich, but just above the poverty line, they still had a lot compared to us. We had nothing. I remember living out of a cooler and feeling hopelessness.

When you're young, there's a grace of God that's on you for protection. I believe there were prayers from our families and prayers from people around us that prevented us from getting seriously hurt and dying, because we all could have died based on what we were going through. It's amazing.

Looking back, what a privilege this was. The experience really helped me empathize with people experiencing poverty and homelessness. It equipped me with passion to fight the good fight for those in need. It helped me to bring great awareness to a growing social issue in our country and share the painful story behind the people walking around without a home, without hope.

At the end of the day, we're all just trying to live in this big world we call home. Some of us have more than others, because we worked for it, and some have it or lack it just because of the country or circumstances they were born into.

But we all deserve to be treated with dignity, respect, and love. Everyone deserves a home to live in, food to eat, and clothes to wear, regardless of their material circumstances, culture, or background. These are basic human necessities and rights. God loves every one of us equally and is the only one who knows our hearts, our journeys, our stories. He's the only one who knows the choices we've made and why. He's the only one who has the right to judge.

And yet through His incredible grace, even He doesn't judge, because He sent His Son Jesus to die for our sins and set us right with Him. As John 3:16 tells us, *"For God so loved the world that he gave his one and only Son, that whoever believes in him shall not perish but have eternal life."* That's how much He loves us, and He asks us to love each other the same way: as we would ourselves. If we deserve forgiveness, so does everyone else.

While we were back with my mom, Dave had to drop out of high school and find a job. As he explains:

In Grade Ten, one of my friends, Pete, moved with his parents to Gillette, Wyoming. I was trying to make a living on my own because I had dropped out of school. Pete, who was eighteen and older than me, told me that they paid more money in Wyoming if you could get into the oilfields. So right after my sixteenth birthday I decided to hitchhike to Wyoming to look for a job.

I had been staying with a friend named Rob. I had a bag of pot, a little bit of money, and a change of clothes. Before I left, Rob actually pinched some of my pot, which really pissed me off. I had almost nothing, and now someone was stealing my stuff? I trashed his house a bit before I left.

So I left Port Charlotte and hitchhiked to Wyoming. The whole trip only took me three days.

In the first car, I got picked up by a couple of sketchy guys, one who was a hitchhiker. They were both over eighteen. There weren't a lot of kids my age hitchhiking.

So we were smoking pot and all decided to share a joint from our stash. Well, the one dude pinched my bag while he was rolling from it. There was nothing I could do about it because they owned the car and were older. They were pretty rough-looking dudes. I probably was rough for my age, too.

When the car overheated, we had to stop. The driver took the plates off the car, threw them in the woods, and then we were all hitchhiking. I don't know why they took the plates off the car. Maybe because they didn't want anyone to see the car or maybe they'd stolen it. Who knows?

Gillette was more than two thousand miles away and I slept when I felt safe. There were a few situations where I didn't feel safe, and a few situations where other guys were trying to come on to me, which was kind of creepy. Thankfully, nothing bad ever happened. I wasn't going to go down without a fight.

I just took the rides wherever they came from. It wasn't the way I had planned on going, but I ended up in Milwaukee. I was almost a thousand miles away from Gillette, at a truck stop, when I noticed a cowboy-looking dude. Typical Wyoming kind of guy. He had pointy boots, hair down to his shoulders, and a cowboy hat. I walked up to him and asked if he was coming from Wyoming or going back that way and he told me he was going to Gillette. So then I got a ride right to my friend's door, which was definitely a God thing.

When I got to Gillette, I moved in with Pete. He and I were living with his mom and stepfather, who was a real long-haired redneck. Pete had a certain amount of fear of his stepfather. I don't know what had happened there, but he was pretty afraid of him.

We were still doing drugs together. We tried pretty much everything. I could go on and on about what we took and how much we took.

One day, we had this bag of pills called crosstops or whiteys, a form of speed. Pete's mom was doing the laundry and we were sleeping. While cleaning out the pockets of his pants, she found the pills and started freaking out—not yelling, but totally out of control.

"Let's get out of here," Pete said. "My dad's gonna wake up."

He was obviously afraid that he was going to get his butt kicked.

That's when we moved out of Pete's house. We moved into a trailer with a couple of guys he knew from work. There were about five of us there.

I only spent the summer in Gillette that first trip. Afterward I hitchhiked back to Florida and it only took me two and a half days. I tried to keep myself clean-looking so people would give me rides.

13.

A LIFE-CHANGING TRIP

Grace allows you to remain whole when evil tries to break you.

AS MY MOM SPIRALLED INTO DEPRESSION, MY SIBLINGS AND I WERE SPIRALLING into drugs and alcohol. During the summer before Grade Seven, I started getting involved with the wrong friends. I met some people over the summer who were older than me, and they were into drugs and alcohol. Sarah was three or four years older than me and had much more worldly experience. From her, I learned how to smoke cigarettes and get high. We hung out at a local arcade.

In August, Sarah came to me one day and said she was going to a Peter Frampton concert. She had an extra ticket because her other friend had cancelled and she wanted to know if I wanted to go. The only problem was that we didn't have a ride to get there, and it was in Tampa, ninety miles to the north.

"How are we going to get there?" I asked.

"Well, we'll just hitchhike. Lots of people are going to the concert."

So there I was, eleven years old, making a major decision that could change my life. Should I go? I was terrified of hitchhiking, but she was older and I should be safe, right? I didn't have anything to go home to, since my mom was comatose on the couch most of the time.

I thought about it and finally said, "Okay, let's do it." I told my mom I was sleeping at Sarah's house, and then off we went to the concert. I was really terrified but didn't want her to know.

We were so lucky. For our first ride, a semitruck driver took us to Arcadia, which was almost halfway. He lectured us on the dangers of hitchhiking, especially for women. He seemed to care and made me feel safe.

But then we had to get out and look for the next ride. This vehicle happened to be coming from Englewood, which was close to where we lived, and they were going to the concert, too, and even offered us a ride home after. They happened to know my older brother, so it felt safe. How lucky was that? We could have been picked up by anybody. We could have had so many horrible things happen to us on that journey, but by the grace of God we ended up at the concert safe and with someone who knew us.

It started raining when we arrived, but luckily we had an umbrella. Nobody else seemed to have an umbrella, but for some reason we did. What we didn't have were drugs, which is essential if you're going to enjoy a rock concert. So we traded the umbrella for some drugs. We didn't know what kind of drugs they were; we just thought they were a couple of joints. We smoked those joints and felt the biggest high either of us had ever experienced. Both of us were blown away by the strength of the pot.

We went up the stairs to watch the concert and worked our way to our seats. While sitting there in that great big stadium of people I didn't know, I felt exhilarated and scared all at the same time. It was kind of cool for someone so young to experience a concert like this. But I was so far from home, so naïve and young. I really shouldn't have been there, and I was stoned out of my face which can really make a person vulnerable.

I happened to look around and, lo and behold, in the next section over was my sister Cindy with her boyfriend—which is unbelievable, really. We seemed to catch each other's eyes and as we looked at each other, I thought, *What is she doing here?* She must have been thinking that her sister was way too young to be at this concert. Cindy, at thirteen, thought she was old enough to be there.

So we ended up walking over to each other and I told her I had hitchhiked with Sarah. Cindy thought this was ridiculous and she was very, very angry with me. She wanted me to go home with her, but they had no room to fit me in their vehicle.

I don't really remember a lot of the concert. I remember knowing some songs and enjoying them. We were pretty sure the joints we'd smoked had been laced with something; there must have been some speed or something else in them because Sarah and I walked around quite a bit at that concert. We had so much energy.

After the concert, we ended up going back to a hotel room to stay overnight with the people who had driven us.

At some point Sarah decided to go for a walk and said she'd be right back, leaving me in the room all by myself. She was gone a long time. Having no idea where Sarah was and starting to become afraid, I decided to go look for her. I had no idea where I was, and it was a big hotel with many floors. It might have been eight stories, but to me it was a huge place.

I walked around calling Sarah's name, going by the pool area and saying her name. The longer I walked around, the more scared I became. I didn't know if she'd left me there. I didn't know if somebody had taken her or done something with her. These are the sorts of things that go through a child's mind. You're scared and you don't know anyone.

As I was walking by one of the rooms, some guy grabbed me and said, "Oh, Sarah's in here." And with that, he pulled me inside. There were tons of people in there and they were all partying, drinking, smoking, and in various stages of undress.

The next thing I know, I'm underneath him and he's attacking me. I started screaming, but he covered my mouth with his. I really didn't know what was going on, but suddenly I felt a horrible pain and I heard him scream, "She's a virgin!"

I was terrified, scared, hurt, and in pain.

When he was finally finished, I got up but couldn't find my pink bellbottoms. It should have been easy because of the colour, but I couldn't see it anywhere. I wanted to get out of there, having no idea what had just happened. People were laughing and thought it was funny. I didn't even know who they were.

Unable to find my pants, I just left and ran back to my room, which took me a while to find because I was so lost and upset. I huddled in a chair, crying, bloodied, and scared, until Sarah came back.

By now it was six o'clock in the morning, but it felt like a lifetime. I just remember rocking myself back and forth on the chair, wondering if anyone was going to come back to the room, wondering if I was going to make it home. All I was wearing was a T-shirt and my bathing suit bottoms.[12]

Sarah asked how my night had gone. She'd apparently been out with some guy all night long. I was crying, in pain, and in tears. When I told her what had happened, she asked me if I'd had my period yet. My answer was no.

"Then you have nothing to worry about," she said. Apparently I couldn't get pregnant if I didn't have my period.

What? I was mortified. I didn't even know how getting pregnant happened… but now I did. She didn't even seem concerned or upset. It was as if this type of thing happened every day. Inside I was dying.

Talk about trauma! On top of that, I didn't know how I was going to go home without any pants. So we started looking around to see if we could find the

---

[12] Remember, I had no underwear, just my bathing suit. In this case, having on a bathing suit bottom was a good thing.

room I had been in. When I found it, I hid while she knocked on the door asked for my pants. Of course they couldn't find them. In hindsight, I think it became a sick kind of trophy for the guy who had taken my virginity.

As we were leaving the hotel to go home, we happened to look up the side of the building at the balconies and saw some jeans hanging over the railing in front of somebody else's room. We both looked at each other and seemed to come to the same conclusion: if we ran by, we could swipe the jeans and I could wear them home.

They turned out to be way too big for me, but that didn't matter. At least I was covered up.

Sarah didn't have any sympathy for my situation. I guess to her it was no big deal, but for me it totally changed my life. What innocence I might have had left was gone and I was traumatized. Nobody talked to me about what had happened, and I couldn't tell anybody because I'd been somewhere I wasn't supposed to be.

I was so sore for the next three days, but I didn't know how to tell my mom. In fact, my mom hadn't even missed me. She was sitting comatose on the couch most days, rocking back and forth. She prayed a lot and occasionally drank wine. She also smoked cigarettes and had coffee all day long. That's basically all she did.

I didn't know what to do. Now I had no clothes, because those had been the only pair of pants I had. Gone were my pink bellbottoms. Thankfully, my friend Sarah ended up giving me a pair of hers.

For months afterward, the naïve young girl in me wondered if that man who'd stolen my virginity was a "special person" who'd been sent to me and who would marry me. That was what happened in the movies, right? He was my knight in shining armour and was going to take me away from poverty, homelessness, and a broken home.

I was so naïve, so innocent... so sad. I had been raped by a complete stranger in the middle of a sick orgy after a rock concert and all the while I put on a brave face. But on the inside I was dying.

14.

HOMELESS BEFORE HOUSELESS

Grace comes through our actions and interventions.

CANADIAN AUTHOR TIM HUFF, WHO SPECIALIZES IN HOMELESSNESS, HAS SAID that many people are homeless before they are houseless. And at the age of twelve, I can honestly say that this was true. I had a house to go home to, but it wasn't a home. I had no supports, no one to tell me to brush my teeth, shower, and get ready for bed. I was basically on my own, living in a house with my siblings who were all going in different directions, each trying to survive on their own, with a schizophrenic mother who was unpredictable at best.

So I stopped going home and started sleeping in the woods with my brothers and couch-surfing with friends. I was looking for someone who would comfort me and help me through this thing called life.

The summer between Grade Six and Grade Seven was a transition on so many different levels. I went from innocent sixth grader to losing my innocence, smoking cigarettes and weed, drinking booze, and partying all the time with my new set of friends.

I did end up getting my period not long after the concert experience. When I told my mom, she asked me if I wanted pads or tampons. I asked her what the difference was and she explained. I figured after my experience with that guy that tampons wouldn't be a problem.

A lot of "firsts" were happening to me but there was absolutely nothing special about them. I had no idea what was going on and I honestly didn't care. When I think back, I was just numb.

It grieves me to think back upon my childhood and see a young girl so violated and hurt. It truly numbed me from my emotions. I tried not to think, not to feel, because it hurt too much. I also think of my own children and how precious they are to me. Parents should be there to keep their children safe and help them through life, whether it's a first boyfriend or girlfriend, their period, or transitioning into junior high or high school. I had no one, and my innocence was taken from me.

We need to do more to help our children who are struggling in poverty. Many of them are in foster care or live in single families whose parents are working hard to survive, like my mom did. Intervention can make a difference. The more often we let bad things happen, the more kids will think that it's normal, when it's not.

If someone is struggling with family issues, we need to look deeper. They need help, and the signs are easy to see. Certain behaviours start to develop, like disengagement from learning, acting out, hyperactivity, and depression. This is where our educators play a pivotal role. They have the ability to discern how a child is adapting and whether they come from a healthy environment. Many educators are very sensitive to this and we need to empower them to help these precious children and spend extra time with them. We need to make sure there are supports and programs in place to help our children succeed, like free breakfast programs and extracurricular activities.

Years later, as I was raising my children, I had the privilege of working as an educational assistant, and I worked with that subset: kids in care or those coming from single families, helping them achieve their goals.

While Grades Four to Seven in my life were a blur, God gave me these years back through my own kids. Through His grace, I ended up helping a class and some special needs children in this age group and got to re-experience those years. Their success was my success. Their joy was my joy. I didn't realize until much later that God had given me those years and those kids for a purpose. It was, in a way, about helping myself.

This reminds me of God's promise in Joel 2:25:

I will repay you for the years the locusts have eaten—the great locust and the young locust, the other locusts and the locust swarm—my great army that I sent among you. You will have plenty to eat, until you are full, and you will praise the name of the Lord your God, who has worked wonders for you; never again will my people be shamed.

We need to do more for, and be more intentional with, our youth. If they succeed, society succeeds. We also need to encourage our kids to help the other kids in their classrooms. That student with a chip on their shoulder needs a friend and unconditional love. They don't need to be bullied, made fun of, or ostracized. They need friends and encouragement, a safe place to share their feelings and situations.

We need to support anti-bullying campaigns. It pains me when I hear of children who commit suicide because of being bullied in school. It needs to stop! Parents, if someone accuses your child of bullying, pay attention and do something about it. As parents, we want to think that our child wouldn't do such a thing, but kids are kids... and unless we take it seriously and confront it, they'll just continue in their behaviours.

It all boils back down to loving your neighbour and caring about those around you, and then teaching the children in our lives to do the same.

15.

HELP ME, SANDRA

Grace allows you to get past the pain.

I HAVE TO DISCLOSE AT THIS POINT THAT MANY OF THE TIMES, DATES, AND seasons I write about may not be accurate. When you're experiencing trauma, going through homelessness, you lose all concept of time and it comes to really have no meaning. The goal is survival.

I had another friend named Sandra who was a bit older and also liked to "play around." I was still very innocent, but I wanted to have friends, and Sandra and Sarah were all I had. Sandra had a friend nicknamed Sloppy Joe, who used to hang out at the arcade. He drove a big truck with a T-bar… and he was a coke dealer.[13] Soon we tried that as well. It was a crazy time and I just followed the people I hung out with and did what they did. Sandra and Sarah tried to set me up with guys several times, but I was frigid and frightened. As much as I wanted to be loved, I wanted nothing to do with guys after the sexual experiences I'd had.

Sandra lived in El Jobean, and we had to walk and hitchhike a long way to get to her house. But I slept at her house many times.

I remember getting really stoned one night and passing out. Suddenly, I woke up to find her brother Bradley on top of me, ramming into me with the sickest grin on his face. I tried to scream, but he covered my mouth with his hand. This was my second experience with a man—again, not one of my choosing. I couldn't believe he was raping me in his own house with his sleeping family not far away. He thought it was funny, but I was horrified and had no idea what to do. I was crying, yet again feeling mortified.

Now that I had my period, I could get pregnant. When I told Sandra what had happened, she replied, "Oh, you don't have to worry. Just douche."

---

[13] Not the soft drink… the drug. I was no longer innocent when it came to drugs.

Just what? I didn't even know what a douche was. There was no sympathy, no caring, no kind words, and not even any shock that her brother would do such a thing. I was sick with guilt, remorse, and betrayal. Every time I saw him after that, he would give me this knowing grin that made me want to vomit. It was a rude awakening into the seedy world of sex. I was suddenly twelve going on thirty.

It's still hard for me to believe that this type of stuff happens every day. According to RAINN (the Rape, Abuse, and Incest National Network), the nation's largest anti-sexual violence organization in the United States, every seventy-three seconds another American is sexually assaulted.[14] For some people this would be shocking, and for others it's just the way life is. Unfortunately, for me it was just the way life was.

But it should be shocking to everyone. This isn't how life is supposed to be. If this book does anything, it should bring attention to the fact that so many children suffer in these types of environments today. Children reach out to the adults in their lives but get abused and taken advantage of by people who know how to prey on the vulnerable.

We need to open our eyes and put a stop to it—the sex trade that preys on young victims, the drug trade, the gangs, and the violence. Just because it isn't a part of your life doesn't mean it's not out there for someone else. They need our help. They need your help. We need to open our eyes and ears to the world around us and not be afraid to be a part of the solution. We need to stand up for our children.

It's sad that at this early stage of my life, my only experiences with men were with my abusive father or men who forced themselves on me. It certainly took away all my innocence. In all honesty, I don't remember being a child… I felt like I was much older. You grow up fast when this is your life.

Unfortunately, it was all I knew. I had nothing else to compare it to.

I feel great sympathy for people, especially youth, living in poverty and homelessness. When a person's focus is on survival, it's impossible to dream and think there could be more. You just hope to get through the day. You don't realize that there's a greater world out there and that God has big plans for everyone, not just the rich and privileged.

We need to be intentional about sharing with people the fact that God has a plan and it's above and beyond anything we could imagine—for everyone. That is God's grace and love for us.

---

[14] "Scope of the Problem: Statistics," *RAINN*. Date of access: March 27, 2021 (https://www.rainn.org/statistics/scope-problem).

16.

WHO REMEMBERS GRADE SEVEN?

Grace comes through education and the church.

SANDRA AND I WERE STILL FRIENDS, DESPITE WHAT HAD HAPPENED WITH HER brother. I had no one else.

For my first day of Grade Seven, we arranged to meet down the street from Port Charlotte Junior High. She was going to help me learn my way around.

When we met at the bridge over a small canal just down the street from the school, we started talking. Neither of us really wanted to go to school, so about five minutes before the bell rang we walked away. We booked it down the road fairly quickly.

Just as we rounded a corner where we knew we'd be safe, we encountered a guy in a car. His name was Sam Spade. I had no idea what was going on, but Sandra was in Grade Nine and totally aware.

"Oh damn, there's Sam," she said. "Just act dumb."

That was easy for me.

Sam rolled down his window. "Hi Sandra. Who's your new friend?"

"This is my friend Judy," she said.

"I bet you didn't know that the school bell rang five minutes ago?"

In her sweetest voice, Sandra responded, "Oh my goodness, I had no idea! We better go, Judy. Bye, Sam. Thanks for letting us know."

We turned, pretending that we were heading back to the school.

"Well, ladies, today is your lucky day," Sam said. "I'm just heading over there. Get in and I'll give you a ride."

So of course we had no choice. That's how my first day of Grade Seven started, with an escort by the truant officer.[15] Port Charlotte had a curfew of

---

[15] A truant officer is someone who looks for kids skipping school and brings them back.

10:00 p.m., so truant officers also looked for kids who stayed out past curfew. There was no reason kids needed to be out that late in a small town of elderly and retired people.

But I learned quickly what kind of car Sam drove, what he looked like, and how to avoid him going forward.

To be honest, most of Grade Seven is a blur and I have very few memories of it, probably because I didn't spend a lot of time at school—and because of the drugs. I rarely knew what class I was supposed to be in or where it was.

I remember two incidents in particular. One was my first day of art class. The teacher's name was Mr. Wiley, and when he called out my name during roll call I answered "Here." He immediately jumped out of his chair and stared down the classroom until he found me at the back of the room.

"Damn, girl, are you another Needham?" he said. "How many of you are there?"

"Eight, sir. There's one more, my little brother Duane."

"What the heck, did your mom have a kid every year? I've had Needhams in my class every year for the past eight years."

"Actually, sir, she missed a year. My mom had eight kids in nine years."

"Well, I'll be damned. That's even more than us black folks. Welcome to my class, Miss Needham. You have a nice family."

While I was extremely embarrassed for being drawn out in class and getting so much attention, it was nice to know that at least one person liked our family. Of course, all of us liked art, so most of us behaved in his class. It's my understanding that this wasn't necessarily the case for the rest of the classes!

It's important to note that when you see children go from being good citizens, athletes, and straight A students to suddenly being disruptive, missing school, and acting out, there could be something wrong. Instead of judging their behaviour as bad or inappropriate, you should try to look a little deeper to see why things have changed so rapidly. We tend to just say, "Oh well, they're turning into bad children." But that hasn't been my experience. I believe that kids start making bad choices when there's no one in their lives to encourage them to make positive choices. They need help on the journey and it's our job as adults to be an influence. Even if we aren't their parents, we have a role to play in shaping the lives of the youth who come into our social circle. We cannot be afraid to rear a child in the way they should go. It's our job as adults.

We had nothing to go home to. Someone should have noticed that.

The other incident I remember took place in health class. While I was a straight A student in Grade Six, this year was much different. Going home to no electricity and no running water was beginning to take its toll on me and my siblings and I got really tired in school. Health class was also boring.

However, I'll never forget the teacher who taught us CPR. One day in class I asked to go to the washroom. The truth was that I needed a smoke break and had planned to meet Sandra in the can to share a cigarette. But when I got there, Sandra wasn't around, so I went into the can and lit up, waiting for her to come in. Finally, I heard her come in and go into the next stall. I passed her the smoke only to find out it was my health teacher.

Crap, I was busted!

Busted meant school suspension, and the principal wanted to have a chat with my mom. Crap. At this point, my mom could still put on a good face, so she picked me up, asked what had happened, and took me home. She was upset, but after eight kids this was probably a minor issue compared to some of the other reasons she'd gotten called, like when my brothers got into fights. They loved to fight. Or perhaps they'd been bullied and needed to defend themselves. It's hard to say.

As soon as we got home, my mom began to dwell on her thoughts, which took her right into another world where I didn't exist anymore. So rather than punishment, I got three days off school. I thought it quite funny that I'd been in health class when I got busted for smoking. When I shared this story with my brothers, we all had a good chuckle.

Those were the two big school memories. I honestly don't remember anything else of Grade Seven other than that my grades went from straight A's to C's, D's, and F's. It made me sad that my grades were falling, but there wasn't a thing I could do about it.

As Duane remembers:

By nine years old, I smoked marijuana, ate mushrooms and had hallucinations, took pills, and drank alcohol. I smoked cigarettes regularly. I was addicted. I took whatever the older kids gave me. I overdosed twice and had my stomach pumped.

I was also in many bad fights. One time I punched and kicked a young boy as kids cheered and egged me on until blood came out of his mouth and they had to call an ambulance. This bothered me for years.

I stole a lot of food, cigarettes, alcohol, and candy, of course. For a couple of years, I remember coming home to no electricity and found my mom sitting at home alone in the dark. She once asked me to go to the neighbour's house and borrow a candle.

There was no food in the house. If I was lucky, there might be something floating in the cooler, waterlogged and disgusting.

I remember staying at friends' homes for weeks at a time, and sometimes even longer. On one occasion I remember coming home and Mom said she was glad I was okay. I told her I had been at my friend Jimmy's house because they had food and electricity. She told me that was good. Since we didn't have any, it was okay for me to go back.

I remember going next door to Mrs. White's house with cereal in my bowl and asking her if I could borrow some milk, as if I was really going to pay her back. Sometimes she would fill my bowl with milk. But eventually we wore out our welcome. She was very old.

One time I came home and saw my brother Doug, who had overdosed. He looked dead. His eyes were wide open and he wasn't moving. They rushed him to the emergency room.

For about two to three years, it seemed like all my siblings were coming and going. We were never all together. As I look back, it seems like everyone was in survival mode.

I was kicked out of two elementary schools for bad behaviour. I got spanked by the principal many times with a wooden paddle, and then I was permitted back. I went to school without shoes many times. When I did have shoes, they were hand-me-downs from my brother and usually stank because none of us had socks.

One time the owners of the arcade invited me to sleep over at their home because they felt sorry for me.

I decided to go to sleep with my shoes on because I knew if I took my shoes off they would stink. I told them that I always slept with my shoes on, but the parents insisted I take them off. So when they finally left me alone, I did.

Within five minutes, I heard the man say, "What the heck is that horrible smell?" When they realized it was my feet, they very discreetly invited me to the dining room for ice cream—it was 2:00 in the morning—and then the daughters said they wanted to wash my beautiful long blond hair and blow-dry it. They begged me to let them do it.

That was how they got me to take a bath. I hadn't had one in weeks.

The next morning, I woke up to find two new changes of clothes, brand-new socks and shoes, and a very cool skateboard lying on my bed.

Looking back, I realized that they treated me with dignity and respect. They never mentioned my smelly feet or made me feel bad. It was very humbling.

Connie was in Grade Ten at the time:

One afternoon my friend Rachelle, who I was living with, got mad at me and kicked me out of her house, so I started couch-surfing. Another friend, Rob, was getting a divorce, so he let me stay with him as long as I took care of his child during the day.

I was supposed to be in the tenth grade, but I quit going to school because I had to take care of Rob's daughter in order to have a place to live—that is, until the truant officer arrived at Rob's house one day. He found out where I lived, knocked on the door, and told me that if I didn't start going to school again, my mom would be arrested since she was still legally responsible for me.

So then I had to go back to school. I tried to go a day or two per week, just enough to get by. I remember not knowing where my classes were. We had no books. We had no schedules. We had no pencils. I don't know how we were supposed to do schoolwork.

I was attending Punta Gorda High School and don't even remember how I got there, whether I took a bus or found rides. That's probably why I didn't go, because I didn't have anyone to take me.

God's grace allows us to forget some things, especially hardship. I was in survival mode, living one day at a time, living on my own, doing whatever I had to do to get by. And that was Grade Ten.

I remember a teacher once telling me, "Connie, you are a B+ student. If you just did your homework, you could be an A+ student." But that was too much to even think about. We didn't have the tools. I was happy with a B. I was happy just to get by, because it was too much work to try to figure out how to improve at school.

But I did know enough that I needed to get my GED, and I did that at sixteen.

That's also God's grace. Everyone in the family ended up getting their high school diploma and post-secondary education despite our beginnings. It wasn't like we had a dream about what we wanted to do, or a passion to fuel our desire to do it. Our education was inspired by survival, and it was God's grace that helped us achieve it.

My brother Duane recalls what happened one day when a lady came to deliver a food hamper during this period:

There was nothing at home to go to. Our electricity had gotten shut off because we couldn't pay the bills, and eventually our water got shut off, too. We had very few clothes. My mom would purchase food with her food stamps and put them in a cooler in the morning on ice, but by noon everything would be floating upside-down in a pool of water. In Florida's heat, usually ninety to a hundred degrees Fahrenheit, it was hard to keep anything fresh.

I remember when Saint Charles Church came and gave us a bunch of food. Someone had put our name on a hamper, and they came to drop it off. When I opened the door, which was hanging off the hinge, the lady looked like she was scared. I would've been about eight or nine years old and I had hair all the way down my back. The lady just handed me a bag of groceries.

"What's that for?" I remember saying.

"That's for you!"

"Really?"

She then went back to her car and I didn't think anything of it. I had already ripped the bag open when she came back with a turkey.

"That's for Thanksgiving," she said.

"I'm looking for food now. I'm starving."

She handed me the turkey.

"How are we going to cook that?" I asked.

"What do you mean?"

"Well, we have no electricity."

I remember that look on her face. First it was wonderment, and then she was horrified. The look said, *This poor family has nothing, not even the basic necessities.*

In that moment, I related God to compassion through this woman who represented the Catholic Church.

"You got no electricity?" she said.

"No."

Within an hour, our electricity was turned on in the house and they left it turned on for November and December. The Catholic Church came back in December and gave us another turkey dinner and groceries for Christmas.

That was a huge moment for me, relating God to something good for the first time. My only other experience of God was from when we used to go to catechism and the nuns beat me. I'd known that wasn't right. They would beat my hands until they were bloody. I remember leaving catechism one afternoon after the nun had beat my hands with a wooden ruler. The nun would slap me with the ruler, and slap hard. One time she turned it sideways and smacked it really hard across my hands, which hurt so much that I went home saying, "God, I'm sorry. I don't want to go to heaven if there are people like that in heaven. I just don't want to go." And that was my conviction.

But having people feed us when we were hungry gave me a glimpse of hope that God was good, that there was hope.

During this time, my mom just sat on the couch. When coming home, we didn't know whether Dr. Jekyll or Mr. Hyde would be there.

Cindy remembers being terrified of Mom. She always got it the worst:

When we were living on Calvin Lane with no electricity and food, my mom wasn't well. However, I didn't know at the time that she had a mental disorder, because I was only eleven. She was schizophrenic and not taking her medication because she couldn't afford to.

She couldn't care for us children or herself. As young children, we were confused about our home and family situation, to say the least. We didn't understand our mother. No one had ever explained to us her condition. No one ever sat us down and explained or comforted us through it.

To me, she was cruel, kind of vicious, and unsympathetic, and she loved to pick on me in particular. She would hurt me intentionally over and over again for no sound reason. I thought she hated me. That's all I understood: I was never good enough.

She was verbally abusive and would scream right into my face: "I hate you. You are so ugly. You are useless." She'd continue ranting at me with an evil look on her face until she made me cry. Then she would laugh and say, "Poor Cindy. Oh, look at poor Cindy crying. Boohoo. Poor Cindy. Let's have a pity party for Cindy. Boohoo." I would try really hard not to cry, and I rarely did, but her enjoyment of my tears was more hurtful than the taunts.

Imagine your mother trying to hurt you like that.

I was so scared of her that I would run to my friend's house a few blocks away and hide under her bed. This happened at least two times to my recollection. My mom would then phone the police and they would come to my friend's house, march into the bedroom, and tell me to come out from under the bed.

Of course, I was too scared to come out. They would finally have to grab my legs and pull me. I'd have to get into the police car for the ride home—and when we got there, I'd be scared to death.

As Connie recalls:

I recall how badly my mom treated Cindy, and I remember the summer we lived on Calvin. I was in a work program for needy kids and had a part-time job at the library. I would give what I earned to my mom, except she let me keep $20, which was enough to get a good-sized bag of pot.

Cindy was stuck for the summer taking care of the house and the younger kids by herself. She would work so hard cleaning, cooking (if there was anything to cook), and watching after the younger kids. She would try to be so sweet to Mom and she never talked back. But Mom seemed to take all her frustrations and anger out on her. I would try to help by talking to Mom, but you cannot reason with someone who is mentally ill. It was painful and we didn't understand it at the time.

Everything started making sense when we realized how sick she had been when we were growing up. We found out later that she'd had a mental breakdown when Cindy was born and spent six months in a mental institution. My Uncle Billy had come from Pennsylvania to take care of her and the rest of the kids. Maybe she never bonded as much with Cindy because of it? Or blamed her? We will never know.

My mom's mental health was deteriorating rapidly. At times she was scary and would scream at the top of her lungs. Other times she had the most beautiful smile that could light up a room. The anger and depression were taking over more and more, though, the despair becoming apparent. She was an undiagnosed paranoid schizophrenic, trying to care for eight kids without a job. She certainly couldn't be faulted. This was her normal.

She read her Bible faithfully and always prayed for us. I truly believe this is the only thing that saved us. I believe that the power of a praying, desperate mother in her darkest hour is an S.O.S. that causes all of heaven to stop, listen, and take action. For all intents and purposes, considering the things that happened to us, we should all be dead.

Prayer is so important. It's something we can all do, and we should make a point of praying daily for each other, our families, our neighbours, our leaders, our politicians, our cities, our country, and our world. It's a gift we can give that doesn't cost a penny, yet it moves mountains and transforms the world.

17.

A WOLF IN SHEEP'S CLOTHING

Grace comes in the form of a wake-up call.

BECAUSE OF OUR HOME SITUATION, MOST OF THE TIME MY BROTHERS AND I GOT wasted and slept in the woods, or we couch-surfed with friends.

We met a brother and sister duo, Bobby and Lisa, in junior high. My brother already knew Bobby from the previous year, but I met Lisa at the beginning of Grade Seven. We hit it off right away. She was really pretty with long blonde hair and she smoked pot, which was right in our wheelhouse.

So often we hung out at her place, and I had a secret crush on her brother. Her stepdad also happened to be one of the biggest drug-dealers in town. We thought this was really cool because he could get any kind of drugs we could imagine in pound-sized bags. Whenever a new shipment came, we would sit around and test the drug. We tried everything from Colombian gold, Hawaiian gold, Mexican gold, Thai stick, and hash. Then we slowly upgraded to cocaine, Quaaludes, uppers, and downers. You name it, we tried it.[16] But I drew the line with anything you had to inject into your veins. Through God's grace and discernment, I knew that shooting substances into your veins couldn't be good.

One day I stood in the kitchen in Lisa's house as she made a grilled cheese sandwich with the fancy, spreadable butter and cheese! My mouth watered as she made it. I don't think she realized how hungry I was, but to this day I can feel the punch of hunger in my gut just thinking about it. It's this deep, queasy feeling that controls your thoughts. No wonder we didn't do well in school. All we could focus on was our hunger.

---

[16] We didn't have street names for the drugs back them. We called them by what they were.

We had been taught not to ask for food… that we had to be offered it. So I would watch her eat and just about die from hunger. Every once in a while she would offer me something and my stomach would do gleeful somersaults.

I spent more and more time at her home, and eventually they caught on to my need. They saw that I wore the same clothes, had no shoes, and rarely showered. I can't imagine what we looked like as our bare feet must have been filthy. Once they discovered how poor we were, they offered to buy us some clothes and allowed us to stay with them. We were thrilled. Their mother Janet was super nice and always very compassionate.

But the father, Barny, wanted an exchange for his generosity and the next thing we knew we became drug mules. It was really quite simple. Once a new shipment came in, he would let us try it for free. Then we would package it up into ounce-sized baggies and each of us would get six or seven bags to sell. If we wanted to skim some off the top of each bag to have our own stash, that was up to us.

We became dealers in the school. I'd carry two ounces in each sock, which was nicely covered by my new bellbottoms, as well as two in my new underwear against my belly. I could roll one bag into thirty joints and sell it that way, too.

As long as we got Barny the money, we had clothes, food, and drugs. With the extra money, we also had alcohol. Drugs and alcohol allowed us to escape our problems—and believe me, we knew we had problems. We saw how other people lived. We saw their nice stuff, nice clothes, and fresh food. We saw all the families who cooked real dinners and ate together.

Meanwhile, we had *nothing*. We "borrowed" food from the neighbours and drove their bikes to get food with food stamps. We chased the milk truck to steal milk. The worst thing was going home high with the munchies and all we'd find was flour and water. No food.

So selling drugs was a small price to pay for having what everyone else had. And the high allowed us to forget.

This allows me to be empathetic and understand the plight of the homeless, and see why there's such a high level of addiction in this sector. Going through trauma makes you feel so unloved and separated from real community. You'll do anything not to feel the pain of abandonment, loneliness, and lack of hope. The world is a beautiful place, but only if you're a part of it. It can get ugly and desolate to live on the outskirts, marginalized and vulnerable, watching others enjoy what you cannot.

Around this time, I started dating Bobby. He and I hit it off right away and he was my first real love. We went everywhere together, laughed together, and partied together. He was the only person I "allowed" to make love to me. Although we were young and reckless, to us it was love, and we felt very strongly for each other.

Sex, drugs, and rock and roll could be fine in safe environments, but unbeknownst to us Barny was also a pedophile. He would get everyone so high that for the longest time we didn't know. We just partied hard. Lisa was a good drinker and could easily guzzle a twenty-six-ounce bottle of Jack Daniels or Seagram's 7. Although we didn't realize it at the time, she was a teenage alcoholic.

We would all get wasted and then the girls would crash in Lisa's room. Barny would also get his wife so wasted that she would pass out. Sometimes she wouldn't wake up for days.

Although we didn't think anything of it in the beginning, strangely she would wake up with bruises and never know where they came from. We weren't allowed to go into her room at all. In retrospect, I think Barny was abusing her. It wouldn't surprise me. We were just too naïve to know.

Many times the girls would wake up, and if they were on their period they'd say, "I had a tampon in last night, and I woke up this morning without one. That's strange." Or they'd go to bed in shorts and wake up in just their underwear or topless or bottomless without explanation.

One night, everyone passed out but me. Bobby and I had gotten into a fight that evening and I couldn't sleep.

While lying on the floor mulling things over, I heard the door open. I pretended to be asleep, hoping it was Bobby. Unfortunately that's when I saw Barny sneak into the room, go to the side of the bed and start fondling one of the girls.

Suddenly, everything clicked and I understood all those nights of wondering what was going on while we were sleeping: Barny was groping us in our sleep. This was a divine awakening from the Holy Spirit.

Although I was frightened, I managed to yell in my meanest voice, "Barny, get the f— out of here!" When he heard me, he immediately snuck back out of the room.

I decided to start sleeping in Bobby's room so I could be safe from Barny. And when we realized what was happening, we told Janet, Lisa's mom. Unfortunately, she didn't believe us. Love is blind.

So my sleeping options were: (1) stay home without electricity and running water, with a mother who was completely out of it, (2) sleep in the woods with snakes, alligators, and black panthers, or (2) stay at my friend's house whose dad was a pedophile. None of them were good options, and none of them were safe.

When I look back, it's crazy to think that nowhere was safe. Even the adults in my life weren't safe.

Sadly, I'm sure this happens to a lot of kids today. There's always someone out there preying on the vulnerable. They know how to detect vulnerable people, and they know who to take advantage of. It's really heartbreaking. This is how kids get into gangs. Back then we didn't call it that, but it was the same idea. The predators can see who needs attention—love and basic necessities—and they are willing to help these people if they help them in return. That help usually comes in the form of selling drugs, sex, violence, or theft, but it gets much worse and can include scaring and sometimes even killing people. I don't think I would have survived if I'd needed to do anything like that.

At this point, due to desperation and hunger, we also learned about the "five-finger discount"—in other words, we learned how to steal. One of us would go into a store and act as a decoy, asking the clerk for help while the other would shove whatever we needed down their pants, whether it was food, cigarettes, or booze. It depended on the day.

We even started huffing gas. Barny and Janet didn't approve of this activity, so we did it in the woods where we sometimes slept.

There was a homeless guy who lived in the woods named Lance. He was a huffer, too, and had a reputation as a druggie. So we would go to the local store, steal gas, paper bags, and rags and then bring them to the woods. We'd huff together with Lance, thinking it was cool because you get high really quick with solvents, and the high gives you a buzz you wouldn't believe. It took away our problems.

So huffing with Lance became another part-time activity—that is, until one day we went out into the woods and found Lance dead. He had literally huffed himself to death.

I sheltered Duane from what I'd seen and wouldn't let him see Lance's body. It's a horrifying way to find someone dead, and an equally horrifying way to die. It will stick in my mind forever. His body was emaciated from lack of food.

At twelve years old, this was once again a hugely traumatic experience for me. I was scared most of the time, although I always put up a brave front. When you're homeless and female, you need to have a tough edge. But this was beyond anything I'd ever thought I would experience. I was terrified to go into those woods alone again. Looking back, it makes me weep.

18.

UNDERSTANDING POVERTY AND HOMELESSNESS

Grace comes through understanding and relationship.

SEEING LANCE'S DEAD BODY WAS A TURNING POINT. I BECAME NUMB TO LIFE, emotionally dead.

I understand why people huff, and having a personal experience with it made me care later in life even more for the people who were sniffers living on the streets of Winnipeg. I understand their pain and why they do what they do. I know that they feel their life is hopeless. They need that high to escape their reality for as long as they can.

The pain of feeling unwanted, unworthy, unimportant, and unloved is terrible, so they do what they have to do to escape. It's the quickest and cheapest high a person can get, and it takes you away from your problems very quickly. The fumes go straight to the brain and deliver you into a different world.

Lance was a reminder that we were playing Russian roulette with our lives as we got deeper into drugs. Most people had known Lance, but they had been afraid of him. What's really sad is that he was an outcast and probably stayed in the woods because he was afraid of people in return.

I want to address another stigma—the belief that people who are homeless or who struggle with addictions and mental health issues are dangerous or mean. This is far from the truth. We tend to make judgments based on our perception. Most of us live in a loving, trusting world where everything is nice and sweet. People have manners and care about each other.

When you're living on the streets, the opposite is true. You're constantly judged based on your appearance. You're constantly stared at, immediately not trusted, and when you experience these things through no fault of your own you very quickly build a protective wall around your emotions. You change from being soft and vulnerable to developing hardness. You develop a tough veneer mainly because you're so hurt by the assumptions people make about you.

I became a bully because I needed to protect my feelings and force people to back off. That's not who I was, nor how I wanted to be. It was just who I had to become in order to survive.

If you walk down the street and pay attention to the people you see, especially people experiencing homelessness, notice that edge first and foremost. However, when you smile and say hello, you'll see that edge diminish. Their faces will relax and you'll see their vulnerability. If you give a genuine smile of warmth, they'll even smile back.

People experiencing homelessness expect you to judge them, so their guard is up. But when you treat them as human beings, when you treat them as people who deserve to be loved, you'll see their countenance change and the true human spirit underneath it.

If you take the time to sit down and chat with them, you'll discover stories of hurt and pain. They'll share with you who they are, and why they are, and what happened in their lives. And you'll discover all that they've endured. They should be admired for their survival, not judged by their appearance or circumstance.

If we could learn to do that with each other, and become intentional in our relationships, we would slowly tear down the walls. That's the ultimate goal for God's kingdom: for us to just be us, God's children, together in community, enjoying a quality of life on earth where we care for each other and give one another a hand up.

That's why Jesus came to this earth. He came to form a personal relationship with each of us and try to understand our pain. He came to walk amongst us and break down the walls so he could see through to our hearts. He came to teach people, not to judge, because we don't know the true heart and intentions of a person. Only He knows. We only see the outside.

Looking back, I realize that our family was lucky. We were brought up with a faith in God. The Lord was my rock and my Saviour. I prayed away all my fears every night, talking to Him.

When you're young, you're afraid of everything and fear the worst things imaginable. When you have no parents to keep you safe, it's ten times worse. Praying to Him was all I had. But it was also all I needed.

I was lucky because I had Jesus at such a young age, and the more I prayed, the more I believe He listened. I know this is why nothing permanently bad happened to me or my siblings, and why we were able to overcome everything that did happen.

19.

DRUGS ARE DANGEROUS

Grace allows you to survive.

ONE OF MY SCARIEST EXPERIENCES OF GETTING HIGH CAME WHEN BOBBY AND I decided to try to raise some money and drugs for the weekend. Barny's best friend Todd had a home, and he needed the grass mowed. He told us that if we went over there and mowed the grass, he would pay us with cash and drugs. So Bobby and I mowed the grass and cleaned up his yard, getting it all nice and neat.

Just as we finished, Todd came home. Barny happened to be coming along for the ride, and they invited us into the house.

They proceeded to form two lines of cocaine and two lines of speed for each of us—eight lines total. We snorted that, and then we smoked every drug he had in his arsenal. We shared two joints each of Thai stick, Colombian gold, and Mexican gold. I was only a twelve-year-old kid, and taking all those drugs in one setting would be a lot for anybody, never mind somebody who was less than a hundred pounds.

Once we were done taking all these drugs, we drove back to Bobby's. My head was spinning like there was no tomorrow. I was completely wasted.

When we arrived, I saw a car in the driveway and immediately thought it was the cops. I started freaking out and insisted we go straight down to the beach and come back later to see if the car was still there.

It was.

I was the only one who was out of control, and Bobby and his dad wanted to go into the house.

When we went inside, I found out that the car belonged to Cindy and her boyfriend. I have to tell you that I don't remember a lot about what happened after that other than sitting in the rocking chair listening to rock music and rocking back and forth all day and all night because of the speed and different combinations of drugs. It was a very frightening time. My face was white as a ghost and I felt nauseous off and on. I'm lucky I didn't OD.

It was another moment of Russian roulette. I was still alive. Once again, God gave me grace and saved me.

One day while out walking with Duane, Doug, Bobby, and Sandra, we came upon a guy's house. We didn't know who he was, but we had seen him around the arcade. He invited us in to smoke some weed. He had plenty and the party was on.

As we were smoking up, he suddenly excused himself to go into his bedroom. The next thing we knew, he came out stark naked carrying the Bible and a *Playboy* magazine. He proceeded to chant and read from the Bible at the top of his lungs. He read about sin while turning to the full-page spread in the magazine. We just sat there and stared at him in shock and horror.

Terrified, we then got up and ran from the house. It was very creepy.

I've seen with my own eyes that smoking and taking drugs leads to all sorts of erratic, immoral, and quite frankly unacceptable behaviour. Drugs are evil, and they bring out the worst in people. They give people an excuse to justify their immoral behaviours. Being high allows them to do things they would never do sober. I've seen violence, pedophilia, and rape. And when they do become sober, they blame the inexcusable behaviour on the drugs. It's a terrible lifestyle.

I believe this is why the world is in such a dilapidated state today. We allow toxic substances that alter our brain and behaviour to take us over. I can't believe the rest of the world doesn't see it. Now marijuana is being made legal. Obviously money and greed have become more important than morals and values.

Drugs can also lead to mental health issues. While I was in my twenties, I found out that my former boyfriend, Bobby, went on a thirty-day high of marijuana, acid, and coke and became a walking vegetable. He was seen daily walking around town unable to control his bodily functions, completely spaced out. He lived in and out of mental institutions and passed away prematurely at the age of forty-two.

Lisa married a guy who used coke and was physically abusive when high. She became a battered housewife. Sandra was never able to quit doing drugs and died in her forties.

None of this core group of friends had a happy ending in life, and my siblings share the same reports of the people they knew. Most of their friends died young as a direct result of their lifestyles.

Thankfully, I quit drugs at an early age. So this is something I try to impress on young people today, especially my kids. Don't do drugs! Don't do drugs! Don't do drugs!

20.

FUN AND GAMES FOR BREAKFAST

Grace comes through diversions and opportunity.

WE HAD TWO PLACES WE WENT TO WHEN WE FELT BORED OR WANTED TO avoid going home. The first was the arcade. Duane and I learned how to shoot pool and play foosball there. We became very good at both, but pool was our specialty—and if I'm being honest, Duane was the better player. The funny thing is that he could barely see over the table; he needed to stand on a milk crate!

We used to hustle people for money so we could eat. Guys would walk in with their professional pool cues, take them out of their case, and get ready to play. Then one of our older friends would challenge the skilled players, suggesting that either my brother or I could beat them in their craft. Of course these guys had big egos and always took the challenge.

My brother and I could easily make $20 a night just winning pool games. We never had money to ante up, though, so somebody in the room would ante up for us. We almost always walked away the victor. All the regulars would laugh as we beat the older players. It was fun, and it gave us focus. Billiards is very mathematical, the angles are interesting, and it was fun to try different shots. We got really good at banking the balls and could very easily clean the table.

Foosball was also very popular, and one time there was a tournament which people had to pay to enter. The teams won money if they came in first, second, or third. One guy, who tolerated me at best, was in a mixed doubles tournament and his partner didn't show up. I was the only female there at the time. I remember him looking over at me with a look that said, *Oh my goodness, I can't believe I'm doing this.*

He invited me to partner with him.

This was a very tall, very large man and I was a scrawny twelve-year-old, so of course I was ecstatic for the opportunity.

Well, he may have only tolerated me at first but he was proud of me when we won that tournament! I had a really quick wrist shot and was able to beat their goalkeeper several times. This man realized that, under pressure, when push came to shove, I could really play.

He gave me part of the prize. I was just happy to have been invited to play.

It's one of my proudest childhood memories. Nobody knew what had happened except me and him, but at least someone was finally proud of me!

Cindy and I also used to play foosball as a team, and we were really good! As Cindy remembers:

I got very good at foosball. Judy and I would play together all the time. I played goalie and she played forward. I was a really good goalie, and a good goalie was hard to find.

Judy and I were between the ages of nine and twelve at the time. We were short, skinny, and cute, but we would go up to the older adults usually, between the ages of seventeen and twenty-five, and ask in a southern belle voice, "Would you guys like to play a game of foosball?" We would bet for money and we always won.

We loved playing the game, and it made us laugh a lot when we completely surprised our opponents. They thought they were just being nice to a couple of kids—and they were. Those were our good times. Our opponents would compliment us and make us feel good about ourselves, which we needed. We definitely rattled a few egos.

Unfortunately, this was not a healthy place for young children to hang out and it led us down the wrong path of drugs and alcohol.

I also remember panhandling for money every day so we could eat. I'm not sure what I looked like to passersby, but I must have been a dirty child with dirty clothes who hadn't bathed in weeks. Dirty feet. Dirty nails. No shoes. Matted hair.

The ice cream parlour across from the arcade was my favourite place to eat. I would either get a hot dog or a hot fudge sundae with nuts. I also smoked, which was an expensive habit, but cigarettes were easy to steal. When I had to, I smoked cigarette butts off the ground. When you have a bad habit like smoking, you find ways to smoke. We had no pride and did whatever it took to survive.

As Duane recalls, he also got into a lot of trouble at the arcade:

I remember getting into fights. I overdosed several times, and I got punched in the stomach. I remember taking Valium. I remember taking liquid mushrooms. I remember drinking hard alcohol, Mad Dog 2020,[17] and stealing from the store.

There was a guy named Doug who had MS and used an electric wheelchair to get around. In the back of the wheelchair, he had a box to put things in. So if you went with Doug to the convenience store, you could open the box and put alcohol in it because no one was going to check Doug. He was the decoy. And we always got away with it.

At the arcade, we got into a lot of bad stuff. Smoking cigarettes, bumming cigarettes, getting older people to buy alcohol for us when we were only children… we would ask people for money, panhandling. "Got a quarter?" was a phrase we repeated numerous times a day. We didn't think anything of it. We needed to eat and this was the only way it was going to happen unless we stole.

I remember stealing cigarettes. I remember the times I OD'd on drugs. When you're young and dumb, you don't realize you're almost dying. Life is a blur and you think it's normal because people are promoting it. The adults in your life are encouraging you to take stuff and you think it must be okay. When you're eight or nine years old, even a thirty-year-old is like a god. They're supposed to be protecting you and making sure you're safe. They're supposed to know better.

I remember getting my stomach pumped several times. I think the adults allowed me to do drugs because they thought it was funny when I was out of it. So sad.

Doug recalls the arcade too:

We met all kinds of bad people, smoked lots of weed, and did lots of mushrooms. I remember one big tall Hispanic guy who was very funny. One day, he came in at ten in the morning with a whole bunch of mushrooms. I was the only one there at the time.

---

[17] MD 20/20—often called by its nickname, Mad Dog—is an American fortified wine. The MD actually stands for its producer, Mogen David. MD 20/20 has an alcohol content that varies by flavour from thirteen percent to eighteen percent. Originally, 20/20 stood for twenty ounces at twenty percent alcohol.

"Doug, look what I got, man," he said. "I got these mushrooms. I got these in the woods. If you want, I'll share them with you. You want to eat them?"

So we both ate them.

The next thing we knew, we were walking around town, talking about outer space and what's after outer space. If outer space ends, what's behind it? If there's a big wall, then there's got to be something behind the wall. We were like, "Wow, this is cool… wow wow wow."

We stopped by a convenience store for a slurpee, freaking out about our talk on space. It was ninety degree outside on a hot summer day.

But soon it started getting really dark outside and my friend said, "Wow, this must be a solar eclipse."

"Yeah, it's a solar eclipse," I said. "Holy smokes. This is freaky crazy. We were just talking about the solar system and now there is an eclipse."

So we were waiting for the eclipse to end, and suddenly we realized the sun wasn't coming back out. We looked at the time and saw that we'd walked all day until 9:30 at night. The reason it was dark was because the sun had gone down!

We laugh about these times now and try to find the humour in our situation. How lucky and blessed were we to ingest these substances and live to talk about it?

The other place we used to hang out was called the Pines, a place where people went to drag-race. People would go out into the middle of the woods, to a place where the cops couldn't find, then park their cars along the edges of the road and race. They smoked weed and brought out kegs of beer. It was a great big party in the middle of nowhere. There would be anywhere from thirty to forty cars out there.

Bobby's dad had a souped-up Charger and a GTO, so he was always racing. We'd go out to the Pines and then just walk up and down the strip talking to people in their cars and watching the races. It was a lot of fun, but I'm not sure we had any business being out there with all the partying that was going on.

Duane recalls:

I remember going in race cars at the Pines, drag-racing at 140 to 150 miles an hour. We had eight- and nine-year-olds doing it and the adults were letting them. Probably a lot of those adults took advantage of us in ways.

I remember riding a moped at nine years old. I didn't think anything of borrowing people's mopeds. I'd say, "I just need to go home for a minute." The cops never pulled me over and I didn't think anything of it. We borrowed everyone's bikes.

Doug, being a bit older, had a job to do at the Pines:

Bobby's dad, Barny, was a big drug-dealer and he used to give me ounces of Colombian to sell for $25 an ounce, and I would sell them for $30. Mexican he would give me for $20, and I would sell them for $25. But usually he got the good stuff, Colombian gold.

So I would deal drugs for him, and we'd go out to the Pines where everyone raced cars. We used to go out in his GTO and I'd hang out a pound of pot and yell, "Pot for sale! Pot for sale!" By the time we pulled up to our parking spot, we would have a whole line-up of people wanting to buy pot. We would sell a pound or two in no time. For every five ounces I sold, I got an ounce for free.

Looking back, it surprises me that these adults would allow us to go out and get that wasted. They certainly weren't good role models in life. But that was just our reality. That was just what we knew.

Meanwhile, Cindy was hooked up with her boyfriend. As she recalls:

We all stayed away from home, since my mom was incapable of showing love. But when I look back now, I realize that I was the fortunate one compared to my younger siblings. I was about twelve years old and had a steady boyfriend. He also was the victim of a very difficult upbringing and we cared deeply for each other. He always treated me so good.

Of course, we did drugs together, mostly marijuana, and we drank a lot! And he sold a lot of marijuana. At times he would have about sixty bags of pot to sell, and he always sold them. He was well respected by the other teenagers. He was "The Man," as they used to call him. He was very tough and most people were afraid of him. I always felt safe with him.

But we were still very troubled kids. This kind of lifestyle just seemed normal to us, and normal it was. It wasn't until I was much older that I came to realize there wasn't anything normal about it. I couldn't find any friends who could relate to it.

My siblings didn't realize that our life wasn't normal, and neither did I. You don't know what you don't know. I certainly didn't realize that most kids my age would've been involved in organized sports, learning how to play musical instruments, and playing games at home. We had no idea what a proper upbringing was. To this day, my upbringing helps me to relate to the people I see struggling on the streets, living the lifestyle they know and not knowing that there's so much more for them, so much better.

So this was life as I knew it. We either stayed with friends in their homes or we hung out at different places getting drunk and stoned. Our only alternative was to go home to a mother who, for the most part, was completely out of it, who most of the time didn't know if we were home and really didn't have the ability to do anything about us anyway.

21.

DAD VISITS

Grace allows laughter, even in despair.

DANNY WAS VERY HANDSOME, WELL-BUILT, AND HAD A LOT OF FRIENDS AND girlfriends whose houses he drifted between. He was a heartbreaker. He worked full-time, too, so he had money and owned a car.

His first girlfriend was his high school sweetheart, whom he loved immensely. Unfortunately, she came from an upper-class home and so they never really had a chance. Although Danny was handsome and athletic, he would never be able to take care of her to the level she was accustomed to. They dated in high school, but then she went on to college somewhere upstate.

Danny could have gone to Florida State to play football, but we didn't have the money and he didn't have the IQ to maintain his grades.

When he wasn't living with his girlfriend—or, after they broke up, with other girls—he lived in his car. All of his clothes were in the trunk and he just slept wherever he ended up parking for the night.

This isn't uncommon for people who are experiencing homelessness. If a vehicle is all you have, it's like having a home.

To be honest, we had no idea where Danny was most of the time. He just showed up once in a while to check in. We were always excited when he came by.

As for my dad, well, he only came to visit one time. I remember the day clearly, because Danny came home and organized us to be ready at a certain time. We were going to go meet him when my mom decided she wanted us to do some chores instead. She didn't want us to go out, even though she had no idea we were sneaking out to meet our dad.

Well, she turned into Mr. Hyde and started screaming at the top of her lungs to prevent us from going. I equally dug in my heels. I hadn't seen my dad in four years and I really wanted to see him. It all culminated in a great big argument where I pulled back and actually for the first and last time in my life totally disrespected her and slapped her in the face.

I can't describe the emotions I felt in that moment. I was mourning a mother who was lost to me and hopeful for a dad who could save me from a deplorable situation. I was so regretful for hurting my mother, and I will never forget it, but in my heart of hearts I knew I had to go see my dad.

So I left the house and met with Dan and the rest of my fellow younger siblings. My mom had no strength to stop me.

Danny told us we were going to walk to meet my dad at a local gas station and then go visit Susie, who lived in North Port. She had a young family and was doing her best to raise them with her new husband. We saw her occasionally and I'm sure she helped my mom out with money whenever she could.

But North Port was far for a young child like me who walked everywhere, so it was hard to visit.

As we were walking to the gas station to meet my dad, who was going to drive us to Susie's place for a family barbecue, my brother teased us. "So, what kind of car do you think Dad's driving?"

We all started guessing vehicles, and finally I said, "I bet it's one of those things that you put dead people in… what kind of car is that called, a hearse?"

Danny just looked at me. "How did you know?"

"No way!" we all chimed in.

"Yeah, wait till you see it," he said. "It's really cool."

We walked up to the gas station and there we saw a long black hearse. The sign on the side said "Princess Tenoka, Lady of Fire and Magic." That's when we found out that my dad had married a fire-eating exotic dancer. In those days, you could have also use the word stripper. For her, it was burlesque, theatre, and drama all rolled into one. She loved to dance and this was a way to do what she loved.

This was the first time we were going to meet our new stepmother. And we got to ride in a hearse! Oh what a day! In my heart I was hoping that everything was about to change. My dad and new stepmother were going to take care of us. I couldn't wait to see them.

I really don't remember much about the day in general. My new stepmom seemed really nice, and kind of funny. We learned she was from Canada.

When we were done eating, my two brothers and I went for a walk and smoked up before going back to visit my dad. I remember thinking we were so different from the young, innocent kids he had left behind. When he'd left, we were chasing butterflies and having fun. Now we were a good year into partying, drinking, smoking, and doing drugs. We were so skinny that you could see our ribcages and most of our dreams had been dashed.

After seeing my dad, I realized that nothing had changed and nothing would change. Life would go on. He was in no position to take us or have us move in with him. He was just stopping by to say hi, and he wanted to introduce his new wife. They were going to be traveling the U.S. in this hearse doing her fire and magic show across the country. Then they were going to go up to Canada. Good for him.

We were going to remain in our home with no money or food. His excuse for not sending child support was that my mom would claim it, lessening her social assistance from the government. He said that the net result would be nothing.

We see that in the system every day. If a father or mother wants to give their children anything extra, it gets deducted from the social assistance allowance and nobody wins. I guess in a sense the child does win, by knowing that somebody actually cares about them and is giving them something special. But when it boils down to the nuts and bolts of food, clothing, and shelter, those things cannot be compromised.

This is a part of the system that needs to change. The only one who suffers in the end is the children. I think we can do better. At the end of the day, if our children succeed, the family succeeds, the next generation succeeds, and everyone succeeds.

While Danny didn't always stay with us at home, after we said goodbye to my dad that night we all went back to the house with no lights or electricity. We used candles at night, and flashlights, because it got dark by 5:30 or 6:00. Danny slept on the couch because there were only three bedrooms and us four kids shared two of them. My mom slept in the third. I slept with Cindy, and Duane shared a bed with Doug.

That night, as Danny was lying in the living room looking around our house with no food or amenities, he said loudly into the darkness, "Man, this place is so depressing. It's been a long time since I lived in this house."

Realizing what he had said and knowing how depressed we probably were, he quickly started telling jokes to keep it light-hearted. We'd had a good day with Dad, but we weren't going anywhere.

"Well, everybody," Danny deadpanned as we waited for sleep to overtake us, "this might be depressing for us, but can you imagine the cockroaches? They can live off the smallest amount of food, and even they can't find anything in this house. At least you don't have to worry about roaches anymore, because they've packed their bags and left the house. They're saying, 'We have had enough! There's no food in this place. Goodbye. Man, you don't even know if it's night or day here. When are we supposed to come out and play? What are we supposed to eat? That's it. We're leaving!'"

As I lay there, so depressed, I had this image of cockroaches leaving the house with their little suitcases. We all burst out into a giggle attack. It's pretty sad when even the cockroaches don't want to stay in your home!

Danny knew how terrified Cindy and I were of cockroaches, but somehow his words made them magically disappear. That was Dan. He always thought of things differently, and laughter was the only way to deal with the situations we found ourselves in. If you didn't have a sense of humour, life could get the better of you.

One thing we Needhams had was a sense of humour. That was a defence mechanism. We tried desperately not to let our situation overwhelm us and devolve into the same state my mom was in. Depression is a horrible disease.

For the most part, the older kids didn't come around Calvin Lane, but I think something changed in Danny that night when he was reminded of how we lived.

22.

THE CHRISTMAS THAT WAS

Grace provides angels of hope.

CHRISTMAS WAS FAST APPROACHING AND OF COURSE WE HAD NO TREE OR decorations and electricity was still off. We had nothing. Duane, Doug, Cindy, and I used to go carolling because that was another way to make money. Even though things were bad, we still managed to put on our cheer and go sing. Singing gave us the illusion of joy.

Duane couldn't sing at all, so we made him the hummer. He really wasn't even a good hummer. Our favourite song was "Here We Come A-Wassailing." Whenever we got to the part of the song that says "We are not daily beggars that beg from door to door; but we are neighbours' children, whom you have seen before," we would look at each other and grin, thinking, *Yeah right.* We knew we were really begging and just hoped no one would notice. But both parts of that lyric were true. We were the neighbours' children, too.

As kids, we really wanted that money to buy presents for our mom and for each other and for our family. Christmas was, after all, still Christmas. Everyone wants to have the opportunity to give. It shows how much you love the person you're giving to. We also realized at a young age that when you're rich enough to give, you're blessed. It means you have more than enough. Being able to give is a blessing.

At Christmas, our friends were busy doing all the normal things they do with family and friends and forgot about us and our situation. They had normal lives outside of the drugs, parties, and stuff that helped us survive. We were the ones who didn't. It was a depressing time for us. We knew we wouldn't have a turkey, and it was hard to be around people who were looking forward to getting presents and having dinners and festivities and fun.

So we hung out at home. When you're living the way we were, in poverty, Christmas was actually the most depressing time of year.

It made me realize that there's only one thing worse than death, and that was living in this beautiful country and being homeless and alone—not being a part of mainstream society, not experiencing the greatness of our world, but living on the streets in the dirt and grime on the outskirts. When you're homeless, you lose all sense of pride. We were existing to die, to see another dreary day and experience the worst that people can be to each other. When you're living without food, clothing, shelter, and the basic necessities, and without the basic human rights people should have, you don't see beauty; you see the street, the darkness, the danger, the evil.

We can do better. We need to show people the hands and feet of Christ through care and loving support. Isn't that what Christmas is all about?

Well, sure enough, Christmas Eve arrived and believe it or not my grandmother sent us something in the mail. She lived in Pittsburgh and had very little money herself, but she loved us. She always sent us a crisp one dollar bill or a small gift.

Before I came home, I had smoked some weed to get through the holidays, and I found her present. It was a little perfume-scented sachet that you put in your clothes drawer. I had no idea what it was. I had never seen anything like that, but it had my initials on it. It was so pretty. I felt around inside it, praying there was some food in there. In my altered state of being so high and hungry, I tore that sachet apart with my teeth to get at the little pill inside. I tasted it, thinking it was food, but it was so bitter. Then I realized it was a perfume pill.

And that's how my sister Cindy found me when she came home. I was already depressed, but now I was even more so.

When she saw what I had done, she burst out laughing. "Judy, don't you know what that is? That's a scented pillow that you put in your drawer to make your clothes smell pretty."

I looked over at my drawer and opened it. "What clothes?"

We both started laughing. I realized this was my only present, and I had just ruined it.

Yes, it was a sad state of affairs. I'd finally gotten a present and ripped it apart. But I had no clothes to put it with anyway, and no food. Cindy and I decided to go to sleep.

As we lay in bed, we heard a car pull up. Suddenly we heard my brother Danny yell from the yard, "Judy, Cindy, Doug, Duane! Get up! Get up!"

We had no idea what was going on, but we started walking out of our bedrooms into the living room. We saw Dan's station wagon backed up to the front door.

"What's going on?" I asked, opening the door.

"Santa Claus came. He came to my girlfriend's house and brought all these presents."

Of course we had stopped believing in Santa, back when we'd had our first non-Christmas. I'm not sure Danny realized that we didn't believe, though. He was so naïve.

We looked into the hatch and saw a whole bunch of nicely wrapped gifts. We were astounded. Shocked! We started crying, because we really hadn't thought Christmas was coming, since it hadn't come for so many years.

"Hurry, hurry," he said. "Let's take it all out of the car."

So we took everything out of the car using our flashlights and brought it into the house while Danny parked the car in the driveway. Somebody lit a candle.

"Danny, we can't open the presents," someone said. "We can't see anything."

He looked at us with his boyish grin. "I know what we can do."

He pulled the car up so it was facing forward, shining its headlights into the house through the front door. Next, he brought in a little tree which he'd so far forgotten in all the excitement and set it up in our living room.

That night, as we opened our presents in the beams of those headlights, it didn't matter what we got or if it was to our taste. Although none of the clothes fit and we didn't like the styles, this was probably my favourite Christmas ever! It's not about the stuff; it's about knowing that someone cares, that somebody is thinking of you, and that somebody loves you. And it's about celebrating with everyone else in the world as if you're normal.

And of course it's about the birth of a little baby named Jesus who brought love, hope, peace, and joy to the entire world.

Since we didn't believe in Santa, Danny confessed later that my dad had sent money for him to go shopping for the presents.

A few weeks later, we got another gift in the mail, this time from my Aunt Candy (my mom's sister) and Uncle Chuck. It took longer than she had thought to get to us and it came in a big box, all taped up, all the way from Alaska where they owned a convenience store.

When I opened the box, it was full of bags of chips, all different kinds and flavours. Nacho chips, cheesies, potato… there must have been about sixty bags. We were so excited because it was food—and trust me, we all chowed down. It was like a mini party. It truly was one of the best gifts we ever received. The note said:

> These chips are expired, and we could not sell them in the store, so we thought that you could use them. Sorry they are expired, but they should still be good to eat. We love you! Enjoy!

All of us caught the irony that the only reason we were able to eat that week was because of a gift from Alaska. We all laughed about it as we ate. It was definitely a godsend!

23.

BILLY JOE AND BOBBY SUE

Policemen are angels of grace.

WHILE OUR LIFESTYLE WAS VERY DIFFERENT FROM MOST PEOPLE, WE STILL FELT like we were just kids going through the motions of life. We had fun, played hooky, and of course got into mischief. The less parental supervision we had, the more trouble we got into. We were kids, and we were bored. And most of the time, we didn't get caught.

We didn't do big things. We would chase the milk truck and try to get some fresh milk. We would steal from the local convenience store, items like chocolate bars and cigarettes and the occasional six-pack of beer. When we stole, it was usually food. I remember thinking very morally that I would never take anything just for me, and I would only take to survive.[18] And we also stole cigarettes, which had become a bad habit for us.

But there are two incidents that stand out. The first one is truly funny and juvenile, and the second is much more serious.

As many people are aware, Canadian geese fly south for the winter. So when it's tourist season, the canals in Florida are covered with geese. As kids, we used to go and play with them, chasing them around and startling them. It was kind of a fun pastime and we'd laugh when they ran away from us with their wings up high.

We discovered that if we took a flashlight and shone it in a goose's eyes at night, it would freeze and we'd have a chance to grab it. So one night Doug, Bobby, and I went walking along the canal with a flashlight and some garbage bags. We decided that we were going to steal some geese.

---

[18] I used to covet the really nice clothes in stores, but I didn't steal those.

It wasn't easy. I held the flashlight while Doug and Bobby tried to grab them. As soon as they did, the geese would try to fly. They were quite strong and made a lot of noise. We didn't want to wake up the people living in the houses, so we had to close their beaks at the same time.

It was hilarious watching my brother try to chase these birds around. He and Bobby got all scratched up, but by the end of that evening we had a whole gaggle of geese. We brought them home and put them into the little shed area that was attached to the house. We got a mom, a dad, and a whole bunch of babies. We thought this was the greatest thing, because now we had pets.

My mom, being out of it, didn't notice right away, which made us feel really sneaky. Unfortunately, geese are loud and eventually my mom woke up to the sound of them squawking inside our utility room. She asked where they'd come from and we told her that the neighbour down the street had given them to us. Wasn't it wonderful?

Since she was always out of it, she believed us. She let us keep them for a couple of days, but then we had to let them go. Her logic was sound. We couldn't afford to take care of them because if we didn't have any food, how were we going to feed a bunch of geese? Plus they pooped everywhere.

We thought Mom had a good point. So at the end of the week, we let them go. But I have to say it was funny.

The other incident was much different. It was the one and only time I got in trouble with the police, and it was once again with Doug and Bobby. We were hanging out in Port Charlotte, which had a curfew of ten o'clock. Sometimes, of course, we went outside of those parameters, and on this occasion we were wondering through a hotel parking lot and happened to notice a camper trailer. As we looked through the back door of the camper, we saw some interesting items: a cooler, which might be full of food, and some really nice fishing rods.

My brothers and I loved to go fishing. We also loved to eat fish. We didn't have food, so being able to catch fish and crab would provide us dinner.

So we decided to break into this trailer and take the fishing rods and the cooler.

"Man, if we could just have those fishing rods, we would never have to worry about food again," Doug commented with a conspiratorial wink. "We would have everything we need to catch our own food. I think that's very entrepreneurial. Don't you, Jude?"

Doug was always very smart. He was a conniver, but he also was a thinker. All of his thoughts had logic and humour, and the logic usually helped justify what we were going to do, even if we knew it was wrong. He could convince anybody to do anything. He always made it seem so simple, so logical, so fun.

Lo and behold, inside the cooler we found bologna, bread, and all sorts of really nice fixings for sandwiches. It was full. Then, of course, there were the fishing rods. We quickly took it all and ran across the street into the middle of a field where there was a great big tree and a bunch of palmetto bushes. We tucked everything into the tree, including the rods. It was camouflaged and we figured we could leave our stash in that tree and come back the next day to see if it was still there. After all, we knew if the police caught us walking down the street with fishing rods at this time of the evening we would be busted, especially after curfew.

The most exciting part of this find was the food, so we proceeded to open the cooler and make ourselves sandwiches. We were in our glory! This was a great opportunity to have something to eat. We were so excited. This really was the treasure.

Unfortunately, just as we were in the middle of making our bologna and mustard sandwiches and chowing down, the police happened to spot us. Now, understand that they were constantly looking out for kids breaking curfew. When they saw us, their sirens went flailing.

I was terrified, as I'd never done anything like this before.

We immediately started running in different directions.[19] As the police chased Bobby in one direction and Doug in the other, I decided to just play possum and crawl under the bushes. I almost got away with it, too, since they were initially only chasing the boys.

They finally caught my brother, then Bobby shimmying up a palm tree.

The only reason I got caught is that they decided to bring the two boys in the cop car towards the tree to see what we'd been up to. As they pulled in, I heard a cop bellow from a loudspeaker on top of the car: "There's a girl in the bushes."

Crap, I was busted!

My brother later told me after that all they saw when they pulled up was the bush shaking like crazy and my big blue eyes staring out from under the leaves, terrified. I was just a hungry and terrified child.

Obviously I had to come out when they saw me, and then they figured out what we'd been doing: eating from the cooler. They didn't see the fishing rods, because they were hidden inside the tree.

---

[19] This was a tactic we always used. We were smart. The police could only catch so many of us when we all went in opposite directions.

They asked a bunch of questions, and we explained that we'd done it because we were hungry and we'd just happened to come across this cooler of food. The police officers were very understanding. I think they could tell that we were frail and serious about our need to eat, so they brought us home.

When we got to the house, it was dark of course. My mom opened the door and they realized that our situation was indeed true. They were very nice. They told her to keep us inside after ten o'clock, and that was the end of that.

It wasn't until the next day that the theft got reported. When it did, the police realized that we'd also taken the fishing rods, which they found when they went back to the tree. Damn! Doug and I had thought we might have gotten to keep the rods and had food for life. Oh well, at least we tried.

Luckily for us, the people from whom we stole didn't press charges. They were just happy to get their belongings back. They actually felt sorry for us.

24.

ONCE A THIEF, ALWAYS A THIEF

Grace comes from being an accomplice and not getting caught.

LITTLE DID I KNOW THAT DOUG HAD BEEN INVOLVED IN MANY MORE OF THESE situations due to the influence of the older men in his life. It is by the grace of God that he didn't get in bigger trouble. As Doug shared with me:

Sam used to take me out to steal stuff for him. We would go to a tire shop, pop the trunk, then keep the guy at the counter busy, telling him what kind of tires he wanted and stuff for motorcycles and cars. While he kept the guy busy, I would take the tires and load them into the already popped trunk.

We did so much of that. He was older than I, so I just did as he said.

One time we went to another store to pawn something when Sam saw a guy come in with really expensive jewellery. This guy had a whole bunch of stuff and Sam was paying close attention as the guy interacted with the owner of the store.

Sam soon found out that the guy with the jewellery lived in Charlotte Harbor, and he followed the guy home.

Two weeks later, when Sam took me out with him to smoke some pot, he said, "Hey, I want you to do something with me." Whatever it was, I didn't want to do it, but he was bigger than I was and he would feed me drugs first.

"No, I don't want to do it," I said. "I don't want to steal things from people."

I knew it was wrong, but he would pressure me all the time. I never really had a choice.

So he took me over to this guy's house in Charlotte Harbor. The guy always kept valuables in the trunk of his Cadillac, which was parked in the backyard close to the water. Well, we couldn't figure out how to get the car open. Since cars didn't yet have automatic buttons to open the trunk, Sam and I decided to use a crowbar.

At the same time, we had to keep watch of the guy inside the house in case he heard us. He was watching TV, and we tried not to make any noise.

Sam got the trunk open high enough for me to get my hand in, and I took what I could. That day, we got three or four watches that were worth about $300 to $400 apiece. That was big money back then.

Three days later, Sam got a hold of me again and said, "Come on, little hippie,[20] let's go smoke some weed."

And of course before I knew it we were at this guy's house a second time. Here we go again!

I didn't want to do this, because I was so scared. The guy had all his stuff in grocery bags right by his back window of the house, including all his gold jewellery. All we had to do was sneak into the house and grab the bags from the window ledge.

Once again the guy was sitting in his living room watching TV while we looked in from the back window. His back was towards us.

The dining room was on the right, and off to the side were sliding glass doors. We jimmied the sliding glass doors to get it open, being quiet about it. The guy had the TV volume on really loud.

Slowly we slid open the doors and Sam told me to go in and grab a bag. So I did. I brought it over to him and then he took the bag and disappeared for a couple seconds.

Then he came back and we did it again—

—until I got to the third bag. The guy had been eating peanut butter crackers in his easy chair, but all of a sudden he ran out of peanut butter crackers. I was in the dining room, which was right by the kitchen, when the guy started to get up…

I didn't have enough time to get to the door!

Sam slowly shut the door and gives me a look that said, *Be quiet.* I quickly got underneath the dining room table and watched the guy's feet as he walked past me and went into the kitchen to make more peanut butter crackers.

---

[20] That was my nickname.

I stayed under there for another ten to fifteen minutes while he made these peanut butter crackers. The whole time, I was scared to death.

Finally, he went back to watch TV again, but now I didn't see Sam anywhere. I was worried that he'd left me there.

Suddenly, I saw Sam come over to the window, open the door, and beckon me to come out. As I left, I took the other two brown grocery bags, thinking, *I'm never doing this again.*

We took off and went to Sam's house. By the time we took everything out of the bags, it was probably between eleven o'clock and midnight. The jewellery pieces all had prices on them. We had pendants, diamonds, and pins… and when we added up the prices it came up to $85,000 worth of stuff. One pendant by itself was $1,800 bucks.

"Okay, I'll sell this and then we'll split it 50/50," Sam said.

Well, our family was living with no electricity and no running water, and I figured this could really help.

The next day, the theft was in the newspaper. Sam had a big smile on his face.

By the time the next week came around, I still hadn't gotten any money from Sam, so I went to him and said, "Hey, I want my money. I did all that work. Where is my money?"

"Oh, my mom saw the article in the paper and found all the jewellery and I had to pack up all the jewels and give it back to the guy," he said. "My mom made me."

"Bull!"

"No, I did. Do you want me to phone the guy right now?"

"Yes."

So we got to a payphone and Sam phoned the guy. He dialled and then said to me, "Here, talk to him."

And I hung it up. I got scared because I was only thirteen years old. I'm pretty sure Sam got away with all the jewellery.

Sam may have gotten away with that theft, but it's my understanding that years later he and his brother went to Florida state prison for armed robbery. His sentence was twelve years.

Had Doug stayed in Florida, that may have been his fate. By the grace of God go we.

Again, here was an older adult preying on a young vulnerable kid. If a young kid gets caught, they go to juvenile detention and get out after a short while. If an adult gets caught, they go to prison. Some of the adults in our lives were smart and took advantage of our age and desperate situation to help them.

The other thing Doug stole was food.

It was almost a daily occurrence to go to the grocery store and steal their bread and danishes. We'd do it in the morning because the vendor used to drop it off outside right before the store opened. If we got there at the right time, we could take what we wanted.

Then after the store opened we used to go in and steal ham. I used to steal ham because it was already cooked and easy to stick down my pants because the package was thin. At the meat counter there were these big mirrors through which I could see if anybody was looking at me. When I noticed nobody was looking, I would grab the ham and shove it down my pants and under my shirt.

One time I was getting the ham and Duane was getting the mustard. When he got the mustard, though, it fell out. So Duane quickly stuffed it back in his pants and nobody ever said anything.

I stole ham from the same spot off and on for almost a year. I thought I was really good, always looking in that mirror.

Much later, when I was older and wiser, I found out that the managers sat behind those mirrors. They could see me the whole time, coming in and stealing food every day, but they never said anything because they knew we were hungry and needed to eat. It wasn't like I was stealing candy. I was stealing food.

By the grace of God, they had compassion and grace for us as young kids in need. It was the only way we survived.

When you see a situation like this—children in trouble or a house that may not be providing a home—we have the opportunity to help or intervene.

Devon Clunis, a former police chief in Winnipeg, once spoke at my church at a leadership prayer meeting. He said, "If we all take care of our own block, if we took care of our neighbours, the ones down the street, next to us, to the left, to the right and around us, if we just took care of them, if we all were responsible for taking care of our neighbours, then the world would be in good shape and a much better place to live." This applies to business neighbours as well. He's right.

Every day, we went home to absolutely nothing. Mom was sick and there was no sustenance or support. Once someone realized we were in need, they should have reached out and helped my mom. Perhaps then we could have channelled our energy into something more positive and fruitful. If that would have happened, maybe things would've turned around for us.

Today we are afraid to get involved. We can't let fear prevent us from being good neighbours. That's who God has called us to be.

This is something I tried to teach my children. In our home, I made sure they looked after our neighbours. We knew a single mother who needed help as well as an elderly couple who were trying to maintain their home. Shovelling their snow and mowing their grass ensured they had the help they needed to get through some of their more difficult times. Sometimes when the outside of a home starts to look a bit rundown, that's the first sign that someone is struggling.

So instead of making a judgment, I encouraged my kids to help. And I told them they weren't allowed to ask for money for the work they'd done. Helping out is just what good neighbours do. I learned that from my personal circumstance and paid it forward.

We all need to do this if we're going to make our world the best it can be. It really costs us nothing.

25.

LAST CHANCE TO BE SAVED

Grace comes through Billy Graham.

MY MOTHER, AS SICK AS SHE WAS, WAS A PRAYER WARRIOR. SHE PRAYED FOR US continually and always had her Bible open. Although her depression overtook her, I believe it was her faith in God that allowed her to get through these dark years.

She did a couple of very important things that were helpful, although at the time they seemed very hurtful to us. The first was practicing her faith. She always encouraged us to have faith and would have us pray over the rosary. She attended a charismatic Catholic church and was a huge supporter of Billy Graham.

Well, one day she discovered that Billy Graham was coming to St. Petersburg, Florida. Although she was out of it most of the time, I think deep in her heart she knew what was happening to us, that we were spiralling into drugs and alcohol.

Although she never said anything directly, this was never more evident than when she told us that we needed to come with her to a church meeting in St. Petersburg. The request came out of the blue. We had been living pretty much on our own and suddenly she wanted us to go to church? We were pretty tough little kids and didn't want to go, but we respected our mother and at this point didn't have a choice. So we went.

While we were at church, the preacher made a call for people to come up and get the "demons cast out of them for their healing." We had no idea what this meant. People had demons? We all looked at each other kind of strangely, wondering what the heck was going on.

My mom insisted we go up one at a time, because she knew for sure that we were following the wrong path and needed help. This was true, but as a twelve-year-old I kind of thought she was whacked.

But we all went up and Billy Graham laid hands on us. We didn't know who Billy Graham was and didn't care. We felt out of our element, to say the least. In fact, we weren't sure what we felt at all.

Later, when we were much older, we agreed that this was a turning point in our lives. Soon after, we all started making better decisions and choices to get out of the lifestyle and eventually follow God. The seed had been sown.

But there was still much to come before we reached our full potential.

My brother Duane remembers a time when my mom sang to him in tongues:

When I was maybe nine years old, I remember Mom praying in tongues in the bedroom. From then on, it was like things started to change. She couldn't change herself physically, but our situation started to change.

One night I went home and asked Mom if I could sleep with her. I never asked, but there was no electricity, it was dark, it was eerie, and no one else was home. She said yes and it was a pivotal moment.

"Son, I don't want to scare you, honey, but I'm going to pray to God in a different language," she said. "A language that He gave me, that only He understands. Okay?"

And I just said, "Okay."

I was used to doing drugs and experiencing some really weird stuff, so nothing could faze me.

She started praying in tongues, and as she started praying I remember feeling the heaviness leave my body and peace come over me for the first time. I'd never felt that before.

She kept praying and praying and praying, and I kept trying to pay attention because I really liked it.

Wow, this is different, I remember thinking.

All of a sudden she stopped praying, and I felt the heaviness start coming back over me. I could physically feel it.

"Mom, can you keep praying in tongues?" I asked.

"Why?"

"Because I feel really good when you pray. Can you pray until I fall sleep?"

"Okay."

She prayed again and I felt all that heaviness lift. That's how I fell asleep that night.

I woke up in the morning and never slept in her bed again, but I'll never forget God's grace and love and the way it made me feel.

The ups and downs of my mom's personality were crazy. But when she was normal and loving the Lord and going to church, she really could be a beautiful lady. In those times, she did her best to take care of us. I can't imagine how tough it was for her as a single mother of eight children. A mother always wants to provide for her children. Knowing that you can't would be a real blow—mentally, spiritually, and emotionally. Prayer was all she had, and in the end all she needed. We truly are blessed that she had the strength to persevere in prayer.

All eight kids in Cleveland:
Danny, Susie, David, Connie, Cindy, Doug, Judy, and Duane.

Mom and Dad's wedding picture.

Dad visits us kids in Florida: Doug, Cindy, Danny, and Judy.
Duane is in the middle.

The Christmas that was. Top row: Connie, Danny, and Susie. Middle row: Cindy,
Mom, and Judy. Bottom row: Duane and Doug, decked out in their new clothes.

My new stepmother, Tenoka, in front of the hearse she and my dad came to visit us with in Florida. The photo is taken in Canada.

Dad and Tenoka at my wedding.

Duane (top left), Doug (top middle and centre),
Judy (top right, bottom right, and bottom left).

David (top left), Cindy (top right), Connie (bottom left),
and Cindy (bottom right).

My brother Danny.

The cabin in Ontario where the four youngest siblings lived

Our first family reunion in 1987, with all eight siblings on the couch: Danny, Susie, David, Connie, Cindy, Doug, Judy, and Duane.when they first moved to Canada.

Our mom, Antoinette Adams, at the 1987 Needham family reunion.

At the Needham family reunion in 1987.
Top row: Danny, Susie, David, and Connie.
Bottom row: Cindy, Doug, Judy, and Duane. Mom is in the middle.

Our family reunion celebration at Assiniboia Downs in Winnipeg, 2014:
Duane, Judy, Doug, Cindy, Connie, Dave, and Danny.

Our second family reunion in 2014, at the cabin:
Duane, Judy, Doug, Cindy, Connie, David, Dad, and Danny.

Judy with Happy, a true hero.

26.

HERE COMES THE JUDGE

Grace allows you to get through difficult situations.

ONE DAY, MY MOM WANTED CINDY AND I TO DO SOME LAUNDRY, BUT FOR whatever reason we weren't doing it quickly enough. Or maybe we weren't doing a good job. The long and the short of it was, she snapped and went into her manic state, screaming at the top of her lungs about how horrible we were.

The next thing we knew, she decided to take us to court for being "incorrigible."

We were in complete shock. One, because we didn't even know what the word meant. But two: our own mother was going to take us to court? It felt very cold, very unloving. We still didn't understand that our mother was sick. We thought she just didn't love us, period, and that she was wicked.

So we got Susie to come with us, because we didn't know what to do. Because she was eighteen, she could represent us. She also phoned our dad for advice, who suggested that we countersue our mom for being an unfit mother, which is exactly what we did.

It was pretty terrifying to walk into the courthouse as a child in a battle with your own mother. It was a surreal experience and one that would mark me forever with feelings of abandonment, dread, and anxiety… and eventually coldness and emptiness.

As Cindy recalls:

I remember when Susie decided for the benefit of us children that we needed to prove our mom unfit. She talked openly with me about it, sharing the details and the seriousness of this accusation, as if I were an adult. I felt uncomfortably sad and full of dread, having to admit this truth in front of a judge in a courtroom.

As young kids, we all felt so unworthy and had personal guilt. Firstly, because we felt like we were good kids considering our harsh upbringings. And secondly, because of some of the things we did that hadn't gone well.

Susie insisted that this was the best thing for us, and also for Mom. Deep down I knew she was right: our mom *was* unfit. But we really didn't want to go through with a court case. To me, it felt like we were turning against our mother. No child wants to do that. It felt just wrong and caused me much distress and anxiety.

Regardless of our feeling, though, the truth was that we were in a bad situation. The reality of it just came crashing down on me. I was very sad and overwhelmed about it all.

Of course, I kept my true feelings to myself. We all did. We didn't know any other way to deal with things. We just had to deal with it. That was that! At least that's how it seemed to me.

So we stood our ground and sued her for being an unfit mother—and we won. The court agreed with us, and the sentence? We had to go into another foster home. What? That wasn't the sentence we had been hoping for.

This time the foster home was in Fort Myers, more than forty miles away in a town where we knew absolutely no one. Going through this again at an older age was even more traumatic than it had been the first time, as I now had to leave some friends behind, like Bobby and Lisa and Sandra and Sarah. I was a lot more aware of what was happening now.

At least I was with my sister Cindy. But all my other brothers and sisters were really far away.

I was to start Grade Eight at a junior high school in Fort Myers, but I don't remember which one. When you're going through transiency and homelessness, it's really hard to remember specific dates, times, and places. Details become fuzzy. It's all about survival.

I had a math teacher who I thought was super cool. I don't remember his name, but he was black and he made math fun. He'd call kids up to the board to do math. He called it Mathland. I was always top of the class, regardless of my circumstances, because math was my thing.

I remember celebrating my birthday in this foster home, even though that was the last place I wanted to spend my birthday. I have pictures of me with a crown on my head. My birthdays weren't special for me, ever. But at least this family bought me my favourite cake: banana. No one had ever done that before.

There were other foster children in the home, and I think the parents only had one biological son. I don't remember all their names.

As we went into this foster home, Connie was living somewhere else:

When my sisters went into foster care the second time, I wasn't home anymore. My mom lost the house, but I was staying at my friend Rachelle's house. She lived with her dad and three brothers, but her dad wasn't around; he mostly lived with his girlfriend in Fort Myers. He would come home on weekends long enough to drop off money for food. I was still working at the library, so I contributed $20 every week.

We were in tenth grade but rarely went to school. Her house became the party house—and without any adult supervision, boy did we party! We would be drinking beer and smoking pot as soon as we got up. The harder drugs were for night time.

Looking back, I know that we wouldn't have made it without the grace of God. I remember this time from the trips I had on different drugs, and the rest is a blur.

One week I spent the $20 for food that I had been supposed to contribute for something else. Rachelle got really mad, because her dad wasn't coming to visit that day and she had planned to use that money for food till he came back.

So she kicked me out.

I had a bike and a bag of belongings, and it was late. With nowhere to go, I rode to where my mom was staying with a friend. But when she opened the door, she told me I wasn't allowed there and there was nothing she could do.

Port Charlotte was sparsely populated then with a lot of woods. I was too scared to stop anywhere so I just rode around all night.

The next day, I was able to get in touch with my friend Rob, who took me in for a while until I met my boyfriend Dale. Then I moved in with him.

Dale was seven years older than me. He worked for waste management and I took a job at an alarm company, trying to make appointments for sales.

One day my mom came to my work and told me that she was either going to have Dale arrested for statutory rape, since I was a minor, or she would sign papers allowing me to get married. I was sixteen at the time.

Since I had no other place to stay and my only other option was being homeless again, getting married seemed like a good idea.

Dale and I stayed married for thirty-eight years, and in the early years we were able to be a landing spot for family members who needed a place to stay to get back on their feet. We didn't have much then, but we had a roof over our heads and food on the table. After how we had grown up, I felt rich.

In all the confusion with Cindy and me, my mom actually forgot about Doug. He experienced something much different during this time. He went home one day to find out that Mom had moved. As Doug shares:

While we were on Calvin Lane, I went home to find out the house was sold and Mom was gone. I was almost fourteen and suddenly had nowhere to stay.

So Connie and Dale took me in. They lived in Charlotte Harbor, and I lived there for a while. I was there catching sharks off the pier.

One day Dale gave me $30 to get him a bag of pot. I knew all the drug-dealers, and I knew who had the good stuff. I took the money and went off to get him some pot, but then I ran into my friends Bobby and Ronny. We ended up smoking half of it and partied all night.

Afterwards I was too afraid to go back to Dale's house, so I went back to Calvin Lane, which was empty since the new owners hadn't moved in yet. I stayed there for three to four weeks by myself with no one knowing where I was.

A guy I knew, Rusty, used to work at the gas station and I would go see him on his night shift. One time I was visiting at one o'clock and decided to walk home.

I was heading back to our old house when the cops pulled up beside me.

"Son, you need to get in the car," said one of the officers. "It's one o'clock in the morning and curfew was eleven o'clock. Not only are we going to take you home, but we're going to meet your parents. You're way too young to be out."

I had to think fast. I couldn't take them to Calvin Lane, because nobody was living there and it was pitch dark and empty.

Finally I told them that I lived across the street on the other side of the highway. I had them take a left onto the access road and then a right onto a road where I knew there were some houses.

I had no idea what to do. I was just winging it.

Suddenly I saw a house with no car in front of it and it looked vacant.

"This is it," I said to the cops. They pulled into the driveway. "The front door is locked. I'll have to go around back and go inside. Then I'll open the door."

As soon as I got to the back of the yard, boom, I took off and ran all the way to Bobby's house! I knew I could cut through all the backyards without getting caught because I was a very fast runner and knew the area. I was used to dodging the cops after curfew.

When I got to Bobby's, I went into the laundry room because it was always open. I curled up there and went to sleep.

The next morning, I was all curled up on top of the dirty clothes when suddenly, boom! I got kicked right in the ribs.

"What the hell are you doing here?" Bobby's dad demanded.

"I didn't have any place to stay. I had to come here."

"Well, get out of here. I don't want you here."

Ironically, as I was walking back to Calvin Lane, guess who pulled up beside me? My sister's husband, Dale.

"Where in the hell have you been, boy?" he angrily asked.

"I'm sorry," I said. "I was afraid to come back to your house because I didn't have all of your pot. I only have half a bag."

"I don't care about the pot. You've been gone for four weeks and we've been worried sick about you! Get your butt in the car!"

I was relieved that he wasn't that mad. I was secretly surprised and happy that someone actually cared about me. It was the first time anyone ever had.

I went back to Connie's house and lived there for a while. I would just go fishing and smoke up. It would've been great to stay there. Connie and Dale were great, and they really cared about me.

God and His angels were always protecting us, even though we didn't know it. So much could have happened to Doug during those four weeks, but by the grace of God he was safe.

As Dave recalls:

What a blessing Dale was during those difficult times. Dale and Connie were always there to provide a place for the homeless. Connie was blood and did what family does, but Dale just happened to marry into our crazy family. More than once, he and Connie were there for me when I needed a place to stay. Dale was willing to open his home to me, Doug, Danny and his girlfriend Lynn, my sister, my nieces and nephews, and even our mom on more than one occasion.

Dale would be the first person to say he wasn't a perfect man and that he had his faults, but when it came to making sure that the Needham clan had a roof over their heads at night, he was an angel and sacrificed a lot for us.

He and Connie were married for thirty-eight years, but unfortunately he had lasting problems with alcohol. He would get well and then slip back. He went to rehab several times but couldn't seem to grasp God's grace to overcome it. He loved God and never turned away from Him, but the alcohol abuse took its toll on his health. He passed peacefully into the Lord's arms surrounded by his family in 2016.

27.

COULD LIFE POSSIBLY GET WORSE?

Grace comes through the Florida Sheriff's Youth Ranch.

I DON'T REMEMBER MUCH ABOUT WHAT HAPPENED IN THE FORT MYERS FOSTER home apart from a day when we were sitting on the bus coming home from school, about a month into the school year, shortly after my birthday. I was very depressed from being away from my family and everyone I knew and loved.

I looked out the bus window with tears streaming down my face. Depression is easy to fall into when you're moving around so much, with no stability or friends. I believe I was emotionally traumatized by everything that was going on and so I'd just stopped feeling. I learned that you never want to show weakness to people, as that makes you vulnerable and can give them a chance to take advantage of you, make fun of you, judge you, and hurt you. So I rarely cried. The tough veneer was best. I learned to mask my emotions. We all did. Then people left you alone.

But on this day I was crying, and quite honestly I was scared about what could happen next. It couldn't get any worse, could it?

Unfortunately, when I arrived home that day I found out that, yes, it could get worse. It had been discovered that my mom suffered from schizophrenia and it was decided we were to become wards of the state. That meant we no longer had a mom or dad to go back to.

Cindy, Doug, and I were going to be moved to the Florida Sheriff's Youth Ranch in Clearwater. This was a group home for kids who were troubled but not necessarily troublemakers, who just had difficult family lives. The people in charge tried to impress on us that it wasn't because of our behaviour that we were going there, but because our mother was sick and couldn't take care of us. No matter how you say it, though, you always feel like it's your fault, so I'm not sure that we truly understood why we had to move there.

Now that the state had custody of us four younger children, Duane was placed in a home next to the house where his friends Timmy and Jimmy lived. The neighbours, Bob and Donna Negrich, had no kids of their own and offered to foster Duane so he could stay close to people he knew. They had a nephew the same age and all the boys played well together.

As Duane recalls:

When I was ten years old, I went to my second foster home. They were great. I'd never had stability before and they taught me discipline. I really needed it.

They had a nephew who came to stay with us, and they later adopted him. We're the same age, and we're still brothers to this day.

They had food in the house on a regular basis, and we all ate at the same table. At first that was awkward, but I began to enjoy that time.

But it never felt like home, because I missed my other brothers and sisters who had all gone in different directions.

These foster parents wanted to adopt me, and I was happy about that, but I missed my siblings so much. I loved my foster parents, and we are still in touch today! I was lucky because they were good to me.

I was never so depressed than on that day coming home from school and learning my fate. It just didn't seem fair. It didn't seem as though anyone loved us or wanted us to live with them. When you're in care, the foster parents aren't supposed to hug you or get too emotional. But I don't think I'd felt a real hug in five years. I can't describe how it felt other than to say I had been abandoned and life felt meaningless. On top of that, we only had a few days to make the transition.

In later years, when she was more stable, Mom told us that she had taken us to court because she hadn't known what else to do with us. We were all out of control, and so this was her way of seeking help. She could see we were into drugs and alcohol, and taking us to court, in her mind, would save us.

In retrospect, it did.

She told us that she'd realized she had to get us out of Port Charlotte. God had told her to get the kids out. That decision helped us in the long run, to get us into a better situation.

It was a very difficult time of transition. The only good news was that I was with Doug and Cindy. It was the first residential group home in Florida that could accommodate siblings from the same household of both genders. All the other groups homes were either all-boy or all-girl. So we were actually very fortunate again. This new model of housing was about trying to keep siblings together.

I hadn't seen my brother in a long time, so I figured it would be nice to be with him again.

We arrived at the Florida Sheriff's Youth Ranch in the fall, and days later we were told that we were among the first group of ten to ever move in. It was a pilot project.

For group homes, it was a beautiful facility. It had seven bedrooms, six bathrooms, a formal living room, a formal dining room, an informal living room, an informal dining room, and a pool—all newly renovated. It was clean and elegantly decorated. It was the fanciest home I had ever seen, and it definitely looked cockroach-free.

Most people would think this was an incredible place to live. If it was your home, it probably would be. But we were foster kids in a group home which made us feel like aliens on a new planet. We didn't feel like this was home. We were living with seven other strange kids and suddenly had to learn how to become part of a larger group. We didn't know each other and yet were expected to get along.

We learned the ropes very quickly. The ranch depended on donations from the private sector to thrive, so we had to be good ambassadors. When any visitor came to the door, one of us was responsible for greeting them with a "Hello. My name is Judy. Welcome to the Florida Sheriff's Youth Ranch. Can I help you? Can I give you a tour?" The same was true for answering the phone. And we all divided up the chores, working in pairs. We would be assigned a room and then were responsible to dust, vacuum, or mop it on a regular basis. If you were in charge of the kitchen, you were responsible for meal planning and grocery shopping, cooking and prep, and clean-up. Everyone had to make their beds daily and clean their rooms and bathrooms before they left for school. We got graded on the chores, and if we achieved less than a seven out of ten we were no longer allowed to swim in the pool or watch TV. The people who ran the facility were social workers, so they were equipped to deal with drama. They also had their own grown kids and understood what kids go through.

We were being taught manners and developing a work ethic. We had consistent discipline, which most of us hadn't had for a long time. Unfortunately, our fate was that we would be released from this wonderful facility at the age of eighteen, given $100 and a bag of clothes, and told "Good luck, kid. I hope you make it."

So basically we graduated to the street.

Having now worked in a homeless shelter for eleven years, I've discovered that about half of people who live on the street became homeless around the age of eighteen, and about half of them went through the foster care system. They never recovered from the trauma of their youth, never obtained a proper education, and never learned how to fit into mainstream society.

This is true of most group homes, which is very sad, especially today. My own children, who grew up with stability, love, care, and a private education, wouldn't be able to make it on their own at eighteen, what makes us think these kids who have gone through so much trauma could succeed under those circumstances?

I'm proud to say that through much advocacy the policy of wards aging out at the age of eighteen is currently under review in Manitoba. In many cases, care is being extended to the age of twenty-five.[21]

As Cindy recalls:

I was sixteen years old when I went to our first group home. Judy, Doug, and I had two sets of group home parents. I didn't want to be at this group home, but I was happy that I was there with my sister and brother.

I was sad, though, because Duane wasn't there. He was in a different foster home far away.

We learned so much at this group home. The adults talked to us and showed respect to us and our feelings. They understood our deepest hurts, our pain, and our unfortunate past. They cared for us and allowed us to express our hurtful feelings, as young teenagers do.

They also corrected us and taught us to express ourselves in a more calm and mature manner. I did my best, but it wasn't easy. We had a lot more to deal with than we realized. It was a very emotional time in our lives.

I have to admit that I contemplated suicide many times at the Youth Ranch. I felt very alone. I remember thinking, *If I die tomorrow, will anyone really care?* The reality was that nobody would, not at that time. And I knew it.

---

[21] Legislative Review Committee, "Transformation Child Welfare Legislation in Manitoba: Opportunities to Improve Outcomes for Children and Youth," *Government of Manitoba*. September 2018 (https://www.gov.mb.ca/fs/child_welfare_reform/pubs/final_report.pdf).

Nights were the worst. That's when all the negative thoughts would emerge. It allowed me to empathize with the homeless shelter workers who worked through the night, caring for people sleeping in shelters. This is when people's demons would come out, when you'd realize how difficult and hopeless your situation was. I admire these workers, as they give the gift of encouragement and hope to people at their greatest time of need. They sit with people, console them, and settle them in for the night.

Doug remembers two incidents at the Youth Ranch that set the tone for his relationships and reputation as a badass:

Not long after I arrived, I got busted along with one of the kids who lived there, Jimmy. Ray, a foster parent, caught us with pot and beer. I remember that he took me by the neck, pushed me up against a wall, and chewed me out bigtime. Then he was yelling at Jimmy.

The next day, the cops came so that the sheriff could scare the crap out of us. He yelled at both of us while we sat in the office. Jimmy, who was three years older than me, cried like a baby.

"I don't see you crying," the sheriff said to me. "Aren't you afraid? You're the big man. What's with you?"

"No, you don't scare me. You just remind me of my dad and my older brothers. My older brothers used to yell at me and my dad used to beat me with the belt all the time. So no, I don't really care. I don't cry when I get whipped by the belt. You just remind me of them. Do whatever you want."

"Okay," he said. "Let's go outside."

He took me out of the office and the two of us had a talk. In fact, he started talking to me really nice.

"You have this big guy in there crying and I don't intimidate you?" he said.

"No. Jimmy's just a big mess. I'm not. I'm not gonna cry over this."

He asked me what I might like to do when I got older, and I told him I wanted to go into masonry. I had a friend who was doing stucco. Well, I didn't know what I actually wanted to do, but I had to give this sheriff an answer.

The next thing I knew, the cop invited me to come over to his house and help him work on some brickwork. He let me hang out with him. He had a big heart and was trying to be there for me.

He was actually a really nice guy, but I wasn't ready to be reformed. While doing work at his house, I remember thinking, *Why did I tell him that? Now he's making me work...*

But at least he treated me well. I got something out of it. It became a memorable moment to look back on with hope.

Unfortunately, wherever Doug went, a fight seemed to break out:

At Dunedin High School, there were a lot of blacks and a lot of whites. You didn't go into the washroom if there were black people in the washroom, and blacks didn't go into the washroom if there were white people in there. You just didn't do it.

Anyway, one day I was in the washroom with a few classmates when six black guys walked in. I didn't quite realize that they were looking at us like they wanted to fight. I wasn't really paying attention to them, because they were in twelfth grade, and I was in ninth grade. They were bodybuilders.

When you're smoking in between classes, you're "hotboxing," so you smoke as much as you can. When you hotbox, you get a lot of saliva in your mouth and need to spit. So I quickly spat on the floor—and ended up hitting the top of one of the guy's shoes. He was six feet tall about two hundred forty pounds.

Then he just kept walking out, leaving me and four other whites standing up against the concrete wall.

Oh good, I thought. *I got away with it.*

The next thing I knew, he came back inside and asked, "Who spit on my shoes?"

He went up to the first guy, then to the second, then to the third. And of course they all said no.

Finally he got to me.

"No, I didn't spit on your shoes," I said.

He moved on as if going to the next guy, then suddenly turned and hit me straight in the head, right between my eyes. I don't remember anything after that. The back of my head hit the concrete wall and I went down.

When I woke up, I had two big black eyes. I don't know how long I was out, but I was completely out of it. The school had to phone the ranch and, luckily, Ollie and Al, the other set of group parents, were there. They were compassionate and gave me a break. I assured them that I hadn't been trying to spit on the guy's shoes… it had been a total accident. It seemed wherever I went, though, something bad happened.

After talking about all the fights he got involved in, Doug was quick to add that he would spend every night crying himself to sleep… but during the day he'd try to be the tough guy so people would leave him alone. This was shocking to hear from my brother, who was always so tough. Fight during the day and cry yourself to sleep at night; I'm afraid that was the pattern for all of us.

28.

TEACHERS HAVE IMPACT

Grace comes from feeling hopeful and special at your lowest point.

I MARKED THE TIME BY THE SCHOOLTEACHERS I HAD, SUCH AS ROY DRIVER, WHO taught social studies. As his assistant, I corrected tests and marked quizzes for him. I also helped him prepare for his classes. He was single, quite a bit older, probably in his fifties or sixties, and had never had children.

Once he discovered that I was in a group home, he seemed to favour me a bit. He took me under his wing and bought me treats, like peanuts and diet soda, which made me feel special. He also paid me for marking tests and papers, even though he didn't have to. Every once in a while he would give me a dollar, or a $5 or $10. It was a really good arrangement.

Roy also went above and beyond with the group home. He had a private beach on Reddington Shores where he sometimes took all of us kids from the group home. While the accommodations were shabby at best, there was a place for us to shower and change and get dressed and go to the beach. On these occasions he always took great joy in buying us ribeye steaks to barbecue, with all the trimmings and salad. He paid for everything. We went there at least once a month.

He even took us out to restaurants sometimes and encouraged us to order anything we wanted. He knew how much of a treat that was. As a matter fact, I don't ever remember going to a restaurant before the age of thirteen, other than at an ice cream place near the arcade. He took us to some really nice places where they had prime rib. I remember my brothers being absolutely astounded when they were told to order anything they wanted.

Roy took great joy in watching my brothers eat. He knew how important it was to them, how much they appreciated it. We will always treasure him as someone who gave us hope at a time when we were really struggling to get through life.

He even went so far as to arrange for one of the schoolteachers to adopt me. She was the Spanish teacher and Roy was willing to pay for me to live with her to get out of the group home. He had always dreamed of one day taking care of a student and sending them to college, and so he wanted to send me to the best college and pay for everything, which was extremely generous. He would have left me his entire estate, too.

To say I was flattered is an understatement. For the first time in my life, someone wanted to take care of me. I was very tempted. The hard part would have been leaving behind all my siblings. They were all I had.

But God had a different plan, and it started at a baseball game.

I will never forget the day the group home was gifted tickets to a baseball game between the Toronto Blue Jays and Philadelphia Phillies. We never in a million years would have thought we'd have the chance to take part in anything so magnificent, exciting, and expensive as a Major League Baseball game. It made me think that anything was possible.[22]

As I watched the game, I remember thinking about Canada. That's where my dad lived now, since my stepmom was from there.

We had been in the group home for a whole school year, and during that time I kept going back in my memory to the day I'd found my mom crying. She'd said that God had a plan, but this didn't seem like a very good plan. I couldn't imagine staying in this home until I turned eighteen, then suddenly being cut loose. To be honest, it terrified me.

I knew that God had a better plan.

So during a discussion with my social workers, I asked them if I could write my dad a letter. It was pretty much full of F-bombs and went something like this:

Dear dad… You are a f—ing a—hole. F— you. You f—ing left us and now we are in trouble… you better f—ing come get us now because mom can't f—ing take care of us anymore and it's your f—ing turn. I don't want to stay in a group home for the rest of my life. If you ever want a relationship with your children you better f—ing help.

Love Judy

---

[22] This incident impacted me so much that when I worked in a homeless shelter in Canada years later, I did everything I could to bring these types of experiences to the people who used our services. We took them to Winnipeg Blue Bomber games, Manitoba Moose games, and other local events. We had professional teams come over to volunteer and serve meals and sign autographs. This gave our clients hope and a message that anything was possible.

The letter was at least a page in length and luckily for us it worked. Unfortunately, I found out later that Doug didn't really want to come to Canada, since he was working hard to save up money to run away from the ranch and go back to Port Charlotte. He had a job lined up with his friend Tommy.

But God had another plan and it involved taking care of his sisters.

Before my dad got custody of us, Dave paid us a visit at the group home. He and our dad had never gotten along. Dave was old enough to remember how abusive our dad was and had intervened many times to stop him from hitting our mother. So when Dave found out we were moving to Canada, he was worried for all of us. As Doug shares:

Dave came up to the group home just before we moved to Canada and said he was moving to Wyoming.

"Listen to me," he said. "You have to watch out for your sisters now because I'm not gonna be around."

Offhandedly I said, "Yeah, yeah, yeah. I will watch them."

"No, no, no… I'm serious. I mean it. You've got to take care of our sisters!"

"Yeah, yeah, yeah."

Then he grabbed me by the shirt and hit me on the side of the head with a thunk.

"No, I'm *serious*," he said with a mean look on his face. "You better f—ing take care of our sisters. Make sure that if anyone comes up against them, you kick their ass. If Dad comes around and does something, you kick his ass. You do what you have to do to take care of our sisters!"

I finally understood how serious he was and what he meant.

Dave was the oldest brother who was actually around and he really cared about his family. Now I would be the oldest man in the family, and he was handing off the responsibility to me. He didn't trust my dad and didn't want anyone to take advantage of our sisters.

Anytime after that when I had to defend my sisters or when I talked to their boyfriends, it was Dave's voice in my head saying, "You got to take care of our sisters. You got to take care of our sisters…"

I wanted to do it, of course, but I'll never forget Dave telling me.

Doug took his role very seriously. It was interesting for me to hear this story from him because in high school I'd thought nobody liked me. I'd had a crush on many of his friends, but it turned out that Doug had kept warning them off. In his mind, it was to protect me. He wouldn't let any of his friends date me.

So Dave moved back to Wyoming. He shares:

Gillette, Wyoming was an oil and coal boomtown in the late 70s, and there wasn't much else to do except party. Along with my friends Johnny and Pete, every week we'd each buy an ounce of pot. We all worked in the oilfield and would smoke a few joints during the day and then have some beers and smoke more after work.

The three of us lived in a mobile home, along with Pete's cousin who had moved from Ohio.

If it was a Friday or Saturday night, we were usually planning on some heavy drinking. We would all pile in the truck and go to the liquor store. If you wanted to drink beer, you'd buy a case of beer for yourself, and if you wanted hard liquor, you'd get a quart of rum or whiskey. As far as experimenting with drugs, if you can call it that, we pretty much tried everything that didn't involve a needle.

Johnny liked to try to get his drugs for free, and the only way to do that was to buy in bulk, deal enough drugs to pay for them, and then consume the drugs he had leftover "for free."

The problem with this approach was that while the cops generally left you alone if you were just a drug consumer, they didn't take a hands-off approach to drug-dealers. Johnny, well aware of this, and having previously been busted in Florida, just couldn't resist the allure of "free drugs."

One day, Johnny decided that he wanted some "free" acid. The problem is that it isn't "free" when you're selling to an undercover cop.

I woke up one morning to a loud commotion coming from the front of the trailer. Next thing I knew I was standing in my underwear with a cop pointing a gun at me. We had been doing acid the night before, and when you do acid you can drink a lot of beer, which I had done... and now I really had to piss. So I assured the cop that I was unarmed and asked if I could take a leak before he put me in cuffs. He was nice enough to say yes...

But unfortunately I couldn't piss. I'm not sure if it was because he was watching me or because he kept pointing his gun.

Soon I was in the living room with my three roommates, lying on our stomachs on the floor in handcuffs. I could tell by the look of fear in Pete's cousin's eyes that he was going to be trouble.

Eventually, after they had thoroughly searched our trailer and confiscated all our drugs and secured our guns, they took turns uncuffing us and letting us get dressed one at a time. Looking back, I can see why they did things the way they did; everyone in Wyoming hunted back then and everyone had guns.

After we were dressed, they had us go out to the street to wait for a bus to pick us up. I had been expecting a short bus, but up pulled a full-sized school bus. It turned out that half the people on the bus were our friends, so we all starting joking and asking each other what we'd been arrested for. I'm pretty sure at least a few of them had gotten a ride on that particular bus more than once.

We proceeded on our way to jail while making stops to pick up some more of our friends and other unlucky victims of their own stupidity.

Our bail was set by noon. Instead of getting his bond set at $500 like the rest of us, Johnny's bond was set at $5,000 since he had been charged with dealing drugs, as opposed to just possession.

A few of us had been smart enough to grab our wallets while getting dressed back at the trailer, and between us we had the $500 needed to get one of us out. We got Pete out first since he had a truck. Once Pete made it home and got his truck, he made trips to ATMs and dialled people for dollars all day until we'd gotten everyone out of jail.

Only Johnny stayed behind bars. He needed a bail bondsman, and they had all closed for the day before we could come up with the necessary ten percent and find someone to vouch for the rest of the bond. Johnny ended up spending the night in jail, which was probably appropriate.

It turned out that I was right about his cousin from Ohio. To get himself out of trouble, he signed an affidavit saying that different things in the trailer belonged to each of us. I had a pot plant hanging in my closet to dry, for which I ended up having to pay a fine. I was only seventeen at the time, but I don't think they even contacted my mom.

From 1976 until 1979, I went back and forth between Florida and Wyoming. Although I'd hitchhiked the first time, on later trips I took the bus, took flights, and sometimes drove by car. Eventually I wised up and realized that partying that hard didn't have a happy ending.

While I was in Grade Eight, going through the motions of school and life and trying to figure out what our next steps would be, my dad and stepmom were working on a way to get us to Canada.

Our real mom also came to visit us at the group home a few times. She loved us very much, but there was a lot of distance and a lot of resentment from us. Doug remembers one time when she came towards the end of our stay:

Mom used to come to the Youth Ranch all dressed up, kind of hippie-ish looking. One time she came with a brand-new car and told us that God had given it to her.

Well, I found out later that she had rented it and then never given it back.

One day she came in to the rental company to get gas, after she'd already had the car for six weeks—and without having paid anything. The company filled the tank, since they were full-service, and then asked if she was going to be returning the vehicle.

She just looked at the employee squarely and said, "Nope. God gave it to me." And then she drove right off!

So they called the cops on her and she went to jail for stealing the car. That's how my dad was able to get custody of us.

On one of her last visits, my mom asked me for my rosary.

"Judy, I know you really loved that rosary," she said. "You prayed with it, and I think God's going to take care of you. I'm wondering if I can have it now because I need some help in my life."

It was an interesting conversation. I really wanted to keep it, but how could I say no to my own mother? I knew in my heart that God was going to take care of me and that she did need the help. This was one way I could help her.

She ended up trading me one of her rosaries for the one given to me by my godparents. I still have hers and treasure it. I do believe that rosary and her incessant prayers helped my mother.

When you're going through homelessness and experiencing trauma, you don't see the beauty of where you live. We didn't see the beaches and palm trees, or the blue water and beautiful creation of God. We only saw the street, depression, hardship, poverty, and homelessness.

Well, through prayer, faith, and belief, in the next few months God picked us up in the palm of His hand and moved us two thousand miles away—going from the warmest, most beautiful state in North America to the coldest city imaginable: Winnipeg, Manitoba, which hits about -40 degrees Celsius in the winter.

Talk about a dramatic change in temperature and culture. This would be a whole new adventure!

29.

TRUE NORTH STRONG AND FREE

Grace allows you to start over.

And the God of all grace, who called you to his eternal glory in Christ, after you have suffered a little while, will himself restore you and make you strong, firm and steadfast. (1 Peter 5:10)

MY DAD HAD TO FLY IN FROM CANADA, GO TO COURT TO ASK FOR CUSTODY, pick us up at the Youth Ranch with all our belongings, and then fly with us back to Canada. It took several days to make all these arrangements, and then finally we were off to the airport. None of us had ever flown on a plane and I remember feeling excited, sad, lonely, and terrified. Terrified, because the only thing I remembered about my dad was that he was abusive. Although he was going to give us a new life in a new country, I had no real idea who he was and how he was going to treat us.

But I was excited because it was a new opportunity, and I would be with my family, with three of my brothers and sisters, and I wasn't going to end up on the street at eighteen. I was sad, though, because I was leaving absolutely everything and everyone I knew. Even though on the outside they seemed to be bad influences, they were all I had. In my own naïve way, I had loved Bobby as my first boyfriend. He'd been my strength during a time when I had absolutely nobody, and he'd loved me back.

I cried and cried, over and over, since the chance of me ever seeing my friends again was so very small. We didn't have the internet or easy ways to connect back then. It was the phone or snail mail, and phone calls were very expensive. With snail mail, it would take four weeks to send a message and get a reply in return.

That's a long time in a child's life. And we couldn't just hop on a plane and go see a friend; that was way too expensive.

My loneliness came from being on my own again. Yes, I had my brothers and sisters with me, but we had all gone our separate ways in the last few years and we didn't have a strong bond anymore. We would need to get to know each other and relearn to love each other.

I cried all the way to the airport. In fact, I cried all the way on the plane to Canada.

Although my dad managed to get us on the plane and to the Winnipeg airport, it turned out that he didn't have any immigration papers to help us get through the border. We were all standing there at the immigration counter with our garbage bags of clothes, carrying all the belongings we had.

"Where are your papers for these children?" the immigration officer asked.

My dad just looked at him. "I don't have any papers for these children. They came from a group home, and now I have custody of them."

He then handed the officer his custody papers.

"Well, sir, I'm sorry, but you can't bring four children through the border without some form of immigration papers to prove that they're yours and they can legally come into Canada."

My father looked at the man with his shrewd, beady eyes and said, "Well, son…" He had a way of belittling people and making them feel bad. He was also the biggest con artist. He knew exactly what he was doing. "Well, son, I just got custody of these children and they're excited to be leaving a group home where they would've graduated at eighteen and been left on the street. Now, you can either let them come into the country or you can send them back to their group home. That's up to you. But I'm not going to be the one to tell these children that they have no place to live. Are you?"

We could see a visible smirk on my dad's face. He knew he had this guy.

The officer sheepishly looked at him, then looked to the other people around him. We could tell he was confused. This was definitely an irregular case.

We glanced at each other, silently freaking out, thinking we were about to be sent back. Tears were streaming down our faces. This wasn't what we had expected. We knew our dad well enough to know that if this man didn't let us in, my dad would ship us back and say he'd tried… and that would be the end of it. He had left us for five years already.

"Listen here, sir," the officer finally said. "You have exactly thirty days to get the proper documentation and papers for these children or they will be shipped out of the country. You have not one day more. Good day."

And that's how my dad got us into the country. I'm sure those tactics wouldn't work today. I'm also sure it was God's divine grace that allowed us to come through in that moment.

But we were through. Welcome to Canada!

Our stepmom picked us up at the airport in a little car. The two adults sat up front and us four children squeezed in the back. It was a good thing we were so skinny! We all smoked cigarettes. Since we'd had permission to smoke at the group home, my dad couldn't really tell us we couldn't smoke now.

Imagine six people smoking in a small vehicle. It was quite interesting!

My stepmom took us to their place on Home Street, which was just a tiny one-room apartment. It didn't have much more than a bed and a TV stand. She gave us each a bag of clothing she had picked up at the Salvation Army, hoping they would fit us. So now we had two bags of clothing.

Then we got back into the car.

"We don't have a place for you to stay right now," my dad explained. "Your mom and I live in that apartment, and there obviously isn't enough room for six of us. So we're taking you out to a cabin where you're going to stay for the next five weeks while I try to find us a home to live in."

Needless to say, we were a bit shocked. We had thought he actually had a home for us.

Instead we were packed back into the car and driven, along with our belongings and some food, towards Ontario. It was now eleven o'clock at night and completely dark. We felt like we were sneaking into the country. It felt very surreal.

Needless to say, I was freaking out. As we drove, we left the city and soon all we saw were bushes and trees—trees, trees, and more trees. We've since travelled this road many times and it's a beautiful drive. But when it's late at night and you're thirteen years old, coming from palm trees and beaches to deep, dark woods, it's quite intimidating, especially when you're with a father and new stepmom you don't know and the only thing you remember is lots of yelling and abuse.

So we drove and drove and drove. We drove for two hours straight. It was one of the longest car rides in my life. Nothing was open because it was so late and we all chain-smoked out of sheer nervousness.

After two hours, we hit a dirt track called Jones Road. It was one of the roughest roads I'd ever been on. We proceeded to travel north up this road for another hour and a half—and the car didn't take it very well, because of all the weight. We constantly heard rocks hitting the bottom of the vehicle. We just looked at each other and wondered where the heck he was taking us.

He's taking us out into the woods to kill us, I thought, terrified. *Nobody has seen us. Nobody knows we're even in the country. We have no papers, and now we're going down this forty-mile dirt road, clunkety clunk…*

My dad finally parked the car.

"Grab all the stuff," he said. "Grab the groceries. Boys, you might have to make two trips. Let's carry it all down this path."

It was now one o'clock in the morning and the sound of crickets was deafening. The mosquitoes were biting like crazy, too.

We started to walk, noticing pieces of boards on the path to cover over the muddy spots so you didn't splash. It was very slippery.

We walked about a quarter of a mile, twisting and turning along with the path, surrounded by bush. What the heck was going on? The scariest movie I'd ever seen was *Texas Chainsaw Massacre*, and of course it came to mind immediately.

At the end of the path, we came to a big lake. A boat was tied up by the shore.

"It's okay, kids," our dad assured us. "We're going to put everything in the boat and then take a ride across this lake about five and a half miles to get to our cabin."

We could barely see anything this late at night, but we didn't really have a choice but to get in the boat. We were literally in the middle of nowhere and had to do what he said.

He had lifejackets for us, which was smart since my dad couldn't swim. He didn't have a lifejacket but made sure we all had one.

Away we went.

Well, we crossed that lake and had to manoeuvre around islands in the dark until we came to an open bay.

"Look, there's the cabin up on that cliff," my dad said.

We looked up and saw a huge log cabin on top of a rocky cliff. Coming from Florida, which is entirely flat, this was new terrain for us. To say we were amazed would be an understatement. This was where we were going to stay for the next five weeks?

We got to the dock and unloaded.

"Now you're going to have to carry everything up the hill," Dad said. "Once you get all the stuff into the cabin, each of you is going to have to come down and get a bucket of water so that we have water in the morning."

Again, we had no idea what was going on, but we did as we were told. One thing with my dad was that you had to do exactly as he said or his temper could flare up at any time. His angry outbursts were strong enough to terrify lions.

So we brought all our stuff up to the top of the cliff and brought it into an old log cabin that had been built in 1913, with moss between the logs to serve as insulation. The first impression of the cabin as we walked in the front door was that it was like a big camp. Right in the centre of the main room was an enormous deer head over a big red brick fireplace. In fact, the whole cabin was painted red. To the left and right of the fireplace were doors that led into bedrooms, and over the top of each doorway were antlers from other wildlife that had been killed.

There was an old oak table in the middle of the main room. We also saw an antique record player, a china cabinet, wicker furniture, and an old couch in front of the fireplace. The floors were all hardwood, although a carpet had been spread out under the table. The dim lantern light threw shadows all over the room, making it cozy but spooky all at the same time.

We put our stuff in the rooms and then went down the hill to get water for the morning. My stepmom gave me and my sister a little bucket to pee in overnight. The boys were told that if they had to go to the bathroom, they should go outside and pee in the bush.

Because we were exhausted, in shock, and frightened, we went straight to sleep.

Well, thank God for sunshine and bright mornings because the next day we were able to get a better look at our surroundings. They weren't too bad. The kitchen was quite old-fashioned. It had a wood-burning stove and a little china cabinet to hold the dishes. There was also a sideboard that held all our food. Pots and pans hung from nails along a wooden beam that crossed from one side of the room to the other, and the pot lids were stacked nicely on the left.

There was a sink and counter to wash dishes, alongside buckets of water to use for washing up. In order to have hot water, my stepmom—or Tenoka,[23] as we came to call her—would heat up a teakettle on the stove to wash the dishes.

In the middle of the room was a four-seat table with a cute little tablecloth, and to the right was a small rocking chair. This would turn out to be my favourite place to sit to talk with my stepmom for years to come.

On this first day, Tenoka was cooking eggs, bacon, and coffee on the wood-burning stove. We could also smell freshly baked bread. It smelled so good that it made our mouths water in anticipation of breakfast.

---

[23] This was her Indian name. Before my dad, she had been married to an Ojibwa chief who gave her the name Princess Tenoka. It was also her stage name.

That's when we discovered that we had no electricity or no running water in this cabin. Well, we were used to that!

We had a wonderful first meal in this new cabin that we were to call home for the next five weeks.

Afterward we decided to explore a little bit, and that's when we realized the cabin was actually quite large, with three big bedrooms furnished with brass beds and lots of blankets and pillows.

When we walked onto the front veranda, the view of the lake was incredible. It was so breathtaking, stunningly beautiful. We were atop a hundred-foot cliff. Behind the cabin were bushes and a path that led to a work shed which housed kerosene, gas, and non-essential items.

Another path that led to an outhouse, my least favourite place. If you had to go number two, you had to use the outhouse. You couldn't use the little chamber pots for that; those were just for peeing and only at night.

The outhouse was made of logs and was home to many different bugs from spiders and beetles to flies and mosquitoes. It was so dark that you needed a flashlight to go in, even during the day. My imagination played tricks on me when it was dark and I could envision three-foot-long spiders crawling everywhere.

My sister and I *hated* that outhouse.

I still couldn't bring myself to trust my dad. I still thought he was going to kill us out here in the middle of nowhere, but at least it looked better in the morning.

He then suggested we write a letter to tell our family back in Florida about our experiences so far. He encouraged us to write that Tenoka had baked homemade bread in the wood-burning stove and served us breakfast on our first morning here.

Yeah, he wants us to make it sound like we're having a good time, I thought. *Then he's going to kill us.*

He did own a gun, something which he'd let us know right off the hop. He also told us to be careful of the bears.

Dad suggested that we could go swimming down at the dock, and he strongly encouraged us to go as that was also where we were to have our baths. We went right into the lake with shampoo and soap and washed ourselves. That's how we cleaned ourselves for the next five weeks.

Tenoka was an avid reader and brought out a bunch of books and novels that we might be interested in reading. I have to say I'd never read books and found this new pasttime interesting. It amazed me that people would come out to the lake and just read books and sit in the sun. That seemed so foreign to us kids.

When we were ready, my dad said he would take us fishing, but only on the weekends. In fact, we were to spend Monday to Friday with Tenoka and he would come out on the weekends. He didn't have a job, and he had five weeks to find one, locate a home for us, and of course get our immigration papers in order. On the weekends he had to bring us food, because the kerosene fridge only held so much at a time.

Tenoka continued to wake us up with homemade bread and treats. We went blueberry-picking and fishing. To be honest, we finally started to learn how to just be kids. We had never really had fun before, and this was an opportunity to have some good old-fashioned fun.

Cindy and I were very quiet, not speaking much. It was awkward spending so much time with a woman we didn't know. However, we did start reading the books and getting into this relaxed lifestyle. The boys loved it. They could go frog-hunting, fish, play in the woods, and see deer and other types of animals. Probably the best news I heard was that there were no poisonous snakes, no alligators, no sharks, no scorpions, and especially no cockroaches. Heck, we could sleep in the woods here without any problem.

Well, almost. I'll never forget the first bear we saw. We happened to be down at the lake swimming one day when suddenly we heard Tenoka screaming at the top of her lungs. Then we heard a gunshot.

We all looked at each other, totally freaking out.

As we ran up the hill, we could see Tenoka standing on the rock behind the cabin with her gun pointed up into the air. She heard us coming and yelled, "Kids, stay where you are and don't move. Don't move. There's a bear. There's a bear!"

She lifted the gun and shot it in the air again. Then she started doing this crazy dance with pots and pans, screaming and yelling and trying to scare the bear away. We only got a glimpse of the animal as it trotted off.

When it was gone, Tenoka said we could come up to the cabin.

That day, we learned to respect the wilderness and the dangers of living in the bush. In those days, seeing bears was very common so we always had to be careful.

We continued to swim, fish, and eat at the lake. We also started to meet the neighbours. The lake was very secluded and there were only about twenty cottages in total. The closest neighbour we had was the Stanley family. They had four children, three boys and a girl: Greg, Mark, Susan, and John. Apparently they'd sponsored us into the country by writing a letter for my dad.

The Stanleys were very excited to meet us. They were nice, which made us feel a bit more secure about being out in the middle of nowhere. They weren't out at the lake the entire time we were there—they only came up on the weekends— but at least we knew some other people now. We got together with them on occasion and played board games and cards. This helped pass the summer. Their cottage was much more modern, built in the 70s. It had propane gas lighting, a real stove, running water and everything.

We met several families from different close-by lakes and discovered many of them had helped to sponsor us into the country. For this we are very grateful.

30.

NEW HOME, SAME BAD HABITS

Grace shines through caring brothers.

FINALLY, AFTER FIVE WEEKS, WHICH SEEMED LIKE AN ETERNITY OUT AT THE LAKE, my dad found us a house in Winnipeg. We then had a couple of weeks to get ready for school, get school clothes, register, and figure out the bus system. We lived on Beaverbrook and I would attend River Heights Junior High. Doug and Cindy would go to Kelvin High School. Duane would go to Sir John Franklin Elementary school right down the street.

This was the first time since we'd arrived that we spent any real time with Dad. Up until now we'd only seen him on the weekends, and he spent most of that time with our stepmom.

When we moved onto Beaverbrook, Doug recalls:

I remember we had just come back from the lake and were living in the new house on Beaverbrook. Judy was doing dishes at the time and the rest of us were watching TV in the living room on the other side of the wall. She kept coming around the door into the room to watch the TV because it was a good show. I can't remember the show, but we were all laughing until Dad yelled at Judy: "Go back and do the dishes!"

So she went back to do the dishes. There were quite a few dishes, because we had no dishwasher. There were six of us at dinner every night.

Judy was about halfway done and then she heard us laughing again. So she came around the corner to take a peek and Dad said, "I told you to get back and do the dishes. Now!"

So she scooted back to the kitchen.

Finally, she was almost done with the dishes and just had a couple of pans left. All the dishes were on the counter drying—and then something else came up on the TV. It was just getting towards the end of the show and Judy came back around the corner for one more peek.

Suddenly, Dad got up and, *bam*, he smacked her in the face. I couldn't believe it. We hadn't even been living in Canada two months when he did that.

I was so angry. So I got off of the couch, walked over to him, and said, "What the hell do you think you're doing!?"

He came over to me with this really mean look on his face as if he was going to smack me, too, but I had my own mean look. I was pissed. After going through foster homes and all the challenges I'd faced, I didn't give a crap about anything.

He came towards me with his fists balled, and I was waiting. As soon as he got up to me, I grabbed him by the shirt, swung him around, and threw him into the wall between two studs. The wall gave way.

I looked him right in the eyes. "You bastard! Where the hell have you been the last six or seven years of our lives? Now you think you're going to turn around and hit my sister? Well, let me tell you, I've been taking care of my sisters and you don't know me anymore. You left me in those homes and I'm different now. I'm going to kill you."

I pushed him again and walked away.

After that, he never hit Judy when I was around. But I'm sure if I hadn't done that then he probably would've started beating us up all the time like he used to.

I wasn't scared about nothing! I was just so cold from living in the foster homes. I was so angry.

There was a girl who lived behind us across the back lane whose name was Colleen. She was the same age as me and was one of my first friends in Canada. She had gorgeous long wavy brownish-red hair and a beautiful smile. Her family had a Scottish background, and she highland-danced and was an incredible singer. Her dad, a cop, was a bagpiper with the Winnipeg Police Department.

She had quite a different upbringing from me, that was for sure. She was shocked when she first heard my story. Her mouth just dropped open and she told me she had never met anyone with such a colourful background.

Colleen remarked that I never seemed to mind walking to school when we missed the bus. For her, it was always a hardship. She probably didn't realize how much walking I used to do.

Another detail of our friendship is that she was frustrated that I could never go out on Saturdays because I had to clean all day. In our house, only the girls cleaned, never the boys. It was different in her house, where everyone pitched in. She used to get so angry with my dad and his chauvinistic ways.

I'll never forget walking into my new class on the first day of school. Thirty eyeballs all stared at me like I was a freak of nature. Coming from Florida, I had a super tan and was as brown as a Canadian bear. I also had a strong southern accent, speaking with an obvious twang in my voice. It could have been all those things, but the real reason they stared was that I was dressed in a floor-length down-filled parka and cougar boots when most kids wore short trendy bomber jackets. To us, the weather here was freezing cold! We didn't want to stand out, so we eventually learned to dress Canadian.

When the Canadian kids talked, I thought they sounded quite British. There couldn't have been a bigger disparity in the sound of our voices. My classmates loved to tease me about my accent, especially with me being new. I also wrote the way I talked, so I'd write things like "y'all" and thought that was perfectly good English. I learned quite quickly that it was not.

I guess some people would say I was pretty, although I never felt that way. I got a lot of attention from the boys, mostly because I was someone new to have fun with.

Doug's first couple of days at school didn't go so well. As he explains:

In Canada, you're allowed to smoke cigarettes outside the high school. One day a couple of days after school started, I was standing outside. There are about nine steps that went down to the sidewalk and Cindy and I were having a cigarette there.

Suddenly, a guy came up to her. He was in twelfth grade, and she was in eleventh.

"Hey b—ch, give me a cigarette," he said.

"I'm sorry, what did you just say?" I asked.

He looked at me. "I just asked the b—ch for a cigarette."

An evil smile spread across my face. "Oh, that's what I thought you said."

Then I punched him in the back of the head, threw him down the stairs, and took a flying leap to land on top of him.

"Don't you ever talk to my sister like that again," I said as I beat on him.

And he didn't.

I did everything I could to protect my sisters, as requested by Dave. I got in so many fights that I can't remember them all. All I knew was fighting.

At the time, I remember thinking to myself that this was a huge opportunity to start fresh. Nobody knew our history. Nobody knew our story. We could just be who we were and hopefully be accepted.

For the first month or two, school seemed pretty good. I tried not to talk about my past and seemed to get by okay. New people are always interesting, especially ones coming from a state like Florida that everyone wants to visit. I could talk about Disneyworld and all the beaches and beautiful things the kids seemed to know about it.

In Winnipeg, my classmates in Grade Nine were just starting to get into drugs. I thought it was kind of funny because I had already taken so many drugs. I laughed when they brought out a joint full of seeds and said, "Let's get high." To be cool, I smoked up a little bit with them.

Eventually I told my closest friends that I thought smoking up was baby stuff compared to what I had done before moving to Winnipeg. Drugs were also way more expensive here than they'd been in Florida. I wasn't sure how they could afford it.

But for the most part, nobody knew my real background. That is, until one day my dad decided that the story about Tenoka becoming a River Heights housewife would be great publicity for her career. She danced in all the bars and pubs in town and made really good money to help support us kids. It was more of a burlesque-type of show, not necessarily the seedier side that people would call stripping. But at the end of the day, it was still a stripping show since she did it topless.

The next thing we knew, the Winnipeg Tribune came to our home to interview the family and ask us questions about Tenoka and what kind of mother she was. They took several pictures of us celebrating my brother's birthday, and of course it ended up in the paper. And suddenly everyone knew that our new mom was a fire-eating dancer.

In 1979, the River Heights neighbourhood was pretty upper class, full of people who looked down at that sort of lifestyle. Mostly they didn't understand it. Quite frankly, most people don't. However, I'll tell you that no one ever worked so hard to bring four children out of foster care into a normal life than Tenoka. Despite what she did for a living, she had love, compassion, and cared for us kids when we were in need. She did everything she could to take care of us and love us and give us a real family, things which we had never really known. For all this, we are eternally grateful.

But we weren't very impressed that everyone suddenly knew about her career choice. Now we got made fun of at school. The boys felt they could come up and grab me by the behind or brush against my breasts; if my mom was a stripper, her daughter must be loose. Several times I elbowed guys, kneed them, and had to push them away. I wasn't afraid.

I was disgusted and disappointed by the change in behaviour. It just wasn't fair.

Another thing that wasn't fair is that we hadn't been given a choice about sharing the story. My dad had thought it would be good for my mom and that was that. Had we been asked, we wouldn't have wanted people to know. Being the new kid in school is tough enough, and we had wanted a fresh start so no one would judge us or look down on us.

We felt compelled to defend our new mom by sharing our story of being in foster care and group homes and how she was the hero who had saved us from devastation. So it seemed like we were going to have to go through this all over again.

Doug remembers:

After the newspaper story came out, I went to math class one day and Tim Johnson, one of the biggest guys in Grade Ten, sat behind me. I had Mr. Emarua for math. He was a black teacher.

As I sat there, Tim whispered in my ear, "Hey Needham, I hear your mom is a stripper. I'm just wondering, does she hook too?" And then he started laughing.

That comment wasn't gonna fly with me. So I jumped up, went flying across his desk, and started beating him up.

Mr. Emarua came over grabbed me. "Hey, what's going on? What are you doing?"

"He's talking about my mama," I said. "He's telling everyone she's a stripper and asked if she was a hooker, too. No one talks about her that way!"

Mr. Emarua took me outside but didn't send me to the principal's office. In fact, he didn't do anything. He just went back in and told everybody to calm down.

Of course, Tim never said anything to me after that. He wanted to be friends, because he knew I could kick his ass.

I got through Grade Nine and managed to earn straight A's and make my parents very proud. I was also able to participate in the district spelling bee, where I came in second place. The only thing that messed me up was the Canadian spelling of different words. That's how I lost the spelling bee. Overall we were still quite proud.

Over the summer, we went to the drop-in at the junior high school and got to hang out with the neighbouring kids. One time, a friend's parents asked what my parents did. I looked at them and deadpanned, "My real mom has schizophrenia, my stepmom is a stripper, and my dad is her manager and is in sales." I just wanted to see their reaction. The cat was out of the bag anyway so I might as well tell the truth. They looked at me strangely and eventually I explained that I'd come from foster care and had just moved to the country. Sharing the truth didn't seem to help me.

I didn't feel like I had a lot of good friends. I had quite a few people I called friends, but when you came from the kind of background I did, you felt the stigma. It was awkward hanging around with people who had good, faith-based foundations of stability and generational heritage. My friends all had accomplishments like dancing, singing, and sports. Most of the families had a piano in the living room. Our living room couch had come from the Salvation Army and Tenoka had reupholstered it herself by sewing new material over the old fabric. From what we were used to, we thought it looked great—until we saw what everyone else had.

I really felt the difference when I went into one of the beautiful, classic homes in the neighbourhood and sat politely at the dinner table. The family would talk to each other and discuss topics of interest. What do you want to do after high school? Where are you going to university? I didn't even know these were possibilities. Our family was always rambunctious. We were like the Beverly Hillbillies.

So the cultural shock was quite incredible. I never felt like I belonged.

Tenoka did try to teach us manners and etiquette, like how to hold a fork, eat properly, and which cutlery to use. She had come from a good background and her grandfather, Douglas Nathanial Stevens, was one of the Winnipeg's old grain barons; her father, John Douglas Stevens, followed in his footsteps. She'd been brought up with a silver spoon in her mouth, with a nanny and everything. Our cottage was one that had originally been owned by her grandfather and a couple of other wealthy local families.

31.

LIFE ISN'T FREE, GET A JOB

Grace comes through independence.

MY PARENTS DID EVERYTHING THEY COULD TO TAKE CARE OF US, BUT IT WAS obvious that they really didn't have the means to provide for us in the way most families could. My dad got a job at a cleaning company and reached out to one of his clients, a local hotel, to see if they would hire me and Cindy on a part-time basis so we could help pay our own way.

So it was that in January 1980 we got our first jobs as housekeepers. I was the only kid in junior high to have a real job. Of course, the other kids probably didn't need one.

I finished Grade Nine with honours, and in the summer Tenoka got five weeks off to take us to the lake. It was her time, and her special place. We learned to love it there; it was a place to find refuge, peace, and rest. A place to find God. We learned to enjoy nature and the beauty of God's creation—the earth, the sky, the beautiful sunrises and sunsets, the lake, the water, the fish… everything He had created.

And of course we got to hang out with all our lake friends, especially the Stanleys. Between us and them, we owned almost the whole bay. It was a carefree time for us to just enjoy being kids.

Doug and Duane did odd jobs, like mowing the grass. Eventually they started working for the people who employed our stepmom. As Duane recalls:

> For a couple of years, things began to straighten out a little. I worked at my stepmom's boss's house. She was the head of the stripper agency.
>
> I worked some really odd jobs, such as running collections. I collected checks from bars on behalf of someone named "Fat Ted." If

they said they wouldn't give me a check, I reminded them that "Fat Ted" was just outside. That's all I would need to say. Sometimes I'd get the check and other times I wouldn't. When they didn't give me the money they owed, "Fat Ted" took action. Ted was a really big guy, three hundred fifty pounds. If he didn't get his check, they didn't get the strippers.

For Grade Ten, I went to Kelvin High School. Doug was a cornerback on the football team. Although he was a small player, his past provided an aggression that made him unstoppable. He loved going after the running backs and tackling them. He wasn't afraid of anything and was probably the best defensive player on the team.

As Doug explains:

In football, I was crazy and didn't care about anything. During practice one day I took two of our own guys out because I was such an animal. I took them out for the whole year because I didn't know how to control my anger. One guy broke his ankle and the other guy broke his leg. I hadn't done it on purpose; they just weren't used to physical contact, and I went in there full blast.

Boomer, one of the players in the twelfth grade, decided he was going to have some fun during the rookie party. He called this one guy over, one of the guys on our team, and sprayed his privates with heat.[24] You could see it was burning and the kid cried.

Then Boomer came up to me, like he was going to spray me.

"Hey, Needham."

"Hey," I said. "If you spray me with any of that, I'm gonna kick your ass so hard you're not gonna know what hit you."

By this time, I had a reputation.

"Well, let's say I spray it anyway," he said. I gave him a mean look, and he backed down. "I wasn't going to do it."

I had such a bad attitude when I came to Canada. I didn't care if I got beat up. I thought, what's the worst thing that could happen? I was either going to get beat up or have a broken bone or black eye. No big deal. I didn't think anything of it. If I didn't do anything when provoked, that would make me a pansy and people would keep picking on me.

---

[24] This is a reference to a pain relief spray. If used on your privates, it cause a deep burning sensation that lasts for a long time. It is very painful if used incorrectly.

Kelvin High School is where I met the love of my life. One day I went to my brother's football game and one of the players, who'd broken his leg, was in the stands. He was one of Doug's friends and his name was Albert. He called me up into the stands and said, "Hey Judy, come sit by us." So I did.

Well, lo and behold, his cousin was there as well. I had brought popcorn and I shared it with Albert's cousin, Joe. I didn't know at the time that this would be my future husband.

Joe and I chatted and had fun. He was funny and very flattering. He always complimented people. That was my first impression, but I didn't think anything of it at the time.

I liked to stay in shape, so I did a lot of extracurricular fitness activities in school. One day while doing my fitness exercises I suddenly saw Joe come up to me wearing his shorts. He had been jogging around the third floor and asked if he could join me.

If you know Joe, this was a huge stretch for him. Exercising wasn't his thing. He must have really liked me! Looking back, the moment reminds me of a scene from *Grease* when the character Danny tried out for athletics to impress Sandy.

"Okay, sure," I said.

When I found out that Joe was dating some other girl, I didn't want anything to do with him. If there was one thing I didn't like, it was a guy coming on to a girl while he was dating somebody else. I pretty much just told him I wasn't interested. If he wanted to date me, he would have to be free.

After that I saw him every day, and every day he complimented me and told me how beautiful I looked, how wonderful I was. It would be an outright lie to say I didn't love to hear these things after all I had gone through. I craved these encouraging words, but otherwise I ignored him.

Then one day he came up to me and said, "Hey, guess what? I broke up with my girlfriend."

"That's nice," I told him. And I walked away.

I think he was shocked. He was in Grade Twelve and I was in Grade Ten. Most girls would have been thrilled to go out with a senior, but I just wanted a person I could trust.

He continued to try to get me out on a date until I finally agreed.

"You need to drive me home, though," I told him. "I need to talk to you before we date."

So he drove me home and pulled over into a parking lot by my house so we could have a chat. I told him my entire life story, everything—from living on the street to being sexually abused, to doing drugs, to everything that had happened to me. I held nothing back.

"I'm telling you these things because if you're going to judge me by these situations or have an issue with my mom being a stripper, then I need to know," I said. "Then it's just not meant to be. I am who I am, and you have to take me with all my baggage."

Joe was very much an Italian mama's boy, and I'm sure he was shocked.

"Well, what happened to you is your past and you had no control over that," he said very maturely. "You were too young. What's done is done. As for your mom, what she does isn't what you do. It's her choice, not yours. So that has no reflection on you. Who you are today is a much better person because of all that you've gone through. So yes, I would still like to go out with you."

Now, I had dated some guys here and there since coming to Winnipeg, but nothing seriously. I pretty much knew after one kiss if they were someone I wanted to continue dating. I was now fifteen going on thirty!

But Joe was the first person I shared my past with in detail. After one kiss, I knew he was the man for me.

Then I had to tell him about my dad.

My dad had some pretty strict rules when it came to serious boyfriends, and one of them was that they had to come to the door and meet him if they were going to take me out, especially if they had a car, which Joe did. They weren't allowed to wait in the car for me. They also had to get me home on time. There could be no excuses. If we were going to be late, we needed to phone in advance of the allotted curfew to let my dad know and give him an estimated time when we thought we would be home.

I was terrified to tell my dad about Joe, but I really wanted to go on a date. So one day I went to my dad and asked if I could go out with Joe. He told me the rules and gave me his approval. Looking back, I realize that he was teaching me honesty, trust, respect, and discipline. He was also teaching me to respect myself.

32.

THIS IS TRUE LOVE

Grace comes in learning what true love is.

ON NOVEMBER 28, 1980, JOE ROLLED UP IN HIS CAR AND PROCEEDED TO COME IN to meet my dad. I was fifteen and Joe was nineteen. He had a moustache, was Italian, and was pretty hairy.

My dad took one look at him and said, "My, you look awfully old to be dating my daughter. How old are you?"

I had told Joe to tell him he was seventeen, because if my dad knew he was nineteen I probably wouldn't have been able to go. So Joe told him he was seventeen.

"Okay," my dad said. "What time are you going to have her home? Where you going?"

After the interrogation, we left.

Our first date was to a hockey game—and it was my very first hockey game: the Winnipeg Jets versus the St. Louis Blues. I didn't understand hockey, although it seemed like an interesting sport. I asked a lot of questions because I wanted to know what was going on. I loved football, a sport I had grown up, but hockey was new to me.

Well, I found out that every date with Joe was going to involve going to a hockey game. We seemed to attend every game that season, and unfortunately the Jets lost every one of them. They were the newest team in the NHL at the time and Winnipeggers were just happy to have a team.

By the end of the season, I had met a lot of new people and had started to understand the sport.

In meeting Joe, I felt like I had won the lottery. I had never been to a professional sporting event with a boy before. I'd never been to restaurants. I'd never even been on a date for coffee, never mind a drive around the city. When I had been with Bobby, we just hung out. This was different. Joe took me everywhere. He truly spoiled me and made me feel like a princess.

My first Chinese food experience came after a Jets game. I remember picking a fortune cookie, and inside the fortune said "You are happily in love." In that moment, I realized it was true. So I saved that fortune cookie and pressed it into a photo album, along with tickets to every event he took me to during our first year together.

Meeting Joe was a divine appointment. He had graduated from St. Paul's High School the year before, in 1979, and was trying to get into university. He had to improve some grades in order to get accepted, which is what had brought him to Kelvin. That's what made it possible for us to meet. Otherwise our lives would never have crossed. I know God had set that up so we could have a future together. That's just how God's grace works.

I also remember meeting his parents for the first time. When sharing my past to people for the first time, I usually gave them the Cole's Notes version—and since the story had already been in the newspapers, I figured people already knew. Most parents were taken aback, but not his parents.

One day I went to Joe's home after school. I stayed for supper and helped clean up. Later in the evening, I sat in the living room and did some homework while his uncle popped over for a visit. It was typical for Italian families to have espresso after supper. His mom made the coffee and we all sat together enjoying the treats.

As soon as we were finished with our refreshments, I brought all the dishes to the sink and washed them. I then sat back down to continue my homework. This was a normal routine for me at home. I had been trained to always help clean up, so of course I did. But I didn't realize this wasn't what most kids did.

Coming back into the room, I noticed the members of the family glancing at each other. It was a bit uncomfortable.

Then they started asking me questions. Of course the first question was, "What do your parents do?" And of course I gave them a play by play: "My mom is a schizophrenic. My stepmom's a stripper." I even told them a little bit about having come up through the foster care system.

They understood English pretty well, but Joe had to interpret some of the conversation into Italian to emphasize certain points.

I will always be honest. I only know how to tell the truth, as that's a character trait my dad instilled in me and my siblings once we came to Canada. I had also learned that it's better to tell the truth and get it over with then get caught up in a story that will get you into bigger trouble later. So if you ask me a question, you're going to hear the truth.

As I told my story, I remember my mother-in-law having the sweetest look on her face. I felt that she was a kindred spirit. Unbeknownst to me, she had her own difficult past. She'd lost her mother at an early age.

Once she learned that my stepmom was a stripper, she looked at me and said in her broken English, "Well, you're a very nice girl. You cook. You clean. You do the dishes. You help out in the home. As long as you take care of my Joey, that is all I care about. You're a very nice girl."

Her thick Italian accent was hard to understand, but I understood the heart—and I understood the compassion and love. That's one thing I will never forget: the feeling of love you felt upon entering my in-laws' home.

My in-laws were always very generous with their food, and Papa Cheech always had homemade wine on the table. They always opened their doors to strangers and fed whoever came through the door. They shared what they had and made it work.

They always showed love and compassion, something we hadn't grown up with at home. This incredible Italian family was addictive, and I was in awe of the love they exhibited. They knew what real life was about, what real love was about, and what real family was about.

I found it very interesting that some of the most educated people, including the parents of my friends or acquaintances, judged me. I could feel their reservations towards me when they heard my story.

Yet when I shared it with this sweet immigrant family, who had very little education and very little money, there was no judgment. I found it amazing that they would just love and accept me for who I was, despite my past, despite what I had been through. They actually loved me even more because of it. It was very gratifying and very welcoming.

When you've gone through hardship and experiences most people don't understand, what you really need is a nonjudgmental response of love, compassion, and support. We all go through difficulties, and we all have to make decisions based on those difficulties, some that we're proud of and some that we aren't. But when circumstances come our way, most of us act out of our best intentions, with the wisdom we have in the moment. We need to be accepted for that.

That's what I felt from Joe's family—unconditional love and acceptance. It was like coming home. This is where I learned that if people can just learn to love each other, unconditionally, real change can happen. It certainly worked for me and my family.

Joe and I dated through high school. While most of the kids were just starting to do drugs and smoke up, Joe did not. This made it very easy for me to quit. I had tried so many drugs already and felt lucky to be alive. I also found that since I was happy and in love with Joe, I didn't need it. It was kind of ironic that I was in high school telling kids that I was quitting dope when they were just trying it for the first time.

It was another blessing from God to be delivering me from this lifestyle at such an early age. Many people make it a part of their lifestyle, but I just plain quit. And the fact that my classmates knew I had smoked in the past allowed me to be cool and popular, able to fit in with any group.

Meanwhile, Duane continued to do drugs:

At fifteen, I got a job at a restaurant. Just before I got that job, I was making some money working for people around the neighbourhood, and I had a paper route. At the restaurant, there were a lot of bad influences. I began smoking marijuana, hash, and hash oil... and I was drinking again.

But the worst part is that I began to sell marijuana. I got my first pound of pot from one of the cooks at the restaurant so we could make some extra money. Next thing I knew I was selling for a couple of people and I was their guinea pig. But I was okay with that because I was making money.

When I was sixteen, we moved to a different house. I was in ninth grade and had a driver's license and a car. After all, I was two years behind in school.

I became one of the "potheads" at school. I remember one night making a stop outside a convenience store to sell marijuana to some of the kids before a school dance. Little did I know that it was a setup. As I pulled up, I gave two of my friends bags of pot to sell. They got out of the car to go into the store...

And then three police cars surrounded my car. They put me up against my car, searched me, and then began to search my car for drugs. I was in tears and so afraid, since I knew I was going to jail. I had over a pound of marijuana in the car—the biggest bag I'd ever had. They looked in the trunk, looked in the hubcaps, and even looked in the engine.

When my friends came out of the store, we made eye contact and with my eyes I told them to split. They took off.

With tears running down my face, the officer showed me more than forty pot seeds he had found in my car. The entire car smelled like pot.

"I know you have pot in this car and we want it," the officer said, yelling in my face.

To my surprise, they couldn't find it. I smiled inside as I watched them search. As the officer leaned into the car, he put his hand on the backrest of the driver's seat. He didn't realize it, but I had pulled the stuffing out of the bottom of the seat and pushed the pot up in it and then restuffed the seat. So when I was driving, I was actually leaning against the bag of pot.

They didn't find the pot, and they didn't arrest me. I escaped the big moment. Tears were running down my cheeks and they knew I was guilty. But they didn't have any evidence.

Duane was very lucky. I hadn't heard this story before; we were again living different lives. The age gap between Duane and me was only one year, but three years of school was a big difference and meant we were in different schools during the years he lived in Canada.

I loved becoming friends with the "nerds," the kids who were considered different. I wanted to set an example to others that everyone deserves to belong and have friends. I always chose to partner with kids whom no one else wanted to be with. I knew what that felt like and I wasn't going to let anyone else feel that way. This was the privilege of being the new kid in town. I always tried to treat others the way I wanted to be treated.

After our past was shared in the newspaper, it felt like this big neon sign had been hung around my neck labelling me as a foster kid, the daughter of a stripper, and a faker in River Heights who shouldn't be there. That's how I felt inside, but it wasn't really how people saw me. In high school, kids are so self-absorbed. Most of them just worry about their own personal issues—boyfriends, girlfriends, sports, activities, etc. While our family story did have legs for a little while, like any sensational story it quickly dissipated. Life moved on and people forgot.

If you're a kid going through difficult times, I want to encourage you. Your high school years are just a blip in your life. This part of your life doesn't define you and won't follow you. Get through it. Tough it out and be strong, not letting your circumstance define who you are. You can overcome anything if you make the right choices and follow the vision God has planned for you.

A big challenge came my and Joe's way was when I got pregnant in Grade Eleven. It was interesting that I'd gone through so much between the ages of eight to thirteen and was spared a teenage pregnancy. But in this relationship of true love, I was finally caught.

I didn't know what to do. My dad wasn't the nicest man, always very angry and extremely difficult to live with. He was very OCD and wanted everything perfect when he got home. He expected dinner to be made every night and put on the table. He expected us to do most of the work—and when he came home, he always wanted a rye and coke. He explained to us exactly how he wanted it, and he expected it to be ready when he walked in the door.

He was an autocratic ruler and a bully who liked to scream to scare us. We lived in fear, although my stepmom was an incredible buffer for many of his outbursts.

How was I going to tell my dad that I was pregnant? I didn't even realize it until I was already about twelve weeks along, because I hadn't had regular periods to begin with. Telling him would take tremendous courage.

Finally, the time came.

At this point in my life, I was pretty self-sufficient. I worked part-time on the weekends and sometimes in the evenings. I had my own money and paid for all my own things—shampoo, tampons, clothes, bus tickets, you name it. If I wanted to go out to eat, it was all on my dime.

I was very independent, but I guess at the same time I was very ignorant. When I went to tell my dad, before I could say anything he just looked at me and told me I was pregnant. I asked him how he had known and he told me that he'd seen the changes in my body. My breasts had gotten fuller, for example. I guess after eight kids he was the expert.

I was kind of shocked that he had even noticed.

"I suppose you're going to get an abortion?" he asked.

"Well, I don't know what I want to do," I said. "That's why I'm coming to you."

My dad had a way of having a conversation where he'd tell you what you were going to do whether you really wanted to do it or not. He summed up all the logical reasons why I should have an abortion and gave me very few reasons why I shouldn't.

A part of me knew it was wrong, but I listened to all his logic about pregnancy. It could ruin my life at this age since I hadn't graduated yet. I'd been given a chance at a new beginning, and this would burn my opportunities of going to college and getting a good education. And I could always have a baby later.

He laid out all the options as if I had a choice, but the options all pointed to one choice, the one he thought I should take.

I felt trapped. I also knew that my dad would be disappointed if I went through with having the baby. His list of pros and cons was very persuasive.

So the decision was made. It was clear that if I had the baby, I would be on my own. It was clear that there would be little support from home.

The next thing I knew my dad was taking me to the clinic to figure out how to get an abortion. There, we learned that the only way it could be done at this point would be for me to go to the U.S. The clinic set up the appointment for me.

"Okay, you need to go and get it done," my dad told me. He could be pretty cold and ruthless.

I can't say I wasn't in agreement, because there was a part me that wanted to go to college and succeed in life. At the same time, I still felt like a torn child trying to figure out what I should do. It's interesting that my dad never really showed any emotion about this situation—no compassion, no love. It was like I just had to go. I had to do it. It would be done and then it would be over and we would never talk about it again. Period.

So that's what happened. Joe and I went across the line and got it done. It was a horrible experience, and a very emotional one for me, because I'd felt the changes in my body and the baby in my belly. I knew I wanted a baby, and I knew Joe was the one, but I had made this decision.

I felt like a part of me died that day, and I didn't know if I would ever get it back.

Joe was very supportive. Guys will never know what a girl has to go through to make those decisions, because it's our bodies, our hearts, and our minds that go through the experience. Men can only be observers and try their best to be supportive.

Afterward, we drove back to Winnipeg.

For anyone in this situation today, I highly recommend that you go to a crisis pregnancy centre for help and advice. Most of them have Christian operators who can help you through the decision-making process and seek ways to save the baby and support the family, which is the better moral option. This is a life-changing decision that needs to be taken seriously and explored wisely.

That same year, Joe and I got engaged. He wanted me to know that his intentions were serious. Now we could take more time to plan a family instead of having it thrust upon us.

To this day, I would love to hold that baby in my arms. I know it was a boy. Looking back, if I'm honest, we would have figured life out either way. God has a way of working things out for His purpose. But at the time I still hadn't given myself to the Lord, and I didn't understand what that meant. I loved God, but that was all I knew.

If I had known God then like I do now, I would have made a different decision. But after all I had gone through, I felt confused, frightened, alone, and unsure of the right decision. So I took the advice that was given.

Joe was more than willing to do whatever I wanted to do. He was prepared to marry me then and there and be responsible for the child. Deep down in my heart, I really wanted to have that baby. I felt the warmth in my belly of a child, and it made me feel that I could really love, care, and nurture a family. I knew I would be good at it. I needed so much to find love and give love. I knew I had that love for Joe as well and that we could have made it work.

What I didn't have was support in my choice.

From the time I started dating Joe to the time I married him, my dad didn't like him. My dad would take me downstairs to the basement and try to convince me that Joe was not the man for me. He would lecture me over and over about how Joe was a bad choice. He said I was way too young to be committing my life to somebody when I was only fifteen, and then sixteen, and then seventeen.

Dad constantly challenged me. If I wanted to go anywhere with Joe, like to visit a relative or friend of his,[25] he said that people would think badly of me, that they would probably think I was having sex and doing inappropriate things with him. My dad said that Joe only wanted me for sex. Imagine that—after abandoning me to the street at such a young age, he was now worried that I might be having sex? I think he was more concerned about what people thought.

Finally, one day I looked at him and said, "First of all, people are going to think what they want to think, so it doesn't matter what I do. Secondly, Joe and I had sex in the first month of our dating, so if he just wanted sex then he got it a long time ago, and he is still with me. Who cares what people think?"

I also knew the difference between sex and love. Joe and I really loved each other. I think in my dad's mind's eye he was hoping for someone better educated, like a doctor or a lawyer. But what I saw in Joe was a man who would do whatever it took to take care of his family. That's all I wanted.

We've been together more than forty years and have been extremely happy. I made a good choice.

---

[25] We went to Roblin, Manitoba to visit his cousin, and later to Thunder Bay, Ontario to visit his family.

That was the pain and joy of high school. I managed to do very well in Grades Ten through Twelve, getting high B's and mostly A's. But living with my dad and dealing with the past had its challenges.

I had a constant rage that needed to be released. Whether it was from fighting my dad, trying to please him, or him saying inappropriate things or picking on my siblings, it burned a hole in my chest. If he wanted something, you wouldn't serve him fast enough. He was very demanding and always angry.

So when Joe would pick me up—invariably late, which didn't help—I would take out my rage on Joe's little car, pounding on the dashboard until all the anger had subsided. Joe had a lot of patience. It took many years for me to gain confidence and lose my anger.

33.

LIFE JUST ISN'T FAIR

Grace sometimes feels absent, but it's always there.

DOUG CONTINUED TO BE ANGRY, TOO, AND CONSTANTLY GOT INTO FIGHTS. HE shares one incident he got into with Joe's little brother, Aggie:

> One time we were going to the liquor store, and it was five minutes before it closed. I was with Aggie and three other girls, and we were all partying. But we were out of beer.
>
> We were trying to pull into the parking lot, but the traffic was backed up because a car had gotten stalled right in the middle of the road. Everyone was honking their horns.
>
> "Screw this," I said to Aggie. "We'll never make it."
>
> So I put my car in park and decided to run down the back lane on foot to get the beer.
>
> It was winter and very icy, so I decided to run toward the side of the lane so I wouldn't slip. There had to be about thirty cars backed up down this alleyway, and they were all honking their horns.
>
> I was about fifteen cars down the line when suddenly Aggie's girlfriend, Leona, got out of our car. Someone yelled at me and I looked back to see her standing with a guy, about six feet tall and two hundred fifty pounds. They were yelling at each other.
>
> This guy was a biker dude, and he suddenly pushed her really hard right in the middle of her chest. She fell back and hit her head right on the concrete.

I stopped running and turned around to go back. Everyone in the cars had seen what happened and started yelling at me, "Hey man, go kick his ass!"

So I went up to the guy and said, "What the hell are you doing?"

Leona got up and kept yelling at him, so I told her to get back to the car. For what it's worth, Aggie never got out of the car. But I wasn't paying attention to him or the other people; I was just looking at this guy.

"What are you gonna do about it, little punk?" the biker said.

I was only five-foot-six and a hundred fifty pounds. He was way bigger than me.

But I was pissed and had no fear.

"I'm gonna kick your ass!"

"No, you're not."

As he came at me, I jumped up and down, karate-kicking in the air. Then, *boom*, I hit him in the face. His glasses went flying and landing on the ground. I kicked him, grabbing him by the head, and started beating the crap out of him. I took his head by his ears and just slammed his face into my knee a whole bunch of times.

Suddenly, he went limp. His buddy got out of their car and started coming over, like he was going to get me. So I waited till he got right to my side, then jumped up and grabbed him by the shirt. I butted him right in the head.

"What the heck are you doing?" I asked.

"I just want to get my friend," he said.

I didn't know what was going on with the guy on the ground, so I stepped back and said, "Okay."

I started to realize I had only one or two minutes to get my beer, so I ran back towards the store. As I went, everyone was cheering me on. All I was thinking was that I wouldn't get to the store on time.

When I got to the doors, sure enough, the liquor store was closed. So after all that trouble, I had no beer.

Defeated and dejected, I walked back. The two guys I'd beaten up were gone and I got back into our car. All the other cars were gone.

"Sorry, guys," I said. "I didn't make it there in time."

Aggie and the girls were standing by the car's open trunk, which had a cooler in it. He lifted the lid and I saw, like, twenty to thirty beers in there, all different kinds. All the people who had been waiting in the cars, who'd already gotten their beers, had dropped off a beer as a donation to me for beating the guy up.

Now we had a whole cooler full of beer. I had only been going to buy a twelve-pack, and we ended up with more than double that.

That was a fight I really hadn't wanted to get into, but I had to. I hated to see any guy hit a girl after watching Dad and his abuse. A guy has no right to hit a girl and should never hit a girl. Period.

But for the first time in my life I got rewarded for my fighting.

Unfortunately, as my life finally started to stabilize, my mom's life down in Florida was getting more and more out of control. As Connie remembers:

With paranoid schizophrenia, our mom heard many voices. She always thought the Russians were out to get her and that they were tracking her.

She once made me walk ten feet behind my parked car to talk to me. I asked her why she had made me walk back there and she said that the Russians were listening through the radio.

"Mom, the radio's off!" I argued.

She said it didn't matter. They could still hear.

You never knew what she was going to say or do. We tried to get help for her, but we were unsuccessful for many years. She wasn't a danger to herself or others, so there was no way to make her get help without her permission.

She would stay with me and my family when she was in town. But then the voices would tell her to go somewhere else and she would just disappear. That was the worst thing about her mental illness, not knowing where she was or if she was okay.

One time she took the last of her money, bought a bus ticket, and went to Oral Roberts University in Oklahoma. She was broke when she got there and slept on the lawn.

She ended up at my grandpa's house in Pennsylvania one time, but after a few weeks my grandpa couldn't handle her anymore. Her mom and her brother were mentally ill, too, and he had his hands full with them. So he put a map of the United States on the table with $400 and told my mom to pick any place to go—and he would give her the money to get there. God bless him, he did his best to help everyone and he somehow always seemed happy. Well, that might have been the beer. But we all loved him and enjoyed being around him.

She was once admitted to the psych ward at the hospital I worked at. They Baker-Acted her but could only keep her for three days. Baker-Acted is a means of providing individuals with emergency services and temporary detention for mental health evaluation and treatment when required, either on a voluntary or involuntary basis.

The staff at the psych ward called me every day asking if I could come over from the main hospital and try to calm her down. She would refuse to come into the building, because she wanted to stay out and smoke all day. She also refused to take her medications.

At the end of three days, I took her back to my house.

The doctor also warned me that her condition was hereditary, so we children had a twenty-five percent chance of inheriting it. This meant the odds were that two of her eight children would get it. I just remember us looking at each other, thinking, *Who's next?* It could have been any of us; it could have been all us.

The doctor also told us that most people start showing symptoms in their early twenties. If we didn't have any symptoms in our twenties, we should be okay. So in my twenties I was watching and waiting, as I'm sure we all were. Thankfully, no one else got it, and when I turned thirty I felt relieved.

When my mom was homeless, Cindy remembers Mom telling her that she would sometimes have to perform sex just to be able to eat or have a safe place to stay. This unfortunately isn't uncommon for women in her situation. The mental illness, combined with hunger and the lack of basic necessities, results in them making choices they would never make if they were healthy and stable. Making these inappropriate choices adds to a person's guilt and condemnation because in their lucid moments they know the decisions aren't right. They get stuck in a vicious cycle of depression and heartache, spiralling deeper into mental illness.

I'm sure many people would have judged my mom's actions and thought she was a hooker or a slut. That is why it says in the Bible, *"Do not judge, or you too will be judged"* (Matthew 7:1). Jesus also challenged those who wanted to stone the woman at the well. Only God knows the heart of people and knows why they do what they do. Thank God that we only have to answer to Him and He knows the heart. If you saw my mom's heart, you would know that she acted out of sheer desperation, sickness, and survival.

My mom even went to the White House once and camped on the front lawn to tell the president that the drugs down in Florida were out of control. She wanted to tell him that drugs were stealing her children from her and the politicians needed to crack down hard.

As sick as Mom was, she was right about that. Drugs were out of control, and they're even worse today. They should be cracking down on drugs, not legalizing them.

As Connie continued to tell me:

Many times when Mom disappeared, she would end up in homeless shelters or on the streets. She didn't always like the homeless shelters. She said that she didn't feel safe because there were so many men there.

So sometimes she stayed in treed areas and parks.

One time, she came back to us saying that she hated black people. This was totally out of character for her. She had brought us up to not have any prejudice at all. She'd taught us that God created everyone and we were all God's children. She loved all people and treated everyone the same.

Eventually she told us that she'd gotten raped on the streets of Tampa by a big black guy who'd beat her up really bad and choked her. As she was being choked, she said God had told her to pretend she was dead, so she had. The guy had stopped choking her, finished his business, and left her for dead.

She said she was completely out of it, but God had told her to get up, get dressed, and go to the hospital for help. Once in the hospital she found out there was a man on the loose who had raped and killed several women who fit the description of the man who had raped her. Had she not played dead, he may not have stopped until she was. By the grace of God, her life was spared.

Later in her life when she became mentally stable and was able to think clearly, the prejudice thankfully left. She told us that she'd had many bad experiences on the streets but wouldn't talk about most of them.

It's a shame my mom had to experience these things. We were on our way to a new country but she was still vulnerable, sick, and being taken advantage of everywhere she turned. It was very hard to get her into a mental institution in those days, because patients had to admit themselves. Unfortunately, many people who have mental health issues don't realize it, so they never get the help they need.

The same holds true today, which is why so many people suffering from mental health issues end up in homeless shelters or on the streets. It's still true that many women who have to share a homeless shelter with men are frightened to stay in them. They don't feel safe. When women stay in these shelters, they become targets. That's why we need to ensure that women have access to separate shelters. Women are the most vulnerable and need to be protected and provided a safe place to stay during their struggles. These are our mothers and our daughters.

34.

THE LOVE OF A FATHER

Grace is knowing God's unconditional love.

But because of his great love for us, God, who is rich in mercy, made us alive with Christ even when we were dead in transgressions—it is by grace you have been saved. (Ephesians 2:4–5)

CONNIE SHARED WITH ME THAT SHE FOUND THE LORD WHEN SHE WAS SIXTEEN but struggled with it. She said:

I remember so vividly going to a church service at sixteen, shortly after getting married and getting born again. When you truly receive Jesus, you don't forget it.

I struggled after that for a few reasons. One, my mom was *nuts*, and I didn't want to end up crazy like her! Two, I was sixteen, didn't drive, and didn't know any Christians… so I did the only thing I knew: go right back into the world.

When I did get a little older and started going to church, it seemed like all I heard about was the Father's love for me, and they would relate it to a natural father's love. I didn't know a natural father's love. I'm sure my dad loved us then, and he told me so many times in his later years, but at that time my experiences were not of love but of chaos, punishment, and abandonment.

An angry and unpredictable *father instills fear in his children and conveys to them that God is a tyrant who lashes out unexpectedly.*

A critical, demanding *dad makes his kids feel inadequate. They see God as a taskmaster who's never pleased.*

An uninvolved *or absent father sends the message that his children are unimportant, and both he and God are too busy for them.*

An arrogant *dad's tough, uncaring nature leads his children to feel unloved and conclude that the Lord doesn't love them either.*

A fault-finding *or abusive father communicates that his child is worthless and God is full of condemnation.*

But a man with Christ-like character provides children with a healthy connection, not only to their earthly dad but also to their heavenly Father.

Unfortunately for us, this was not the case. We knew all of the other fathers, but not the Christ-like one. We knew yelling and screaming, and we knew discipline, but we didn't know love.

My father also abused us verbally, which affected us mentally. When my sister was twenty-five, he saw her for the first time in ten years and the first thing out of his mouth was "It looks like you put on a lot of weight." He didn't give her a hug. He didn't say "I love you." He didn't say "I missed you." That was it: "You've gained weight."

So the love of the Father was foreign to us.

One day, my pastor asked me about my dad. We had been talking about him coming down and getting the younger kids and taking them to Canada.

"Did that bother you, that your dad didn't take you with him?" my pastor asked. "You were sixteen and probably should have gone too."

And I said, "No. I think I was the lucky one because I was left behind!"

I really, really meant it. Plus, I had been married to Dale when he came.

I sought and asked God for a revelation of His love. When it came, it was life-changing. His love is above and beyond what you can ever imagine. He's always with you and He never forsakes you. There is no need He can't or won't meet, and He delivers you from all your troubles. He delivers you from the pain and sadness of everything you've been through.

After that I was able to love myself, love God, and love my dad. I was able to see the pain and rejection my dad had gone through that made him who he was.

This opened the door years later for me to share the Gospel of Jesus Christ with him. He had come to visit us in Florida and stayed with me.

He kept me up several nights asking me questions about God, forgiveness, and salvation. We were able to pray together and God washed away all the bad memories and replaced them with His goodness.

God is faithful and His goodness endures forever!

David meanwhile was starting to party way too much in Gillette, so he decided to move back to Port Charlotte. What had started as getting high with friends and having a good time had gotten a lot more serious, and some of the players in the drug scene were changing as well. As he recalls:

My dad said one thing about drug-dealers that I will never forget. He said that they would give you the drugs for free to get you hooked and then you would have to buy it. I didn't believe what my dad had told me, and up till this point in my life I had never experienced anyone trying to pressure someone to do drugs.

But that was about to change.

Due to our heavy drinking and drug use, there were times when we needed a little pick-me-up. Our drugs of choice for those occasions were little white aspirin-looking pills called crosstops, and a white powdery substance called crank, which is a less potent form of meth. We would pop the crosstops like vitamins and snort the crank whenever we needed a little boost.

Well, one time this guy Rich was trying to talk Johnny into shooting up some crank. Johnny kept telling Rich no, but Rich just went on and on about what a great high it was.

I'd always had a rule that if you stick a needle in your arm, that's going from having a good time to being an addict.

The pressure got to the point that I became pissed off and told Rich to leave Johnny alone. I didn't like to see anyone try to tempt others to go from snorting to shooting up. It was almost like watching the devil at work.

Instead of a close group of friends getting high and having a good time, we were starting to see weird people show up. I was always very selective about who I wanted to do drugs around, but the times, they were a-changing.

One time when I was doing acid, a guy named Tom kept trying to irritate me. It's really stupid to irritate someone who's tripping on acid.

It got to the point that I had to tell Pete and Johnny to stick by me and not leave me alone with him because I was afraid I was going to kick his ass. The idea of getting in a fight while high on LSD scared me. I was afraid of what might happen to him.

After that I decided to stay in Port Charlotte and quit going to Wyoming. All the older druggies were pretty weird and I didn't think it was a good thing to be able to drink almost a quart of whiskey at eighteen years old.

Thank God for working in my heart. That's the only explanation I have for getting out of that lifestyle when I did.

Rich, the pusher, died very young in a car accident. He was probably high on something.

Meanwhile, Danny was having his own struggles with drugs which shocked all of us.

Because of his athleticism, we thought he was careful about everything he ate and never ingested anything harmful to his body. He was always Mr. Perfect.

However, after we moved to Canada we discovered our assumptions had been wrong.

Danny phoned my dad one day to tell him that he was in prison and that things were really bad. He was crying and scared. At the time, Danny was in his early twenties and had tried to sell cocaine to an undercover cop.

We all felt Danny was too naïve to get into that type of business, that somehow he was being taken advantage of. The cops thought so, too, but he got busted for trafficking in Fort Lauderdale and now faced at least ten years in prison. He desperately needed help.

My dad quickly called all the business leaders in our hometown who knew Danny well and got letters of support from them. They all believed this incident was totally out of character for Danny.

My dad then dropped everything and flew down to Port Charlotte. He picked up the letters, went to Fort Lauderdale, and managed to bail Danny out of jail.

But when he arrived, to his horror he realized that Danny had gotten addicted to drugs and was going through withdrawal in his cell. It was a painful revelation, but at least the experience was enough for Danny to quit drugs. It wasn't long after this that he started seeking the Lord.

35.

WHAT CAREER SHOULD WE CHOOSE?

Grace comes in knowing right from wrong.

CINDY AND I WORKED OVER THE SUMMERS, WHICH HELPED US BUY NEW CLOTHES for the upcoming school year. One time we had to pick up my stepmom from work with my dad. It was a Saturday and he had picked us up from our work at the hotel where we were cleaning. My mom worked at the clubs downtown and we had to pick her up.

As we sat in a coffee shop, I remember my dad looking at us. We were talking about work and how much we got paid.

"You know, you have really nice bodies," he said. "If you wanted to, you could become strippers and make way more money than you're making now. Strippers make about $1,000 per week. And you don't even have to work full days."

My jaw dropped. I couldn't believe my dad would even suggest it. I was fifteen and Cindy was seventeen. What type of father encourages their daughters to become strippers? This was a far cry from my Christian mother in Florida, who would have shuddered at the thought.

"I cannot believe you just suggested that," I challenged him. "Are you serious? You would want to see Cindy and me up on stage taking our clothes off?"

"Well, university and college are expensive. You can have those bills paid off in no time. You could do your work around classes. Your mother does it. No big deal."

To say I was disgusted would be an understatement. But to him it really was no big deal. That was his lifestyle and morality. Mine were different.

I continued cleaning at the hotel, was promoted to supervisor at eighteen, and paid my way through school and college.

I graduated from high school and went on to Red River College where I took business administration, majoring in accounting and minoring in marketing. Originally I thought this would be a great career choice, because no matter where a person lands they need to understand business and finances. It could even allow me to open my own business.

One day while looking at the course selections for the business program, I came across a mandatory course on public speaking. This course absolutely terrified me. Having grown up the way I had, I was very shy and didn't like to draw attention to myself. I immediately removed myself from the business administration program and changed my application to go into chemical technology. I was also good in chemistry and thought this would be another really good fit. At least there was no public speaking required!

The summer passed, and then two weeks prior to school starting I looked at the chemical technology program I had enrolled in and asked myself, *What the heck am I doing in chemical technology?* I'd thought I wanted business administration. So I immediately put myself back into business administration.

On the first day of school, the very first class was public speaking. I was called up to introduce myself, and in that moment I remembered why I'd transferred out. Now I was stuck. I had to go through with it.

That was probably the only part of the program I didn't enjoy, and I promised myself I would never use it. But I managed to do well, because I had been taught that if you're going to do something, you do it to your best ability. This would become an asset in my future endeavours. God always has a plan.

I managed an average of eighty-six percent.

Most of the time I had straight A's or A+'s, but in the winter months my grades took a nosedive. I think it was the cold weather, long bus rides, and lack of sunshine. I seemed to get more depressed in the winter months.

Overall, though, I have to say that this time in my life was really positive. I worked hard to get good grades. I paid for my education myself, and if I got student loans I gave the money to my dad since the interest rates at that time were very high. He used the money to take care of us, then ended up paying the loans back on my behalf.

He was still a very difficult man to live with. Quite honestly, we couldn't wait to get out of the house. He was a hard man and oppressive, but at least he didn't hit us anymore.

Since my stepmom worked over the dinner hour, I usually made dinner and did the dishes. Every weekend we had to do chores, including cleaning all the cupboards in the kitchen inside and out, vacuuming, bathrooms, etc. I couldn't wait to get married and move out.

During my last year of living at home, two instances stand out. The first involved Duane, and the second involved Cindy.

Duane came home from high school one day in December before the Christmas break with straight B's on his report card. He was so excited and proud because he'd worked really hard at his marks. Achieving straight B's was an incredible accomplishment for him since he really struggled in school.

But when he came home and showed the report card to my dad, my dad only saw the absences. Dad chastised and ridiculed him, telling him how disappointed he was. He'd expected to get an "I'm proud of you, son." But instead his face fell.

Dad walked away very angry and disappointed.

I tried to stand up for Duane. "Hey Dad, look at his report card. This is the best report he's ever brought home!"

The next thing I knew, he backhanded me and I was out cold.

As Duane explains:

My dad was always a hard man to please. I tried real hard to get good grades for his approval. School didn't come easy for me at all. It was probably because of my upbringing, or lack thereof, and skipping classes.

I finally got straight B's. Best report card I ever got. I was so excited that I showed it to my sister, Judy. She was so happy for me.

When my dad got home, I couldn't wait to show him my report card so he would be proud of me too. My sister was smiling because she was so proud of me and she knew I couldn't wait to show him and he was going to say "Good job!" for the first time in my life.

Nope. He saw that I'd skipped a few classes and started yelling at me. Judy tried to step in and explain to him that I was really trying, and with that comment she got a backhand to the face. She dropped to the floor like a fly.

I looked down at her and then looked at my dad, eye to eye, for the first time in my life. I began to walk toward him.

He put his hands up. "You want to fight?"

I pushed him in the chest, feeling an amazing strength come into me. He was dancing around with his fists up in the air and a big smile on his face.

I looked at my sister, who was still out, without turning my back to my dad. I didn't trust what he might do to me.

I again rushed at him, and with this rage of strength I pushed him back, making him lose his balance. He fell all the way into the back wall of a closet.

Then I saw my sister moving and knew she would be okay.

I looked down at my hands, then up at my dad. I thought that if I went after him again, I might kill him. I felt such power and strength that I decided I had better go for a walk real quick.

As I sat on the steps to put my shoes on, I thought that things would cool down.

Nope. My dad grabbed me by the back of the head and began to slam my head into the floor, over and over again.

My stepmom came running from the kitchen and jumped on my dad's back with her arms around his neck. She told me to leave the house, to protect me.

I remember running outside in -20 degrees in the snow with nothing on but a pair of shorts. I ran for miles to a friend's house for help. I didn't come back for a day and a half. I stayed there until I got my own place.

With my face bloodied, we both ran out of the house. Duane was in bare feet and ended up at his friend's house. I ended up going to Joe's house. I didn't go home for a few days. I was too afraid.

My dad's temper was like a firecracker. You never knew when he was going to explode, and you had to walk on eggshells all the time. It wasn't a good living experience. He didn't know how to handle stress. At least my stepmom always stood in the gap and tried to bring down his temper, but this lifestyle was devastating and inspired both Duane and I to want to move out as quickly as possible. Although Duane didn't come back, I had to wait until I got married.

The other incident happened the following spring, during my last year of college. I was working really hard to pay my way through school and prepare for my wedding, which would take place in August. I had to save money for my dress and all the many things that go with a wedding—and since Joe was Italian, it was going to be a big wedding.

Spring break was coming, so I told my dad I would clean the house, but my week became filled with work opportunities. I was excited about this, because I needed the money. On the one evening I had off, I really wanted to visit with Cindy, who had been married and out of the house for more than a year.

When I told my dad about this, he got pissed off. He wanted me to spring-clean the house. My dad, the neat freak, liked everything a certain way. If we wanted him to be pleasant, we had to keep everything as perfect as possible or he would blow his stack. I was more afraid of his anger than anything, so I said I would clean the house. I told Cindy that if she wanted to visit, she would have to come over.

I still wanted to go out with my sister and begged her to help me. I figured if she helped we could get it done more quickly and then still go for coffee. I told her about my stressful week, that I'd just finished midterm exams, and that I was trying to work more to save for my wedding. She really didn't want to come but very reluctantly agreed. She made it clear she was only coming because I sounded so stressed. She knew I needed a break.

So that night, Cindy and I worked really hard at cleaning the kitchen. Every so often our dad would come in and make sarcastic comments. It was very immature. He kept taunting me, though, and by his fourth round into the kitchen I finally grabbed him by the scruff of the neck and said, "Look, if you want me to clean this damn kitchen you better stay the hell out of here. I'm tired of you coming in and out, making fun of me. I'm cleaning the kitchen. You asked me to clean the kitchen and I'm doing it. If you want me to finish it, get out until I'm done or I'm gonna kick your ass."

It was the first time I had stood up to the bully and it felt really good. As Cindy recalls:

I was in shock! At that very moment, I was standing on the kitchen counter cleaning out the top of the cupboards, helping Judy out of sympathy.

But this was too much. You didn't challenge my dad. What was she thinking? Now I felt like a little mouse in the corner. What was I going to do, jump off the kitchen counter and hurt myself? Was he going to come after me? I was terrified of him and had nowhere to go. I figured I'd have to jump on top of him.

I knew it wasn't over, so I waited quietly in shock, not saying anything.

Oh my gosh, she's going to blow, I thought. *He's going to blow!*

There was a long moment of complete silence during which you could literally hear them both breathing hard, staring at each other eye to eye. It was scary quiet.

Then, without a word, he sheepishly walked into the living room.

We were shocked. This couldn't possibly be over.

But he never came back. The bully got bullied that day and was defeated. Judy and I were in control of the kitchen.

When I look back, this was probably a defining moment for Judy, because it was the first time she was able to get control of her life with our father.

My dad had no consideration for the things I was going through—studying for final exams, preparing for a wedding, and working full-time weekends and evenings to pay for everything. It was always about him and what he wanted. That was just how he was.

Well, that was the first time I stood up to the bully and it felt really good. Cindy said I looked five inches taller than him that day.

While I was proud of myself, I was also very sad. He was my dad. You shouldn't have to be afraid of your dad, and yet we lived in fear. It was no way to live.

That's the last memory I have in our home because that August I married the man of my dreams and moved away.

Duane had left earlier and experienced even more trauma. As he explains:

I ended up getting my own place and living on my own. I began to sell pot and live a partying lifestyle without any adults. This wasn't a good place to be without any guidance.

Seven months after living on my own, going to school full-time and working full-time, I decided to skip school. Usually when kids skip school, nothing good happens—and this day was no exception!

My friends and I decided to go to my place after lunch and huff cooking spray. We'd done this before on several occasions to get a cheap high. We didn't have any cooking spray in my apartment, so we all put in some money and then flipped a coin to decide who would go to the store and get it.

Steve, my very best friend, lost the coin flip.

As we were huffing, it came to Steve's turn. He huffed… and then didn't pass it on to the next guy. As I looked at him, as stoned as I was, I noticed the blank look on his face. His eyes were wide open. He just stayed in that exact position as we giggled and laughed.

As a joke, I took my cigarette and put it up to his knee. I actually burnt him, but he didn't respond.

Suddenly, I pulled Steve onto the floor and saw blood coming to the surface of his skin on his forehead. His face began to turn blue and foam came out of his mouth.

Steve was dead.

My other friend and I looked at each other and ran to call 911, but it was too late.

My other best friend and I stopped hanging out. Both of us were in shock. I was angry, outraged, and confused all at the same time. It felt like nothing was real. Not even me. I was numb.

Thank God for Mr. Otto at Kelvin High School. He started talking to me on a daily basis and gave me some guidance to help me get through Steve's death.

I talked to him about working out with weights and he came up with a plan for me. He asked if I would like to help create a weight room at school. I helped with ideas and flyers to get some weights in the school. I don't think I did much, but he made me feel like I did.

It was finally a way for me to take out all the frustrations and stress in my life, something that was going to help me and not hurt me. If I wasn't in class, I was in the weight room. I found peace and satisfaction working out.

I played high school football for three years and my dad only showed up for one game. I broke the record for most single tackles on our team and played both offence and defence. I also played as a running back, punt returner, kickoff returner, and safety.

The one time my dad came to watch me play, I had the best game of my life. I wanted to make him proud.

But nope, when I came home the first thing he said was that he had gotten tired of hearing my name over the loudspeaker. The cheerleaders were cheering every time I made a big play.

My heart dropped. I would try to encourage myself by remembering what my coach had said: "You had a heck of a game."

I went back home for my last year of high school, knowing that I needed to graduate and get an education. I loved working out and even competed in a bodybuilding contest at school where I came in second place.

Doug, who was in college studying to become a mechanical engineer,[26] had his very last fight:

I went to the bar with my friend, Chris. I also had a girl with me. At one point I went to the bathroom to take a leak. The urinals were on the right, the sink was in the middle, and there were three stalls to the left. A couple of guys were smoking up in the stalls.

When I finished taking the leak, I went to the sink to wash my hands. As I walked to the sink and crossed the doorway, some guy kicked the door open; it banged me in the back of the head.

"Like, holy crap!" I called out. "What are you doing?"

As I turned around, the guy said, "What the hell do you think you're going to do about it?"

"Dude, you just kicked the door in and hit me!"

Two other guys then came up to me and encouraged the first guy to kick my ass.

"Let's just chill out," I said. "I've got a girl here tonight. Let's just go and have a good time."

But he looked at me and said, "You're not going anywhere!"

I recognized the look in his eye and thought to myself, *Okay, here we go.*

So I hit him in the face. As soon as I punched him, the bouncers appeared. The bathroom was right by the front doors, and so they came in and broke up the fight.

I left to spend time with my girlfriend. For the next thirty minutes, though, this guy followed me around, bugging me to go outside and fight him. My friend Chris was egging me on, too. "Just go fight him, Doug! He's bothering us. Take care of him."

Well, the guy was about six feet tall and I was five-eight.

"Dude, I really don't want to fight," I told this guy. "I have a girlfriend here tonight. I'm having a good time. I don't want to fight."

He just started calling me names in front of my friends and embarrassing me in front of my girlfriend.

---

[26] Doug took this course, since it's what Dad had taken in school and encouraged him to do. But while taking the course and working hard at a local gas station to cover the costs, Dad challenged Doug, saying he would never pass the course, which drove Doug crazy. The course was very difficult and Doug worked hard to pass. When he finally received his diploma, Doug went home, shoved it at Dad, and said, "There. I got it. Done. Goodbye. I'm moving to Florida." And then he left. He never did go into this field of work. He took it just to prove Dad wrong.

"Okay, dude, let's go," I finally said.

We went outside, but Chris was so drunk that he just stayed in the bar, watching by the window where it was nice and warm.

I waited for this guy to make the first move, dancing around him so he couldn't catch me. When he came at me, I did a flip and then grabbed him by the head and started punching.

Suddenly, he went limp and fell down.

One of his friends then started coming towards me, and I thought they were going to try to take me next.

"What are you guys doing?" I asked.

"Hey man, nothing. We're just going to get our friend."

So the fight was over and we all left.

I didn't know it at the time, but this was the boyfriend of a friend of mine, Suzanne. The following Monday, I went to college and she came up to me.

"Hey Doug, I need to talk to you."

"Hey Suzanne, what's going on?"

"Did you get in a fight on Friday night with a guy at the bar?"

"Yeah, why?"

"Well, the guy you beat up, you broke his jaw in five places. He's all wired up. He almost died drowning in his own blood. He's in the hospital, and he'll be there for a couple of months."

"Aw, man, I really didn't know that... that's freaky."

Then Suzanne added, "Well, he was also my boyfriend."

"Suzanne, I'm so sorry. I didn't mean for it to go like that. I didn't want to fight him. He followed me around the bar all night and gave me no choice."

After I'd told her the whole story, she said, "I know. I just wanted to let you know he's not gonna press charges."

Press charges? He was the one who called *me* out.

Anyway, that was the last fight I ever had because I hurt him so bad. I felt terrible. What would have happened if he had died?

I've had to repent about that. I pray that he healed well. I've done that a few times with a few fights I've been in. I pray for them all, because I've beaten up a lot of guys. Even though to me it was always their fault, I never wanted to be responsible for really hurting someone.

I didn't really look for trouble; I just responded to it. I had a no-fear attitude. After going through foster care and group homes and being abandoned by my dad, I just had a lot of pent-up anger.

I've realized that Doug measures his life and remembers his experiences based on the fights he got into. He always had a survival instinct. I can't imagine how he must have felt being abandoned by his father, then coming home at thirteen years old and finding out that nobody lived there anymore, that his brothers and sisters had gone and so had his mother. His abandonment caused a lot of anger, and it came out through all the fights he got into.

He was a fearless little guy who moved around a lot and got picked on all the time because he was always the newbie—and so eventually he had learned to fight. And fight he did. The anger was so raw, so rough, and so consuming that he needed an outlet for it. He told me once that he cried himself to sleep at night and fought fearlessly during the day. He also had to become the man of the family at a very young age to protect his sisters.

Doug desperately needing a father, yet when he found his father he'd realized he was still abusive. He still didn't have a father to look up to, and now he had to defend his sisters.

He did resolve his anger issues, but it took a long time. It wasn't until he found the Lord in his late twenties that he started to repent and change.

What's miraculous is that God got us all through as we turned to Him for support, love, and help. Through Him, and only Him, we were able to save ourselves. Only through the grace of God did Doug get better, surviving the fights he got into and the drugs he ingested. God gave him a supernatural strength to overcome his challenges and survive.

I'm glad Doug was able to get off his destructive path, because we always worried about him. Learning more about his life has given me a better insight into how going through foster care and instability affects boys differently from girls.

Youth for Christ is an international organization that provides great programming for young people and a safe space for them to enjoy athletics with positive Christian role models. Young boys need positive male role models in their lives, especially those without fathers. Getting involved in sports becomes an outlet for them and helps them work through anger, frustration, and nervous energy. We need to support organizations that reach out to youth and provide opportunities for people to change and experience the love of Christ.

36.

MOVING ON UP

Grace comes from accepting Jesus.

...for the Lord your God is gracious and compassionate. He will not turn his face from you if you return to him. (2 Chronicles 30:9)

AFTER MOVING BACK TO FLORIDA, DAVID STARTED TO THINK THERE MUST BE MORE to life than getting high all the time:

When I moved back to Port Charlotte from Wyoming, I remember going to a New Year's Eve party at a friend's house. The important part is what happened the next morning.

I hadn't partied hard the night before, because I just hadn't been getting wasted as much lately. I woke up before everyone else and felt just a little hungover.

My friend's trailer was in a rural area, so I decided to go for a walk. I remember looking up in the sky and saying, "God, if You're real, if You're really real, I need You to reveal Yourself to me."

That was when my life started to change. Looking back, I realize that God had always had His hand on me, but I finally reached out to touch Him.

Change came slowly. It takes a long time to unlearn bad habits.

I was living out near Punta Gorda when I met my future wife, Cindy. I met her at a friend's house. We started talking and realized we were both looking for a roommate. We decided to move in together since she needed a place to stay, and I was tired of having to hitchhike from rural Punta Gorda to Port Charlotte every day to go to work.

We ended up being more than friends and were soon married. We still didn't own a car, so when we were first married I used to put all our dirty laundry in a duffel bag and hitchhike to a laundromat that was next door to a grocery store. After finishing the laundry, I would go to the grocery store. Afterward I'd call a cab to get a ride home. That way I only had to pay the cab fare one way.

Ten and a half months after getting married, our first son was born. Jeremy changed everything. I could survive by myself, and Cindy could survive by herself, but Jeremy needed us to take care of him.

Realizing that we had a child on the way, I decided that I should get my GED, since I had only been to half of the tenth grade. I was supposed to take the GED test over three days starting on April 7, 1981, but Jeremy was born that day. I ended up having to double up the next day, but I passed the exam, and at age twenty I had the equivalent of a high school diploma.

I was still working construction—block work, stucco, or whatever paid the most. I never cared how hard the work was; the hardest work usually paid well since no one wanted to do it.

A counsellor in junior high had told me that I tested in the ninety-ninth percentile on standardized tests, and based on my scores I could be whatever I wanted to be—even a doctor, she had told me at the time.

Well, that was encouraging, but there never seemed to be any hope of me going to college, let alone becoming a doctor. Where would I ever get money to go to college?

Being on my own at fifteen, I had learned early on to have a savings account for when the unexpected happened. When you have no one to turn to for help, you better have some savings, or you can end up on the street.

Unfortunately, my mom knew that I always had a little money stashed away. I remember her asking me for money after Jeremy was born. I had helped her out plenty of times before, but this time was the toughest. I had a newborn baby and an eighteen-year-old wife, and my mom wanted me to give her some of my meagre savings.

It made me feel hopeless, especially knowing that I would never have enough to solve her problems. But maybe I could have enough money to build a future for my own family.

Talk about emotional turmoil. I loved my mom, but I had a young family who depended on me now. I ended up giving her some money, but I remember how tough it was.

Around this time, we started attending a little Baptist church in Punta Gorda. Those Baptists never ended a service without giving an altar call for those who want to decide to follow Jesus, and I can still remember the day God revealed Himself to me, in answer to my New Year's Day prayer from a couple of years earlier.

One day they had an altar call and I knew God was talking to me. It was clear that God was leading me to His Son. So I got up from the pew and went forward and accepted Jesus.

It didn't make me perfect, because God had a lot of work to do. It takes a long time to transform, but it started when I was twenty-three.

37.

ST. IGNATIUS SAVES

Grace is a gift from God through a relationship with His Son.

Whoever conceals their sins does not prosper, but the one who confesses and renounces them finds mercy. (Proverbs 28:13)

WHEN JOE AND I WERE PREPARING TO BE MARRIED, WE DECIDED THAT SINCE HE and I had both been brought up Catholic, we would get married in the Catholic Church. The challenge was that I hadn't received all my sacraments. I was missing confession and confirmation, and in order to be married at St. Ignatius Church, I needed to complete these two very important sacraments.

Confirmation meant making the choice to follow the Lord and to raise our family in accordance with His teachings. I loved Joe so much and saw how he'd turned out and wanted my kids to be like him.

I wasn't sure about confession, though. This scared me. I remember taking the courses, but I hadn't attended a church since coming to Winnipeg other than the odd time with Joe. My family never went. But I took the course, and it finally came time to complete the sacrament of confirmation. I had to go to confession to do it.

I'll never forget going in front of the priest. I was absolutely terrified! I was a vulnerable, guilt-ridden young woman of eighteen. I knew my faith was weak and that I'd have to confess my background. With all the bravery I could muster, I confessed to the priest all that had happened to me—growing up in foster care, living on the streets, not going to church, skipping school, stealing, doing drugs, skipping and quitting catechism. I told him about my mom, and I told him about my dad. I told him what my stepmom did for a living and how this had played a role in my upbringing. I even told him about the abortion.

When I was finally done, he asked me one question: "My daughter, during this time that you were going through all these trials and all these tribulations, did you ever turn to God to help you through it?"

My mouth dropped open wide. "Father, without God I would not be here today. He was my rock. I prayed every night that He would deliver me out of my situation. I prayed every night that He would give me a better place to live. I wore out my rosary saying the Our Father and praying to Jesus, asking Him to help me. As a matter of fact, He's the only loving Father I've ever known!"

He looked at me so compassionately and said, "My daughter, you probably have more faith and have a better relationship with Jesus than three-quarters of the congregation who comes to church every Sunday. That is all Jesus asks is to have a relationship with us. You clearly show you have that better than most. God has forgiven you. We are all sinners. During your deepest, darkest hour, you chose to have a relationship with Jesus. That's what Christianity is all about. It's not about rituals. It's not about going to church. It's not about all of the sacraments, although they are important. It's about having a relationship with Jesus and trying to be more and more like Him. After what you've been through in your life, my daughter, you have surely done that. Go and sin no more. If you want to go out into the pews and say a prayer, feel free, but I think you've been through enough."

Those were the sweetest words ever spoken to me. That was the day I committed my life to the Lord. I realized that I had been saved, saved by grace, saved by God, and committed myself to having a relationship with Jesus.

That Catholic priest showed me my salvation. It was the first time anyone in the Catholic Church ever talked to me about a relationship with Jesus. It helped me to understand why I loved Joe so much, as his faith was very deep.

Sure enough, St. Ignatius became our home church. Not only did I put all my kids through school there, but I worked in that school and learned to love the Lord once again through living and learning about Him every day. I have to say that this was a very charismatic Catholic church. I now attend a charismatic Evangelical church because I find the messages more inspiring and the worship deeper. I also feel my relationship with the Lord deepening. But every step in one's spiritual journey is important and this church definitely made an impact.

Just before our wedding, Joe's mother threw me a surprise bridal shower. I was overwhelmed by the number of gifts I received. It really showed how much people cared and loved me. I would burst into tears whenever someone did something nice and never felt like I deserved the things they did for me.

After opening all the gifts, I had duplicates and triplicates in toasters, salad bowls sets, towels, and sheets. When we moved into our apartment, I had so much stuff that I started giving it away to my sisters and brothers.

As I was packing away the extras, Joe came into the apartment and said, "What are you doing?"

"Look at all the stuff we have. Honey, we don't need all this. We just need one of everything. So I'm going to give it to my brothers and sisters."

"What if one breaks?" he asked wisely. "What if we need a gift for somebody else down the road?"

I never thought that way. When you grow up with nothing and you suddenly have so much, you just want to bless people. You want to give because you know what it's like to be in need.

"When it comes to that, we'll buy a new one," I said. "There are people who need the stuff now, and we're going to share."

And we did. And we still do.

I did keep one extra of some of those things, but generally, we aren't a family that collects tons of stuff. We use what we have, and what we don't use we give away. That's the way it should be.

38.

THE BEST DAY OF THE REST OF MY LIFE

Grace allows new life, adventures, and family reunions.

JOE AND I MARRIED ON AUGUST 24, 1985. I FELT FREE! WE HAD MORE THAN TWO hundred fifty people at the wedding; ten of them were from my side and the rest were all Italians.

Doug, Duane, and Cindy were in my wedding party. I felt like a princess, a Disney princess, with all their joy combined! I was happily in love and excited for my future. I really had made it!

We moved into our apartment—we didn't live together before we got married—with new furniture, appliances, and household items. I had everything I'd ever wanted. I felt so blessed.

From then on, my life couldn't have been more perfect. I ended up getting a job, first for a small business where I learned accounting. This gave me great confidence and experience. I went on to work for Air Canada, where I got to travel. This was divine because it allowed me to visit all the relatives I'd never known I had. In Pittsburgh, I found out that we came from a long line of Peduzzis. My great-great-uncle Reynold had been Mario Andretti's mechanic.[27] He also was an inventor, responsible for inventing the machine that makes Turtle chocolates. One of my dad's cousins is the mayor of Trafford, Pennsylvania. My family there gave me such a warm reception, with more than fifty people in attendance. My grandmother had set it up and it made me feel like I had a place to belong.

Working at Air Canada also allowed me to return to Florida in 1986 for a family reunion with my siblings and my mom. This was the only time all eight of

---

[27] Mario Andretti was a well-known race car driver in the United States.

us were together after our family broke up. We videotaped it all. At that time, we were too raw and fresh from foster care and its devastation to share our stories, so we just had fun.

My mom passed away early at the age of fifty-seven, so this was also the last time we were all together with her. I'm so grateful we had that time. God works in mysterious ways.

We visited all of Joe's relatives as well. Before we had kids, we travelled across Canada from Toronto to British Columbia.

Meanwhile, my sister managed to get our mom into a mental institution and back on her medications. Once back on her medication, she became completely normal and I brought her up to Canada. It was truly a blessing!

Many people with mental health issues can live normal lives with the proper medication. We must advocate for those we can help, and empower them to be the best they can be. The health system insists that taking medication should be optional for any patient over eighteen, maintaining that it's a personal choice—but I believe healthcare workers should allow families to intervene when an adult family member is sick, especially when that person doesn't realize how sick they really are.

Shortly after I got married, Doug and Duane moved back to Florida. As Duane explains:

Two weeks after graduation, I moved to Florida. I was now nineteen years old and I moved in with my oldest brother Dan and began to work with him. Within one month, Doug moved back too. We had nothing to stay in Canada for and needed a break.

Danny had become one of the best tile setters in the Port Charlotte/Punta Gorda area. His reputation was so good that Doug and Duane learned the business from him, and now they're doing phenomenally well in the trade.

The three of them were best friends, and it was such a blessing to see them together. I'm sure the stories they could tell would be full of love and laughter. Duane adored Dan and did everything for him, because he never forgot what Dan had done for him.

While we were in Canada, Danny also learned to play professional rugby and became a bodybuilder. He won Mr. Southwest Florida and managed to inspire Duane to get involved as well. Danny could do anything in sports and succeed. He was exciting to watch.

39.

A GIFT FROM GOD

Grace allows forgiveness.

For if you forgive other people when they sin against you, your heavenly Father will also forgive you. (Matthew 6:14)

THREE YEARS AFTER GETTING MARRIED, JOE AND I DECIDED WE WERE GOING to have children. I was terrified—not of having children, but because I still felt guilty for having had an abortion in my teens. I felt that maybe God wasn't going to bless me with children. Maybe He was angry at me. I was still angry with me. But we truly serve a loving God, and I eventually learned that this isn't how God thinks.

After trying for a while, it still wasn't happening and I started to feel sad and frustrated. I had invited my dad and stepmom over for dinner one evening and we had a few drinks. That's when I discovered that my dad was easier to be with when you didn't live with him. Nothing out of the ordinary was happening, we were just having drinks with dinner… and suddenly I was beyond drunk.

In my drunken state, I started to freak out, cry, and share all my pent-up feelings with my dad. I shared how angry and hurt I was from the way he had treated us, how hurt I was that he had abandoned us. I got really emotional and shared all my feelings about everything that had ever happened to me. I really told him off and I think Joe was in shock.

To be honest, I barely remember the conversation. I just remember that it happened. And then I went to bed.

This conversation was pivotal. It allowed me to release my feelings and forgive my dad. Forgiveness is so important. The only way any of us children could have survived without lasting damage was to forgive and have forgiveness in our hearts. If you don't forgive past hurts and whatever grudges you hold, you can never joyfully move forward. Lack of forgiveness will be a stumbling block for your future.

When you're hurt, you have only two options: you can either relive it or release it. Reliving the hurt only perpetuates the pain. But releasing hurt is the path to inner peace.

I realized that in order for me to truly move forward with a new family, I needed to forgive my dad and everything that had happened in my past. I needed to let go of all the anger and bitterness that went with it.

We need to repent and forgive every day. God promises that if you confess your sins to Him, He will forgive you instantly, freely, completely, and permanently. Forgiveness should be the first thing on our lips every morning. We need to forgive to heal our hearts, minds, bodies, and soul. We also need to do it for God and for our relationship with Him. As Matthew 5:7 says, *"Blessed are the merciful, for they will be shown mercy."*

About a half-hour later, as I lay in bed, Joe came in to check on me and asked if I was okay. I remember feeling the presence of God all over the room.

"Yes, honey," I said. "Everything is going to be fine. God told me I'm going to have a baby. Everything is perfect."

Two weeks later, I found out I was pregnant.

I know that this night the Lord gave me the opportunity to cleanse my mind, body, and soul of anger and bitterness. He showed me how to forgive my dad for the past so I could start my family right. He showed me that He loved me and forgave me for my past transgressions, including the abortion. He also showed me how to forgive myself.

Nine months later, I had my first son, Raffaele Steven, named after Joe's dad and mine. When you have your first child, you never think you will love the next child quite so much, yet each child is so unique. David came next, then Michael.

Having three boys was a handful! They are very physical and they run everywhere, in different directions. They were also mischievous and adventurous… accidents waiting to happen. To say my hands were full would be an understatement, but I was so happy. I loved being a mom and was blessed to be able to stay home with them and care for them myself.

Meanwhile, God made a way for my brother David to go to college. He is now a radiologic technologist in Rapid City, South Dakota. As Dave recalls:

My first wife, Cindy, and my sister Connie both started working as housekeepers at Medical Center Hospital in Punta Gorda. Eventually, they were both able to become medical laboratory technologists, through on the job training and by passing the necessary exams. Lab techs, for short.

One day in 1982, Cindy came home and told me that I should apply for the Radiologic Technology School at Medical Center Hospital. Although I had dropped out of school halfway through Grade Ten, my grades had been all A's and B's... except for that F in biology! Crap, I wish that teacher hadn't been so boring. I could hardly stay awake in that class.

The program had sixteen applicants for that year's class and only four students would be selected, so I didn't feel extremely confident about my chances. But I filled out the application and all the necessary paperwork, then took a required standardized test and waited to see if I would have the opportunity to be interviewed.

To my surprise, I received a call to set up an interview. I assumed it was a one-on-one kind of deal, since that was the only kind of interview I had ever experienced. I have to say that I was a little intimidated when I was led into a small conference room where two radiologists, the chief radiologic technologist, and two radiologic technology instructors were already seated.

After we had all introduced ourselves, I found out that the main reason I had been selected for an interview was because of the standardized test I had taken. The chief radiologist said that they had been giving that same test for some time, and I had scored higher on the test than any previous applicant. Given the fact that I had only finished half of the tenth grade, my score was especially intriguing and so they had decided to interview me.

All I could think was, thank God for six years of Catholic school! After that, testing had always come easy to me.

They proceeded to take turns asking me all kinds of questions, including how I had managed to get an F in biology. I told them I had been fifteen years old and the teacher was boring. I guess they remembered what it was like to be fifteen, because I ended up getting accepted into the program.

I graduated in 1985 with the highest GPA ever recorded at the school.

Our son Tom was born shortly before my graduation. Back in the mid-80s, Florida didn't have many social supports for families and children. Cindy, like most Floridians back then, had also moved there from up north, and we decided to move our family somewhere with more infrastructure for families, and where we might have snow for Christmas.

We narrowed our search to Morgantown, West Virginia or Rapid City, South Dakota and started looking for jobs in either area.

The first job that came up was in Rapid City, where we moved in 1989. I've been here ever since.

Cindy and I ended up divorcing in 1994. Her dad was an alcoholic and her mom had had a tough upbringing. Combined with my background, we just didn't have the skills needed to make it work at a young age.

I married my second wife Donna seven years later after I had grown up a little bit more. We have been happily married ever since.

40.

CINDY FINDS THE LORD

Grace saves a whole family.

He has saved us and called us to a holy life—not because of anything we have done but because of his own purpose and grace. This grace was given us in Christ Jesus before the beginning of time... (2 Timothy 1:9)

CINDY SHARED WITH ME HOW SHE FOUND GOD:

My mom was a schizophrenic. She heard voices and was paranoid about a lot of things. She always thought the government or the communists were listening in on our conversations.

She was also very religious and believed in God with all her heart. She always said good things about God and told us that God had a special plan for all eight of us, her children.

But sometimes she said things about God that didn't make sense. She often distorted the truth about Him because of her mental illness. So when we were young, it was very difficult to believe in God. I for one was very confused, to say the least. I guess I did believe in God, but that was all. No more, no less.

After I came to Canada, I wanted to forget those years and forget about God. I needed to work on self-improvement, start our lives over, and forget the past. I had a fresh start and a new life!

I got married to a wonderful man, and we have now been married thirty-five years. But it wasn't until I was twenty-eight, and pregnant with my first child, that I started thinking about God. Was He real? How real was He? What was real and what was truth?

Until this point in my life, every time I'd thought of God it had reminded me of my mentally ill mom. I mean, my mom was mentally unstable so how real could God possibly be, right? All I knew was that I wanted to know the truth with a stable mind.

I guess I was searching for the truth. I watched a lot of Christian services, pastors, and some Christian programs. They all seemed strange to me. I couldn't discern who was correct about the word of truth. To be honest, I thought they were all quacks. And I knew I wasn't the only one in the world who thought this way.

But somehow, deep down, I knew God had gotten us this far. Also, in spite of her mental illness, when my mom had been doing well and speaking of God, she believed it with all her heart.

I decided that this had to be between me and God, so I became a closet Bible reader for about a year. I would read my Bible at home by myself and before reading I would pray and pray: *God, open my eyes and ears and give me Your understanding. Holy Spirit, please help me to understand Your Word.*

I read and I read and I read. Even though I didn't really understand it, I kept reading.

If you open your Bible and start reading, believe me, you won't understand it on your own. But I was determined to pray and read and give God a good chance.

So I read the New Testament and most of the Old Testament, which I found very difficult to comprehend. But I did my best. I did my part. Deep down, I really needed to know the truth.

Anyway, I had a neighbour next door who was very close to my age, and she was a Christian. She had invited me several times to go to her church, but I wasn't ready. I wasn't yet sure about all this.

Well, I finally decided to at least try going to the women's Bible study. It was a Baptist church and there were about fifteen women in the room. The woman leading it read some scripture and then asked some questions to the group.

Now, I hadn't been to church since I was a young kid, so I was quiet. I wasn't in my comfort zone. I just sat and waited for someone else to answer the questions.

I was surprised when nobody answered the questions. It was very quiet.

Question by question, I got braver and just started answering them—and it seemed that I was the only one talking. The leader would just smile after and then move on to the next question.

Afterwards, while sitting at a table having coffee, the leader came right up to me with this huge big smile on her face and said, "You have the power of the Holy Spirit in you." I had never met this woman before. She didn't even know me.

I just smiled back at her, feeling shocked. Even after she walked away, I was kind of in a daze for a few minutes. It freaked me out. How could she know something like that when I didn't even know?

It finally sank in that she had given me confirmation that I had actually understood the Bible and that the Holy Spirit had been teaching me all along while I was reading the Word of God.

I began to feel really happy inside, and it took quite a few days for this to really get into my spirit. God had been there while I was reading.

My next-door neighbour then invited me over to do a Bible study with her, and now I had some confidence.

When I went over, she had a book with scripture readings and questions to answer. As I read each question, the answer just flowed right out of me. It came so easily. I didn't even have to think about it.

She was so excited with my answers and kept asking me, "What was that you just said, Cindy? Say it again." She was so pumped up about what I was saying, and she kept writing down my words. She wrote down everything I said.

I couldn't believe it. I was so full of joy. This woman had grown up in the church. She was stable, friendly, and came from a good home. Her husband was a Christian and their parents were Christians. They were very respected in the community. God had answered my prayer and revealed Himself to me.

God is good. He knew my unbelief and my doubts about Him. But because of His great grace, mercy, and love, He helped me believe in Him.

I really feel that God wanted me to share this testimony, because He understands our thoughts and our unbelief and our doubts.

I still find my story so surreal. I find it so hard to believe that it actually happened this way, but it did. This world is pretty crazy sometimes, and it's often difficult to believe in anything.

I hope this inspires people to take a chance. Give God your doubt and your unbelief. Give Him your anger, pain, confusion, and whatever else you need to give Him. He knows how you feel anyway. Just pray that He helps you to believe. If you do your part, God will do His part.

41.

DANNY FINDS THE LORD AND LAYS DOWN HIS LIFE

Grace is found through brotherly love.

DUANE EXPLAINS HOW OUR BROTHER DANNY FOUND GOD, AND HOW IT ultimately affected his life:

A hero is someone who saves your life. You see someone pulling another person out of a crashing plane, out of a runaway train, or out of an out of control car… and we call them heroes.

Dan Needham is my hero because he saved my life.

When I was six years old, my parents went through a divorce. By the time I was nine, I'd OD'd a couple of times on drugs and alcohol. I ingested stuff nobody should ever put into their body. I should not even be alive today. When I was sixteen, my best friend died in my hands from doing something stupid.

While I was living in Canada, I would talk to Dan on the phone. I hadn't talked to him in about two years because I was so young and he was much older. But all of a sudden I was bodybuilding and we had that in common. I talked to him about how to get into shape for a bodybuilding contest.

While we were talking, he said to me, "My helper just quit. I can offer you a job right now for ten bucks an hour."

I had no definitive plans after high school, so I got on a plane, came back to Florida, and worked with Danny doing tile work for three years. Danny was the installer, and I was his helper.

When I was twenty-two years old, I had an anxiety attack that lasted two and a half years. I was so full of fear and worry that I literally prayed to God to die. I wasn't holding anything back. Every time I woke up, I said, "God, why am I still here?"

I was so full of anxiety because of evil in my life. There were so many things I was doing wrong. I was reaping everything I had sowed and I knew it was because of those choices I'd made.

During this time, Dan was spending time with my mom. All of us kids thought she was crazy when she started talking about Jesus. We just thought it was a figment of her imagination, that she was off her rocker.

One time she asked me to say the sinner's prayer over and over again. I said the prayer several times, but my life didn't change, because I didn't say that prayer with my heart.

But Dan spent time with my mom that nobody else did. And guess what? Dan got saved. Boy, did he get saved. He had been coming over the Punta Gorda bridge one day and the power of God came on him and made him start laughing—hard. He had to pull over his van because he couldn't drive anymore.

He got out and kept laughing, holding his stomach. As he looked around, he thought, *This world is a joke!* He realized that everyone was running after the wind. Danny got it. He had found the fountain of youth and His name was Jesus.

One day he was talking to my mom and they went back and forth about the Lord.

"Danny, the kids are all lost, but they don't know it," she said. "God put it on my heart to put it on your heart that you need to get Duane saved, because if Duane gets saved, the whole family will be saved."

While I was working for Dan, he was making about $1,500 to $2,000 a week. Then I got my own license and started working for myself.

After six months, I lost my own helper and needed someone to take his place, and I told Dan about it one day.

"I want to be your helper," he said to me. "I don't want any more responsibility. If you pay me eight dollars per hour, I'll do it."

"Okay, dude, seriously?" I said, thinking this was pretty weird. "Sure, you can be my worker."

I'm going make some money now, I thought to myself. *I'm going to abuse this guy.*

Remember, I was in the world chasing the dollar.

So Dan quit his job and came to work for me. For more than three months, he preached the gospel to me from morning till night. I'll tell you what I told him: "Take Jesus, take the Holy Spirit, and get out of my life."

But Dan was persistent and he finally talked me into listening to Christian music. I had been listening to my own on the job, like AC/DC and Black Sabbath. I didn't know anybody who listened to Christian music. To me, Christian music didn't even sound like music.

Well, I fought with him about it, and every day was a struggle. Eventually, I got really angry and cast him out. I cast Jesus out and I cast out the Holy Spirit. I'd had enough!

That same day, I invited Dan to join me for lunch.

"Dude, I'm not going with you," he replied. "Just go by yourself."

I didn't know what Dan was doing for lunch, but I happily left.

When I was gone, Dan got on his hands and knees and said, "God, get me away from this guy. He is worse off now than he's ever been. I don't want to work for him anymore. I don't want this job anymore."

When I came back from my lunch, I saw Dan on the jobsite talking to a man we both know, Morgan. I pulled up in my truck, put my foot up on the dash, and lit a cigarette.

Now, at this point I'd been having anxiety attacks for years and had spent more than $4,000 taking myself to the emergency room, getting pills, Xanax, you name it. I wasn't able to sleep for more than two hours at a time, but my condition got worse as I put more stuff in my body. I was doing the wrong things and I knew it.

I was trying to find some way to get myself out of this hell I'd created, but I didn't know how.

So Dan and Morgan were laughing with each other and I decided to walk over. That's when I heard them talking about Jesus, the Holy Spirit, and the disciples. As I listened, all of a sudden I felt this heaviness leave my body.

I got scared and went back to my truck. By this time, the heaviness was back on me and I didn't understand why.

A long time before this, my mom had given me a piece of paper with a prayer written on it. The prayer was: "God, open my eyes and my ears and give me Your understanding."

How did I memorize that? I didn't. I'm not that smart. But in that moment, the Holy Spirit reminded me.

So as I watched Danny and Morgan, I noticed a ball of joy around them.

I don't understand why they're so happy and I'm so miserable, I thought to myself. *They're laughing. They're holding their stomachs from laughing so hard. I haven't laughed like that ever.*

Little did I know that they were talking about me and praying for me to get saved.

I walked back over to them, standing close, and suddenly the heaviness lifted again. I'd never felt this way before.

When I walked right back to my truck, I said, "God, if You really sent Jesus to die on the cross for me, I am asking You to please open my eyes and my ears and give me Your understanding."

Remember, Dan had been preaching to me constantly and I had fought the truth, like so many unbelievers do. Some people fight it to their death and then go to the wrong place.

Soon Morgan left, and I looked over at Dan. As I watched him, a surge of joy hit me.

"Come on, Duane," he said. "Let's go to work!"

I don't know what happened to me, but as I looked at myself I saw that the Holy Spirit and the joy of the Lord was all over my body. I got out of my van and ran right past Dan into the house we were working on. I ran all the way into the master bathroom.

"Dude! Dude!" I said.

Dan followed me in. "What?"

"I don't know!" I ran right past Dan again and went into the garage. "Oh my gosh, this place is a joke!"

Without stopping, I ran out again. Dan couldn't keep up with me.

I went back into the house where Black Sabbath and AC/DC was playing.

"Dude, shut that off," I said. "It's devil music!"

I didn't have one scripture in me. I didn't know the Bible at all. But I went over and I pulled the plug.

"Dan, I can't believe it!" I said. "It's all over me. I can't believe it."

"What's all over you?" Dan asked.

"I just went out and asked Jesus to come into my heart."

"You did what?"

"I just asked Jesus to open my eyes and to be my Lord and Saviour."

"What?" He grabbed me by the collar and started shaking me. "You did what? I got to make sure!"

"I asked Jesus to be my personal Lord and Saviour and to come into my heart, dude. And the Holy Spirit is all over me."

Then Dan looked up to heaven and said, "Oh my God! Hallelujah!" Without hesitation, he took off the kneepads he'd been wearing and threw them to the ground. "Good, cuz I quit!"

And that's why he's my hero. He saved my life.

How many people would quit their job like Dan did to come work for me, to sacrifice everything? He had found the fountain of life.

Dan Needham was infectious, and within six months of knowing him anyone would be saved. That's his legacy. And since then, every one of us has been touched and saved.

I tried drugs, alcohol, antidepressants, and anxiety pills. They didn't work. But then I found Jesus and the fountain of life. It doesn't matter how old you are. It doesn't matter what you've done in your past, or your entire life. It doesn't matter what you've done wrong. Jesus forgives. Once you accept Jesus, you'll find the fountain of life. Dan showed me.

Once Duane found the Lord, he made the focus of his business bringing customers to the Lord. Winning the soul of the customer for the Lord was more important than winning the job. That's why he is so successful. He puts God first.

Once Dan found the Lord, he became very simplistic in his lifestyle. He was on fire for the Lord and his relationship with Jesus gave him the most joy and happiness. He shared Him with everyone he met—in bars, with hookers, drug-dealers, and strippers, with doctors, lawyers, and seniors. Above all, he shared his love for the Lord joyfully with each member of the family, including our dad, who was a non-believer.

Danny loved us all so much. He learned quickly that worldly things didn't matter. What really mattered was loving God with all his heart, mind, and soul and loving his neighbour as he did himself. And Danny did that every day.

He was also a minimalist. He owned four shirts, all the same style, and different colours. The same went for his shorts, socks, runners, and of course his famous headbands; he reminded me of a ninja when he wore those. I will always remember him as Ninja Dan.

These things were all Dan needed to keep him happy… along with his stash of food. He didn't accumulate wealth, possessions, money, power, or any other worldly trapping. He just accumulated joy and love. All his old addictions passed away, replaced by his one true and only purpose: loving the Lord, his Saviour, and taking care of his family and friends. His love for the Lord was by far his greatest addiction, equalled only when he met his son Jeremy,[28] his wife, and his grandchildren.

Danny didn't become a participating father until two years before he passed away. He had been estranged from his son shortly after he was born. Jeremy had actually thought that Danny was dead.

I think, for some reason, Danny thought his son was better off without him. But by God's grace, Jeremy decided to look for Danny's family members on Facebook one day and discovered that his dad was very much alive.

Their reunion brought us all to tears. It was by far the greatest human experience Danny ever had. I never saw him happier or prouder than when he told us about his son. Danny's life became complete that day. It was like he finally had everything he'd ever wanted. When he spoke of his family after that, his face shone—and after meeting Jeremy, I can see why.

We are so blessed to have Jeremy as part of our family. He is the spitting image of his dad and has the same love of Christ in his heart. It had come full circle, something that only God can accomplish. Our family history has truly been one miraculous experience after another.

---

[28] Danny and David both had sons named Jeremy. They were named after Jeremiah in the Bible.

42.

PRAYER MOVES MOUNTAINS

Grace allows change.

SHORTLY AFTER DUANE ACCEPTED GOD, DOUG DID THE SAME. AS HE EXPLAINS:

I gave my life to God right after Duane did. My mom asked me to give my heart to the Lord, and I did it—but only to please her. To be honest, it really had no effect on me at the time.

Later, I did it again, this time at church. When I did it at church, I suddenly felt a part of the church family. I really needed a family at the time, because we were all living in different places. I really needed a Father.

When I accepted the Lord, I felt the presence of God come over me. Suddenly, I really wanted to change. I went to church with my mom and the Holy Spirit connected with me. I realized that my mom had been right all along.

Change didn't happen overnight. We're all a work in progress, and I work on myself, being a better husband and father, every day. Nobody is perfect. God just wants us to try to be the best version of ourselves possible. And we have to make an effort daily.

But from that day forward, I made the commitment to change.

My mom had prayed and prayed for us all to be saved before she passed away, and we were. That was her one wish. What an incredible gift.

The prayers of a mother can move mountains! As we were all living in different cities, the only thing she could do was pray. She was very obedient in her prayer life.

43.

MIRACLE ON BELLEMER STREET

Grace provides miracles.

AFTER I HAD MICHAEL, I BECAME A STAY-AT-HOME MOM. WHILE STILL PREGNANT, we'd started looking for a new home since we only had a two-bedroom place and the second bedroom was too small for three children. We looked for more than a year, the challenge being that we only had one income. The housing market was booming and we had put in offers on two different homes and lost them. All we wanted was a three-bedroom bungalow with an eat-in kitchen and a dining room, in a good neighbourhood, close to schools—but it appeared everyone else did, too.

One home had been constantly advertised in the paper, but it was in St. Norbert, a suburb outside the city. In those days, it seemed very far away since there wasn't a lot of development in the south end of Winnipeg. Buses weren't as frequent either. We also hoped to keep our kids at St. Ignatius and we only had one reliable vehicle to make the long commute.

I prayed constantly for the right home, but almost everything we found seemed out of reach. And when Michael was born, we still didn't have a new home.

One day I was in the south end of the city with my real estate agent, in the Fort Richmond neighbourhood, when she received a phone call. After the call, she said to me, "Hey, it appears we finally got the keys for a bank foreclosure in St. Norbert. It's really close by. Do you want to go take a look?"

This was the one that had been advertised for the last several months. Joe and I had driven by it several times and it looked very small, with no garage. The grass was overgrown from being abandoned.

Joe was out of town on a business trip, so I thought, *Well, what the heck? I have nothing to lose.*

When we got to the home, we were the very first people to view it. As I walked through, I was amazed. Not only was it only two years old, but it had absolutely everything on our checklist. Most of the homes we'd looked at previously not only cost much more, but they needed new roofs, carpets, furnaces, etc. That was major work which we couldn't afford. This home was brand spanking new and everything was perfect. It had a dishwasher (our current home did not), an alarm system, air conditioning, and a fireplace. It also had three bedrooms on the main floor, so we could have all the kids close by, and an en suite in the master bedroom. It even had a dining room and eat-in kitchen, as well as a huge backyard. With three boys, this was a Godsend. The basement was unfinished, but all the exterior walls were complete and the plumbing had been installed for a laundry room and third washroom.

The agent said that if we wanted it, we needed to get our offer in… and we needed to get it in *now*.

I had no idea what a well-constructed home looked like, and Joe wasn't around to see for himself, so I brought my brother-in-law for a second look that same evening. He was familiar with construction, and when he looked over the house he was amazed. It was an energy-efficient home, the windows were triple pane, and all the floors had been built with two-by-sixes instead of two-by-fours. He said he had rarely seen such a well-constructed home and encouraged me to bid on it.

The real estate agent and I put together the offer, and we faxed it to Joe for him to sign. He had no idea what he was getting himself into, and he thought I was putting in an offer on a piece of junk. After all, the home was $30,000 less than all the other homes we had been trying to bid on, due to it being a bank foreclosure.

By God's grace, we were the first to make an offer, and since we had a bigger down-payment than the other folks who bid, the bank accepted our offer. We've lived in that home ever since, and it has been more than enough for us. It was a gift from God!

That was the relationship I had with God. He answered so many of my prayers and gave me so much. I knew this was from Him.

44.

HOMELESSNESS COMES IN DIFFERENT PACKAGES

Grace allows a full circle of care.

JOE TURNED OUT TO BE ECSTATIC WITH THE HOUSE, AND WE MOVED IN AUGUST right before school started. Life was good.

Unfortunately, that September we received some bad news: Roy Driver, my old teacher from Florida, was ill. He had befriended our group home and took us on outings. I was told that he had developed a cancerous tumour in the brain and had one month to live.

Joe and I didn't have any money to travel, because we were pouring everything we had into the house. But since we had saved some money on the purchase, I decided to go visit Roy so I could see him one last time. We had kept in touch over the years and he'd been very good to my family every time Joe and I had visited Florida. We'd always made a point of spending time with him when we could, especially since he didn't have any family.

Joe knew how important he was to me. Michael, being a baby and still being breast-fed, would have to come along.

So I hopped on a plane at the end of September and flew to Clearwater. Connie met me there and we proceeded to go to the senior's complex where Roy was staying.

When I walked into Roy's room, I was shocked. Here was this wonderful man who had helped so many people and touched so many lives for so many years, and he was lying in a bed with absolutely no personal belongings around him—no pictures, no clothes, no underwear, no socks. When I asked the woman taking care of him where he'd gotten the clothes he was wearing, she said they were from past residents who had passed away.

My sister and I looked at each other, horrified. How could this man who had done so much for so many people be living like a John Doe in his last days? He looked like he was homeless. Having been a schoolteacher for so many years, he certainly had money.

We decided we were going to fix this. If he was going to die, we wanted him to die with dignity and love.

First we had a lovely visit with Roy and shared Jesus with him. He assured us as best he could that he did know Jesus. Then we went to his home to get him some clothes, pictures, and personal belongings. I told him we would stop and buy him lunch on the way back and asked him what he wanted. He asked for a Big Mac with French fries and a Coke.

"Done," I said. If he didn't have long to live, we were going to make sure he lived well.

On our way back from his house, we also bought him new underwear and socks, as well as all the treats we knew he liked—Coke, peanuts, cookies, and granola bars. We picked up a case of bottled water. All around his room, we placed pictures with him and us, and with him and my nieces and nephews. We wanted him to be surrounded by the people who loved him. He enjoyed his McDonalds food and drank his Coke so fast that he didn't know what hit him. He looked very happy and thankful, though.

Afterward the nurse at the front desk said to us, "You do know that Roy is diabetic?"

Connie and I looked at each other in terror. "We're so sorry. We had no idea. We just gave him a burger, Coke, and fries for lunch."

She just smiled. "Well, at his age and with the diagnosis he has, I'm sure it's okay. I'm sure he really enjoyed it. But we can't give him most of the stuff you brought. What should I do with it?"

Connie and I told her to share it with any of the residents who could have it.

We then went back and had a wonderful day with Roy. We sat by his bedside, held his hand, and prayed with him. Unfortunately, he wasn't really able to respond to us too much. We weren't sure how long he would be around and we wanted to stay through the night, but I still had baby Michael to worry about so we decided to go to a hotel and come back in the morning. At the hotel, we prayed for him and went to sleep.

At four o'clock in the morning, we received a call from the nurses to say that Roy had passed peacefully in his sleep. To be honest, we felt a little guilty and thought that perhaps the sugar high we'd given him could have affected him.

Then we realized that in the end he had gotten exactly what he wanted, which was family around him in his last hours, and his favourite meal.

We were very grateful to have been able to show him how much he was loved and appreciated. Everyone deserves to know that they have someone with them in their last hours.

It's so meaningful that God gave me the opportunity to go back and spend time with Roy. If anyone deserved it, he did.

The last couple of days were spent clearing his estate and talking with lawyers. He had left everything to my niece. This was quite a lot, and it would help establish her future.

We hadn't really understood that our family was all he had. Had we not shown up, he would have died alone. God is good, and we are blessed to be a blessing.

Looking back, it makes me think of those who are homeless. Unfortunately, many people on the street pass away and in their final moments have no one with them. Each of us was someone's baby. We were loved enough to be born, and so we should be loved enough to have someone with us when we pass away.

Working in a homeless shelter, I was grateful for the staff who were able to be there for people in their final hours. I and many of the staff and volunteers also attended these people's memorial services afterwards. It's an incredible gift to offer dignity in life and dignity in death.

45.

AN ANGEL GOES HOME, ANOTHER IS BORN

Grace provides angels and takes them home.

ONE DAY, MY HUSBAND AND I WERE WATCHING *THE GODFATHER.* IN IT, THERE'S a wonderful scene where a father walks his daughter down the aisle on her wedding day.

My husband looked at me and said, "Honey, I want to have a little girl to walk down the aisle."

I was exhausted and already had three boys under the age of five. My hands were pretty full. But this was a tough plea to reject. It wasn't that I didn't want to have another child… I just didn't know if I had the energy. I'd always thought in my heart that if my mom could have eight children, I could have four.

"If I get pregnant before I turn thirty, then fine," I told him. I was twenty-eight at the time. "But we're not actually trying."

On my thirtieth birthday, Joe threw me a big surprise party at a community club with all our friends and family. I remember walking around two-fisting my drinks and laughing because I knew I wasn't going to have any more children. Thirty had been my deadline. I thought that was that. I was off the hook. Because of my promise to Joe, he would have to go get fixed.

Not only does God have a sense of humour, but He knows what we need better than we do ourselves. His ways are always higher, stronger, and better than our ways.

Two weeks later, I found out I was pregnant with our beautiful baby girl, Angelina Antoinette Merrilee,[29] named after our mothers. Even as I was proclaiming that I would have no more children, the Lord had already blessed me with a baby girl.

---

[29] Merrilee is Tenoka's birth name.

If ever a family needed the softness, warmth, and beautiful light of a little girl, our family did. The boys were tumbleweeds, constantly fighting, and Angelina brought peace and joy to everyone's lives. She taught us how to be gentle and how to relax. I am forever grateful to God. All of my children are blessings, and I know God has a special plan for each one of them!

Unfortunately, my mom never got to meet Angelina. I was pregnant with her and going into my second trimester when on December 1, 1995, we received a phone call from my brother saying that our mom had been diagnosed with cancer. She was only fifty-seven and had less than six months to live.

I'll never forget that date, because December 1 was also Duane's birthday.

Cindy and I immediately decided we would go visit her one last time. It was Christmas and we both had children, though, so we had to decide whether to book the flight before Christmas or after. Since our siblings didn't think her death was imminent, and the price was so expensive before Christmas, we booked our flights for Boxing Day, the day after Christmas. This would give us time with our kids to enjoy Christmas and then allow us to enjoy the rest of the season with our family and our mom.

Unfortunately, God had a different plan. We received a call Christmas Eve informing us that Mom had fallen into a coma. We all started to pray that she would recover enough to still be able to visit on Boxing Day. Then, on Christmas Day, we received a call from my brother telling us that Mom wasn't going to come out of the coma, that she was braindead and her organs were shutting down. He needed a consensus from all the kids to take her off life support.

We knew she didn't want to be on life support. It was in her will. We also knew that if there was a day she could pick to go to heaven to be with her Lord and Saviour Jesus Christ, she would have picked Christmas to do it.

So we all agreed to let her go. It was a tough emotional decision, but an easy mental decision. This was God affirming to us that she was blessed and highly favoured, and that she was His child.

It also affirmed how blessed we were to have Him in our lives. She was going to be celebrating Christ's birthday with Him. It was December 25, 1995, the biggest celebration of the Christian year. What an honour and what a gift!

Cindy and I ended up cancelling our Boxing Day flight as our intention in going to Florida had been to take care of our mom, not to bury her. We knew she was in a good place with her Lord, and going there wouldn't change anything or have the impact we wanted.

We were so proud of our mother! My last memory of her is of a beautiful bombshell with a joyful spirit. Before she passed away, she had gotten back on her medication and returned to school where she had been at the top of her class. She had become an executive assistant at a major bank, and with her income she'd bought her own place. It was a nice little trailer that had everything she needed. She'd furnished it with brass and glass items and delicate decorations, which she'd loved. Those were things she hadn't been able to have with eight kids. She had lived like a princess in the end.

For the next few years, it was very difficult to go back to Florida. When you go home, you want to see your parents. I still had my brothers and sisters there, and I loved them dearly, but it wasn't the same. She was gone now.

I wept and mourned for three days straight. My children remember that on Christmas Day I cried uncontrollably. On the fourth day, I rejoiced for where she was and what was yet to come. My mom had chosen to go home on Jesus's birthday and there was so much to celebrate in this.

Six months later, Angelina was born. Unfortunately, Joe lost his job around this time, and for three months we had no income. The banks weren't prepared to help us in any way, but eventually he was able to get a job at half his initial salary.

After going through homelessness, nothing could dampen my pioneering spirit. I realized that even if we lost the house, we would still have each other. If we had to move into an apartment, we could do it. Every man wants to be able to take care of his family, but Joe and I agreed that we would both do whatever it took. Joe was struggling, but I reminded him that he had more than two hundred relatives and friends who would help us if we needed it. That was a huge blessing, and one I hadn't had. Most people who experience homelessness or go through insurmountable difficulties don't have that kind of support network to help them in their time of need. That's often how they fall through the cracks.

46.

A HEART FOR CHILDREN

Grace allows you to reflect and feel blessed through hardship.

I FELT BLESSED TO HAVE BEEN A STAY-AT-HOME MOM, BUT TO HELP OUT financially I decided to open a home daycare. That way, I could still stay home with my children. Plus it didn't make sense to pay to put three kids in daycare.

Coincidentally, or perhaps divinely, the woman two doors down was looking for a babysitter. So I took her two children in and watched the neighbours' kids before and after school. I was able to stay home and take care of my children and hers in a way my mom never could. I wanted them to have fun and just be kids—swinging on swing sets and going to parks, swimming pools, and the zoo.

Our home became the local community club and all the kids hung out in our backyard. My children s birthday parties were celebrated with classrooms of kids. It was easy to find twenty or thirty kids at these parties because I could never turn anybody away. I wanted everyone to feel special, and I wanted everyone to know how much I loved my children and how special they were. My kids were and are my life. They are the most important thing to me. I was determined to gift them the life I'd never had, one of love, peace, joy, and happiness.

When Michael was in Kindergarten and Angelina two years old, the woman I babysat for decided she was going to stay home with her kids and work from home. I was devastated, as we relied on that income to pay bills.

So as God would have it, I ended up going to work outside the home. Luckily, there was a job opening as an educational assistant at my children's school. It would be half days, would work great around the kids' schedule, and I could spend even more time with them and get them to their outside activities. Wow! It was also much more economical because I would work during the hours they were in school and didn't have to pay for daycare.

By His divine grace, God put me in a classroom of fourth-graders and I stayed with them until they finished Grade Seven. Looking back, as I've written earlier, I realize God used this as an opportunity for me to "redo" my own early grades, which I don't remember much about. Through this, I was fortunate to meet and help some of the toughest kids in the class, those who were also experiencing family difficulties and poverty. Coincidence? I believe it was a divine appointment.

I'll never forget Jonathon, a student whom I helped in math. He was experiencing a divorce in his family and was starting to get into trouble. It was affecting his grades. I was good at math, and this was a subject he needed to learn, so we were a perfect match. I tutored him in Grades Seven and Eight. I also connected with his mischievous nature and sensed that things weren't right with him, and that he was starting to get into drugs. I feel that we developed a really good relationship, a trusting relationship. He was very bright.

If I'd had my way, I probably wouldn't have passed Jonathon out of Grade Eight. Instead I would have given him one more year at our school, but the new curricula had a no-fail policy. In his final year, he was able to get a pass in math, fifty percent, and graduate to high school.

During his last month of school, he treated me rather rudely. In retrospect, I'm sure it was because he knew he was moving on and from his perspective he was probably going to miss the friendship and attention. From my perspective, I was equally sad. It felt like he was one of my own children who I wasn't going to see again. Unfortunately, that's life as a teacher.

One day, Jonathon was so rude in the classroom that as a teacher I couldn't let it pass. The whole class had witnessed his vulgarity, and it had been specifically geared towards me. I knew I had to do something about it, and on top of that I felt extremely hurt. I had spent so much time trying to help this child.

I mulled over what to do, feeling so angry inside. I have to say it takes a lot to get me angry, but I was extremely angry with this boy. So I made a lunchtime appointment with him in my Grade Eight classroom.

The night before our meeting, I prayed, thinking about Jesus's walk on the earth. While thinking on His death at the cross, the Holy Spirit whispered to me: "I know you're angry at this boy, and I know he's hurt you. I know that hurt goes especially deep because of the relationship you have with him. Imagine how I, Jesus, felt hanging on the cross with the whole world condemning me, every person in the world hating me. Not just *one* person, but *every* person in the world. Imagine how I felt taking on all of their sin, and all of their anger, and all of their transgressions. Imagine how I felt taking on the entire world's pain and suffering. This is just one boy. In my final hour, I chose to ask my Father to forgive *all of you*, for you know not what you do. Tomorrow you are going to go into your meeting and tell him My story, and you're going to forgive him."

Since this was a Christian school, I could share this story. And I did. If there was one thing I could give Jonathon as a final gift, it was unconditional love, forgiveness, and a relationship with Jesus.

I had some recently baked cookies and I brought him a bunch. I told him the story of Jesus and the cross and how I forgave him for his behaviour, just as Jesus forgives us. I prayed with him and prayed that he would seek a relationship with Jesus to help him through his high school years and his future.

I didn't know what happened to him after he left, but I do know that I did my best to help him to know Jesus. Jesus was my strength during my struggles. He is why I'm here today, so this was one gift I could give.

I recently found out that Jonathon is clean from drugs and has a partner and a little girl. Praise God!

That job really was a divine appointment. By His grace, I was able to go back and enjoy those years with my kids and bond with all their friends as Mrs. Richichi.

As I watched my children go through school, they were able to develop a group of friends who progressed with them, year over year. They then went on to high school with some of the same students. They continue to treasure these friendships today.[30]

That's what stability looks like. That's what a real family home and background is supposed to look like. I never had that. Most people experiencing homelessness or who have gone through foster care and group homes don't have that sort of connection in their lives. That's the challenge. It's so easy to fail without a safe network of friends and family. When you have no one to share life with, it is very hard.

The Grade Seven teacher at our school, Mrs. Probetts, had also taught my husband when he was in school, at the start of her career. As a matter of fact, she is now a close family friend and she helped me edit this book. When you can share the joys of life along with the hardships, with real friends, that's what makes it all worthwhile. Real friends are a part of that inner circle that encourages you and gives you hope.

---

[30] I've also kept connections with all the parents of my children's friends, and we continue to get together every month, to encourage each other and go through life together—they are Amabelle, Carole, Theresa, Chris, Miriam, and Brenda, great friends without whom this journey would've been so much harder and certainly far less enjoyable.

There are so many God moments in my life. Some of them I could see and feel in the moment, but others I couldn't see until I'd gotten much older. I couldn't possibly write them all down, but the formation of our family is definitely among them. Joe's and my ability to manage all our children and their activities is divine. The ability to send them to St. Ignatius school and then St. Paul's High school, both private christian schools was definitely another huge blessing. We didn't miss a thing with them as they grew up. Our careers allowed us to be a part of their lives from the beginning to the present. Even Joe losing his job and getting a new one at half the pay afforded him the opportunity to become a soccer coach for them, since he no longer travelled so much. It made me realize that money isn't everything, but quality of life is. For this I am eternally grateful.

47.

MOM WAS RIGHT, GOD HAD A PLAN

Grace allows you to use your pain to find your passion.

EVENTUALLY I REALIZED THAT I NEEDED TO GET BACK INTO THE CAREER I HAD studied for, which was accounting. The kids were getting older and their activities getting more expensive. We could really use the money.

My neighbour was a lawyer and had his own business, and I had helped him with many of his real estate transactions. He knew I was good at accounting, and so he invited me to become his accountant. I had never worked with an automated accounting system before, since I had studied in the pre-computer age, but I assured him I could figure it out.

I spent hours reading over computer manuals. As a matter of fact, I did so on a family road trip to Florida, managing to learn the accounting system on the way. I ended up doing very well in my neighbour's law firm. They really took a chance on me, and for that I am grateful. I learned a lot. Good friends are hard to find, but that friend and his wife, Ken and Bobby, are definitely among the best I've had.

From the law firm, I went to a travel agency and worked for three years as one of their accountants. I was looking for purpose in life, as my kids were getting older and I was trying to figure out what I wanted to do—and what God's plan was. I didn't want to work for an organization just to make money. I really wanted to do something to make an impact in people's lives.

I went to church, prayed about it, and also had the church pray over me. Shortly after that prayer session, I got a call from a head-hunter regarding some job opportunities.

I went to one interview that felt like the right fit. It was a job teaching people in local businesses how to use accounting software. It combined my love of people and my love of numbers. It was also a job I could do out of my home, which would afford me more time with my children. For example, I would still be able to go to their soccer games.

But then one Saturday, I saw in the paper an ad for an accounting job at Siloam Mission, a homeless shelter and soup kitchen. When I saw this, it really tugged at my heart. But my mind said, "No way." The last place I wanted to work was in a homeless shelter with homeless people. I had lived that life and knew it was very difficult. I didn't think I wanted to look at it every day. Twenty-five years had passed and I now lived in the suburbs, living the good life.

Secretly, I told God that if He wanted me to apply for that job, my head-hunter would have to phone me about it. Sure enough, he called me up the next day.

"Judy, I have this opportunity for you that I think you might enjoy," he said. "Because of your background and your faith, I think it will be a good fit."

There was a pause and I blurted out, "It's Siloam Mission!"

"How did you know?"

"Oh, I just know."

Now, being obedient to God and knowing that I had prayed to understand His will, I knew I had to go for the interview.

I went through the first interview, still not convinced it was for me. I was leaning towards the other more worldly and glamorous job, the one about teaching accounting software.

I agreed to go for a second interview at Siloam, but I felt a little afraid. I had a thought: *What if I run into one of "those" people? What am I going to do?* Well, I was all dressed up, walking out of the building after the interview, when I suddenly saw one of "those" people hanging out in front of the door, right where I had to walk by to leave.

My heart started to beat really fast and I panicked. What would I do? I decided that I would do the same thing I'd do if this person was one of my friends; I decided to say hello and smile.

So I walked out the door and, with my biggest and most cheerful voice, said to the man, "Good morning, sir. How are you today?"

His eyes were downcast, his shoulders slumped. Slowly, his eyes lifted up and our glances connected. I looked deep into his eyes and watched as a grin suddenly came onto his face—first expressing shock, then relief, and then joy.

"I am great *now*," he replied very sincerely. "Thank you."

I had looked him in the eye and acknowledged him as a person. This made me think. If all I had to do was say hello and recognize this person's existence with a smile, if it would cause this level of response, what could happen if I actually started helping them? It was very humbling. I felt confident that this was something I could do. If not me, then who?

I thought to myself, *Judy, you can go through the downtown area with blinkers on and pretend that the problem doesn't exist. If you close your eyes and don't see it, it's not real, right? But it won't go away unless you do something about it. You have to be a part of the solution.*

People don't come from other countries to take care of our impoverished because Canada is one of the richest countries in the world. We are the land of the privileged and we're supposed to be doing it all right. So truly, if we don't do something, who will? We have to take care of our own people.

I thought back on my own past and all the small kindnesses that had encouraged me in my life, like receiving a food hamper at the right time, being given a word of encouragement for being good at math, someone offering me a real smile of warmth, giving me a couple of bucks for a meal, or being gifted a rosary by my godparents. Those were the things that gave me hope and kept me going.

Then I thought of my credentials, which spoke for themselves. I had been a poverty-stricken youth, dependent on food hampers and the generosity of others for sustenance, a drug addict, a drug-dealer, and a homeless person, without hope. I was the product of a messy divorce, living with someone afflicted by schizophrenia. I had been sexually, physically, and emotionally abused. I had lived the same life of these people Siloam Mission ministered to every day. I had survived and achieved far more than anyone had expected. My education had gotten me in the door to perform the job, but my credentials provided the passion that would allow me to be successful at it.

I knew this was the plan God had for me. Homelessness doesn't have to be a life sentence. If we rally around and support each other, we can make change happen.

Out of obedience to God, I accepted. I learned that you don't always get to do what you want, or what you think you want. It's not about you; it's about serving God and making the world a better place.

48.

GOD PLANTS A VISION

Grace allows you to realize your blessings.

I STARTED THE JOB AT SILOAM MISSION ON AUGUST 21, 2007. WHEN I WALKED in, there hadn't been an accountant there for more than a year. An external firm had helped them get the books in order, but they were still behind. My job was to get the books in shape for the next board meeting, which would be held in October. That meant completing several bank reconciliations and staying on top of the mission's current operations. I also performed all the regular operational tasks, such as accounts receivable, accounts payable, payroll, etc.

To say that I was overwhelmed would be an understatement. But since I'd felt called to take the job, I knew I had to do whatever it took, and I knew God would walk with me and empower me to succeed. I worked many nights until ten or eleven o'clock. Thankfully, with God's grace, I was able to learn the job and get the organization caught up to help move things forward.

Almost every floor in the building was empty, and we were accumulating a lot of gift-in-kind donations that took up space, like clothing and exercise equipment, wheelchairs and walkers. These were bulky items that needed a permanent home—fast. The second floor was under construction to become the new shelter. The Saul Sair Health Centre was also under construction. The drop-in centre was the only area currently functioning, serving breakfast and lunch and the odd dinner throughout the week.

Shortly after starting, I remember going to the staff lunchroom, which was on the third floor, to make a personal phone call. As I stood in the corner to make that call, I looked outside the window. I had a panoramic view of the entire inner city. In that moment, I had a vision that Siloam was going to own the entire block.

The Bible says that people perish for lack of vision, and when I looked across the street that day, I had a vision—and it was strong. Although I didn't share it with anyone until much later.

When I finally got the books caught up and realized we were severely in debt, I didn't think about the vision for a long time. But God's thoughts are higher than our thoughts. Throughout the eleven years I worked there, we ended up purchasing the building next door, the building behind us, and the building kitty corner to ours. To date, the mission owns almost that entire block. That was His vision, not mine.

After high school, I hadn't shared my story for twenty-five years. Why? Because there was no need. I was successful, living a good life and raising four beautiful children. Nobody needed to know. It wasn't a way to introduce myself. That part of my life was past, gone, over, finished.

Most people who met me during these years were later shocked to hear my story. I began to share it in order to help others, because the people we served at the mission couldn't share their stories. Their lives were very painful, and sharing would cause them to relive it.

Another reason I chose not to share my story is that it wasn't only mine to tell—it was also my children's story. They needed to be okay with it. They were all in high school, a pivotal age.

But sharing my story, I realized, actually could have an impact on the way people thought about homelessness and poverty—about people in need, people who are different, people who are bullied, and people who don't socially fit in or feel like they belong. I had been that person, and I had overcome it. So I shared my story so they didn't have to share theirs, so they could have a voice through me.

I wanted people to see that homelessness, poverty, mental health issues, and addictions can happen to anybody. We are all one job loss, one divorce, one health issue, one calamity away from being homeless. Often it's not the people we expect.

I also shared my story so that people could see how amazing God is and how important it is to have Him in one's life. Because without God in my life, I don't think mine would have had a happy ending. As Palm 22:22 states, *"I will declare your name to my people; in the assembly I will praise you."*

We had six different leaders during my tenure at Siloam, each playing a different role in the organization's acquisitions. I never shared my vision of owning the whole block, but it just happened. I was able to use my vision to confirm that we were going in the right direction, that what we were doing was in line with God's plan. When He's in something, you're guaranteed a win, and of course Siloam is successful today because of His grace.

Every business should have a vision, and it should be something far above and beyond anything that seems attainable. It should be deeper and greater than simply the things an organization does or the things it sells. It needs to be *visionary*.

For example, a TV salesman doesn't just sell TVs. He brings the world to people who might be shut in their homes. He brings imagination and creativity to someone who's new to our country and growing in a new culture. He brings education to the toddler watching shows like *Sesame Street* to learn letters and numbers. He creates an opportunity for families to gather in their living room to enjoy things they have in common. The TV salesman allows all of us to experience the world and be a part of it through the product he sells.

Siloam Mission serves meals and provides opportunities for change to people experiencing homelessness. But that's not the total vision. The vision is about connecting people from all walks of life—donors, volunteers, business owners, philanthropists, widows, men, women, church groups—bringing them in to connect and serve meals to those experiencing poverty and homelessness. It's about allowing people to be a part of the solution through their contributions. It's about creating community and sharing disparity amongst different groups of people. Each stakeholder should learn, grow, and get better from the experience.

That's the bigger vision. Yes, it's about helping people out of homelessness and helping them succeed. But it's also about changing the culture of community so that everyone is able to change for the better.

When people get engaged and give to a cause like homelessness, or curing a disease or mentoring children at YFC, they stop thinking of themselves and their own personal issues and look beyond themselves to realize that others have it much worse than they do. If we focus on others, we stop thinking of ourselves. We become more creative, more productive, and more caring. We become much better parents to our children, better spouses to our husbands and wives. We learn to appreciate what we have as we look into the eyes of those who have not, realizing that this could be us. Then we change just as much as they do, from the inside out. We learn to be grateful for what we have and grateful for what has been given. It becomes a never-ending circle of giving.

The people we help are amazed that people care enough about them and their issues to take the time to give. They learn how to build healthy relationships with us. They learn to trust. They get treated with dignity and respect, and learn to give back dignity and respect. These people in need eventually rise above their circumstances and want to achieve more. We help them to be accountable to each other, to give them hope that others care, to give them a reason to wake up in the morning. It's a community of people blessing each other through their differences and love.

When I started at Siloam, it was a tiny soup kitchen that was just completing a new 110-bed shelter and health centre to provide a safe place for people to sleep and get their needs met. It served up to two hundred people per meal, offering breakfast and lunch, but not every day. The needs continued to grow, but there weren't enough funds at that time to keep the doors open twenty-four hours a day.

When I started, we closed each day at three o'clock. I left at four-thirty. In the winter, when it was -40 degrees, I would see a line of people waiting to get into our shelter. The line wrapped around the building and people would stand outside for five or six hours in the frigid temperatures waiting to get a bed.

My heart wept. It was so sad see this line every day—and I promised myself I would never stop weeping, because if I did it would mean I had lost sight of the importance of humanity. We should all cry when we see the lack of dignity people are forced to endure during their toughest struggles.

The leadership team at the time was determined to do something about it. Nobody should have to stand outside at -40 waiting for a meal and a bed. In Canada, we can do better, and I am proud to say that after eleven years of service we were able to achieve that and so much more.

We had a team called M.O.S.T. (Mission Off the Street Team). This was a team of men who worked under the tutelage of someone who had skills in construction, plumbing, and electrical. The manager would teach the guys trades and skills so they could eventually obtain employment and transition out of homelessness.

I decided that if I ever needed any work done, I would call this team and employ them. I would rather pay them over other professionals so I could help them in their effort to get off the street.

Sure enough, the opportunity came for me and Joe to redo our bathroom.

"Honey," I said. "I want to bring in the M.O.S.T. team."

He was flabbergasted. This wasn't long after I had started working at Siloam and he didn't like me working there to begin with. I'd been working a lot of extended hours and he was fearful for me. I had assured him on many occasions that everything was fine and that people experiencing homelessness were just people. I'd reminded him that homelessness could happen to anybody and that he shouldn't be so judgmental.

We needed to get our bathroom done and these were good guys. The price was right, too.

Joe finally agreed to allow them to come into our home. He came back from work early one day to check them out, and as he walked by one of the guys he realized that he recognized him.

"Joey?" the guy said.

"Larry?"

All of a sudden, they gave each other a big hug. Larry had been Joe's buddy from junior high and high school. In fact, he'd been deemed most likely to succeed by his classmates. Not only had he been good at hockey,[31] but he'd excelled at soccer as well. He had been given an opportunity to play international soccer in South America, and that was the last Joe had heard of him.

We found out from visiting that Larry did play international soccer for a while, but then he blew out his knee, got addicted to painkillers and eventually cocaine, and came back from his experience a broken man. Now he was using the services of Siloam Mission to rebuild his life.

Well, not only did Joe change his mind about the people at Siloam, but he changed his mind about my working there. Larry opened his eyes to the fact that anybody could become homeless, even people he knew. It's usually the people we grew up with, who we lose touch with, people who thirty years down the road maybe don't have quite the life they thought they would. Or perhaps it's people who have faced some difficulties in life and need help.

Later on, we were able to reconnect Larry with his family. He entered programs that stabilized him and he became drug-free. He also came to know the Lord. Today Larry is doing very well in the community and we are proud to call him a friend of the family. He even taught my son a few soccer tricks.

After doing the accounting for three years, a new CEO, Floyd Perras, came in and decided to make me the Director of Development. I knew that God was pushing me to do something more for the cause. We were doing well, but I could see a lot of missed opportunities to raise money. Floyd saw my passion and encouraged me to use my marketing skills to move the organization forward.

With much prayer, I stepped out of accounting and into my new role as a fundraiser. I was terrified. In my accounting role, I had worked with CCCC

---

[31] At one point, he was drafted by the Winnipeg Jets.

(Canadian Centre of Christian Charities) and helped the mission get the CCCC's seal of approval that certified us as an exemplary Christian workplace. I shared a little bit of my testimony with their CEO, John Pellowe, and gave him a tour of our facility.[32]

Two days after I decided to take on the role of Director of Development, John phoned me up and asked me to be a keynote speaker for the CCCC's conference in Winnipeg that fall. I was beside myself. My initial reaction was "Absolutely not! No way! Nope!" I didn't want to speak in public.

But this was a test and a challenge to see if I could actually do the job. I told him I would think about it.

I had never before shared my testimony in public, nor did I think I wanted to. This was a huge decision, because once again I would have to put myself out there and become vulnerable.

However, I realized that this wasn't about me. It was about the mission. It was about what God could accomplish through me for the mission. It was an opportunity to put Siloam in the spotlight and reach hundreds of people working for organizations in our city to help them see what we did, how we did it, and why we did it. It was also a way to break stereotypes as to who the homeless are. After all, I didn't fit the bill as someone who had been homeless.

So I prayed about it and felt God lead me to say yes. I would be addressing Christian leaders across Canada who could probably help us improve our brand and move forward.

I put together a forty-five-minute presentation, and to be honest I was terrified. But I shared Siloam's story, and then I shared mine, as well as my role at the mission. I shared that I did what I did because I believed in taking care of people who are vulnerable, who need help, who suffer from mental health issues, and who otherwise would be unhealthy. I also shared that it's what God has called all of us to do.

The positive response I received gave me the confidence I needed to continue sharing my story and the stories of the people we served. It was also where I met Tim Coles, the current National Director of Youth for Christ, whose infectious smile and positive attitude later inspired me to join the organization. Both of us have served on the CCCC board because we believe in their great work.

Siloam now serves three meals a day to more than four hundred people. The waiting line is contained inside the building, so no one has to be outside.

---

[32] I encourage anyone looking to support Christian organizations in Canada to check if they are a part of the CCCC, as a way to identify their commitment to excellence in ministry. This organization works hard to help others succeed.

The health centre offers everything from optometry to podiatry to dentistry, chiropractic care, physiotherapy, massage therapy, and traditional medicine… everything a person could possibly need to get their health needs met. Programs were also expanded to include case management and spiritual care support.

The staff works with about two hundred clients, helping them to transition out of homelessness. They offer eighty-five units of housing in a self-contained building. The housing offers three meals a day, clothing, shelter, healthcare, case management, and spiritual support for the price of $580 to $600 per month, which is what somebody typically receives on EI assistance. This means that instead of living on the streets with this money—who can live in Canada on $600?—people can enjoy stability, food, clothing, shelter, and a place to call home.

Floyd, myself, and our capital campaign team led by Janet Mcleod and Garth Manness also raised the funds to complete a 55,000-square-foot expansion project to add fifty emergency shelter/transition beds with a private sleeping area for women, because at the time of my leaving we were turning people away in the middle of winter. The expansion grew our drop-in centre from one hundred fifty seats to four hundred and will eventually provide main floor case management support for easy access. Having main floor access is critical.

Seeing the opportunities for help and seeing people get help is contagious. No one wants to admit that they need help, but once a person sees someone else succeed, it becomes possible for them. It truly will be a one-stop shop for people in need of finding spiritual, mental, and physical care.

49.

TRUE HEROES OF THIS WORLD

Grace allows you to see beauty in the broken.

DURING MY TENURE, I MET SO MANY PEOPLE WHO HAVE SEEN AND EXPERIENCED so much pain. They are everyday heroes who have overcome a lot of tragedy, drama, and pain.

Rose, Sharon, Big Al, Bob, and Happy are just a few of these people.

Rose endured residential schools, sexual abuse, and physical abuse and lived on the street for twenty years suffering from addictions. The abuse she experienced caused her to turn to alcohol and drugs for solace, which led her to the streets for years and years.

When I met Rose, she had just moved into Siloam's housing facility. We were serving Easter dinner and she had dressed up. She looked beautiful in her blue T-shirt, blue nail polish, and matching necklace and earrings.

I introduced myself and asked if she was dressed up because of this very special holiday meal. The response she gave me is one I will never forget: "All my life I lived on the streets. I suffered physical abuse, mental abuse, sexual abuse, and incest, and I survived residential schools and addictions. All I wore was black, all I saw was black, and all I felt was black. Now that I have my own home, I want to wear colour again. Today I'm wearing blue, yesterday I wore purple, and tomorrow I'm wearing pink!" She beamed with pride.

That is truly the difference between living on the streets and living in a place where you belong and feel loved. You go from living in black-and-white to living in colour again.

When Rose showed me her room after the meal, I saw all her clothes neatly lined up in her closet, one outfit for each day of the week in a different colour. On her dresser was jewellery that perfectly matched the outfits, and on her window ledge was nail polish that also perfectly matched. She radiated joy and happiness. She had moved in on Monday, three days earlier, and now she found herself living in community, even starting a puzzle club with the other residents.

Sharon, who lived at the shelter for years before finally moving into affordable housing, volunteered by making coffee at the drop-in. She suffered from mobility issues and had three children in foster care. Once stabilized, she went back to school but struggled to pass. But she never gave up and continued to be a mother for her children, even though they didn't live with her.

The kids went to a weekly Bible study at the local church and were raised to become incredible young men. Despite their circumstances, these boys were very proud of their mom. The last time I saw them, they proudly told me that Sharon had finally graduated from Grade Twelve. My spirit soared. I was so happy for her. She had survived amazing trials to triumph in the end. Her children are now leaders in their church.

Big Al was another favourite resident of mine. He worked in our employment training program for almost a year picking up garbage. He lived in our shelter as a community member trying to lift himself out of poverty and homelessness. At the drop-in centre, he was known as the Scrabble king and a wordsmith. Everyone knew he would win every game because he was so intelligent when it came to words and definitions.

Unfortunately, Big Al passed away from pancreatic cancer. At his funeral, there was a picture of him with some Winnipeg Blue Bomber football players. It had been taken when they came for a meet-and-greet breakfast at Siloam. His parents had said that moment was the highlight of his life. He was a huge football fan and meeting the players had really inspired him.

We were shocked to learn from his family that not only was Big Al extremely intelligent, but he was a chartered accountant and had worked for many accounting firms across the country, including a major investment firm and a national bank. He could have worked anywhere.

But he was never so happy as when he found Siloam Mission, according to his parents. It was the one place where he felt he belonged. He'd had a hard time fitting into the business world and struggled with the cliques. It just wasn't him. At Siloam, he was one of the guys. Everyone loved him unconditionally and accepted him for who he was.

Again, I was shocked. This man could have been my own boss but instead he chose to clean up garbage on the street. It's often not about the job, the house, or the money, but rather about belonging and feeling safe just to be yourself.

Then there was Bob, who almost died one day while living in his truck. I'll never forget it.

In the middle of February, I got a call from my good friend John who told me about a worker of his, Bob, who hadn't shown up for work. In fact, this worker hadn't shown up for three days. Due to union rules, if an employee didn't show up for three days, if there was no valid reason, he had to be terminated.

Bob was a good hard worker and had been working with John for over year and a half cleaning produce coolers. He was a simple man, well-respected and liked, and someone who did what he was told.

"So I had to terminate him," John told me. "I have his last paycheque and his personal belongings from his locker. I asked a friend of his to show me where he lived so I could give him his things. When I got there, I was astounded to find out that Bob had been living in the back of his truck. I lifted up the back hatch of the truck and looked in to find Bob lying down in there. He had a space heater plugged into the garage and had insulated the entire truck with garbage bags and blankets. He had everything he needed in there, but it's definitely not a place for someone to be living in the middle of February. The smell coming out of that truck was strong. I couldn't believe anyone could live in there. When I asked Bob why he hadn't come to work, he said that he hadn't been feeling well lately and didn't think he could make it. He had severe pain in his side. Well, I told him he should go see the doctor, and if the doctor gave him a note he could come back to work and keep his job. He said he would think about that. He was concerned, though, because he didn't have a current medical card. He was afraid to go to the doctors because he didn't think he was covered."

I told Johnny to tell him about Siloam, to tell him that we could take care of him. Our health centre was free and many people came to us without medical cards. We could get him a note from our health professionals and save his job.

Unfortunately, Bob refused the offer, telling John that he didn't need help and that he was doing just fine on his own.

Later I said to Johnny, "Well, we can at least give him clean stuff." And I proceeded to fill bags with new blankets, sheets, clothing, soaps, shampoos, and conditioners... things to help him maintain his hygiene. I also gave John a brochure and encouraged him to try to bring Bob over to the shelter.

Still Bob refused.

A week later, John received a call from Bob's friends. It turned out that Bob could no longer get out of his truck. He was in so much pain that he couldn't move.

"Judy, I'm bringing him in, whether he wants to come or not," John said. "Can you please be ready?"

We had no medical doctors on site at the time, but we had the manager of the health centre. I told her what was happening, figuring that at least Bob could touch base with us, and if we needed to send him to the hospital, we would.

It took an hour to get Bob out of the truck and over to Siloam. Needless to say, the guy was in bad shape. He could barely walk. When we brought him into the health centre, the manager looked him over and immediately called for an ambulance. Bob would have to go to the hospital.

His clothes were a wreck, so John and I immediately took off his old filthy coat and gave him a brand-new one so he would be better presented.

"Bob, you're going to the hospital," I said. "Are you okay with that?"

He looked at me so dejectedly. "Well, you know my situation. I have no health card."

"That's okay. I'll come with you and I'll talk to the triage nurse to make sure you're looked after."

When the ambulance came, Bob and I went immediately to the hospital. At the emergency room, Bob was put in a wheelchair and I proceeded to tell the nurse Bob's story. I described him as a well-respected man, a hard worker, someone who had a lot of people rooting for him.

"We don't have a current health card for this gentleman," the nurse said.

"I understand that. Could you possibly find one that he used to have with an old address on it? Perhaps we can find him that way and use his old one?"

She ran a search and we were able to come up with his expired card.

"Would you please accept this gentleman and help him?" I asked. "We recently found out he has been homeless for over a year and a half, living in his truck. He's been living in inhumane conditions for a very long time and it would be really nice if we could spoil him a little bit. Make him feel special."

We both knew that if Bob hadn't come in, he would have died.

The nurse smiled. "Of course."

Bob was admitted and the staff immediately looked after him. The next time I visited, the staff told me that they'd had to drain forty litres of fluid out of his body. The foreskin on his penis had closed and all the bodily fluids that should have been leaving his body had been retained. On top of that, he had five blockages in his heart that had been causing him tremendous pain. The doctors thought he may have had a heart attack while lying in the back of his truck, since his heart capacity was less than twenty percent. At that level, they couldn't operate. As well, he now had pneumonia.

The cause was an infection by mould spores growing inside the truck from all the condensation that resulted from constant hot and cold passing through the vehicle. The truck was uninhabitable.

The hospital staff gave me a bag of his old clothes and said they were full of bedbugs and that Bob couldn't use them anymore. He would need new clothes in order to stay at the hospital.

Now, I didn't know this man from Adam. I wonder what would've happened to him had we not been there to get him in and advocate on his behalf.

On my way back to the mission to get the clothes, I decided I was going to spruce him up a bit. So I got him the best clothes I could find: brand-new jeans, a black leather belt, a nice mauve Italian dress shirt, leather shoes, the works, as well as underwear, socks, shampoos, conditioners, and other hygiene items. I brought this all up to his hospital room.

Bob stayed in the hospital for almost two weeks, and every time I visited him he was very happy and grateful.

"I can't believe this place," he would say. "They're treating me like a king. I get three meals a day, and they come by with cookies and juice in between. I've never been treated so well."

I'm sure he felt like he had won the lottery.

By the end of his hospital stay, Bob had received excellent care and learned about his heart and how his living conditions had been working against him. Now he was able to make wiser choices.

I went to visit him one last time on a Friday night after an exhausting week. I hadn't wanted to take the time and would have preferred to get home and be with my family. But I did stop by the hospital and there he was, sitting in bed, all dressed up in his brand-new clothes, freshly showered and changed. It looked like Bob was going home, which worried me because there was no one at the mission to receive him. I was also worried because I didn't want him to go back to his truck.

He looked somewhat dejected, so I asked him what was wrong.

"They don't want me anymore," he said.

Immediately I understood why he felt this way. "Bob, it's not that they don't *want* you anymore. It's just that they can't *help* you anymore. They've done all they can do and now you need follow-up care. That's why you're being discharged. They want your bed for someone who needs the bed more than you do."

As I explained this to him, I knew that he needed to be able to stay in the hospital at least a little longer so that he wouldn't go right back to his old lifestyle.

I talked to the nurse and his social worker, explaining the situation, and asked them if he could stay until Monday. On Monday, the mission would have staff on hand to receive him. By God's grace, they agreed. For this, we are eternally grateful.

When Bob connected with the mission, we needed a few days to fit him in, since we had a line-up. Fortunately, he had enough money to stay at the Salvation Army until we were able to get him in.

He stayed at the mission for several months, eating his three meals a day, getting a good night's sleep, and staying in the shelter.. He followed up his medical appointments with the health centre. During his time with us, he also connected with our case management staff. We were able to file his income tax and help him apply for a disability pension since he was sixty-two years old and entitled to it, having worked all his life. He hadn't filed his income tax for the last seven years and we were able to get him a GST rebate and a really nice tax return, as well as his pension, which enabled him to upgrade his living conditions into a home where I believe he still lives today.

Essentially, we saved his life, and for that I am extremely proud. It took tremendous team effort from all departments to meet his needs, but we did it. Bob came back to visit one Valentine's Day and brought chocolates to everyone who had helped him, to say thank you. That was indeed a special day.

That's what homeless shelters and missions can do for somebody experiencing homelessness. Every community has one. People need to be stabilized, to get proper healthcare, nutrition, and rest to truly turn their lives around. When you're living on the streets or sleeping under stairs, or in stairwells, or on the ground, or even in vehicles, there is no stability. There is no proper care. And so you eventually deteriorate.

Bob had become homeless after his mother died and her home was declared unfit to live in, leaving him with nothing but his truck. It's a reminder that behind every person, there is a story.

Finally there's the case of Happy, an East Indian fellow who suffered from schizophrenia. When Happy was on his medications, he was a very happy man. He came to our health centre every day for his daily dose of medicine to keep him on track and mentally stable.

Happy played the piano at the drop-in centre and made the most beautiful music. He didn't have much, but what he did have was his words. He chose to use them every day to empower and encourage the people he met. Whether it was the patrons using our services, the donors, volunteers, or staff, Happy had a beautiful word for every person he came across, and he was always excited to tell you how special he felt you were.

Happy passed away the same day he was supposed to finally get his new home. He had been set to move out of the shelter and get his own place when he was unfortunately stricken with cancer. At his funeral, there was standing room only, and not a dry eye in the place. People remembered what an incredibly gifted man he had been, and how special he had made them feel.

At the end of the day, people don't always remember what you do, but they always remember how you make them feel. Happy gave the people he met the best gift of all; he made people feel loved, accepted, and special. It was the greatest gift he could give, and he gave it happily.

Finally, although she didn't use Siloam Mission's services, I cannot leave out my mom, Antoinette Adams. She suffered from mental health issues and lived in and out of homeless shelters. Most of her life, the challenges she faced were beyond her ability to cope, but through it all she prayed. She prayed for her family, for each of her children, their circumstance, and their futures. Through her prayers, she saved us all.

There are true heroes in this world. Rose, Sharon, Al, Bob, Happy, and my mom are just some of the ones I've learned from. They're people who have overcome so much tragedy and pain most people never experience, yet they were willing to be a part of their community, make an impact as best they could, and achieve their best. Not all of us will become doctors and lawyers. Not everyone will become a rocket scientist. But we all have a gift we can share, and each of these heroes did just that.

If we look back through the New Testament, we can see that Jesus encountered many people who lived similar lives, and He used their stories to teach us. Every person is important in God's kingdom, because every person can teach us something about ourselves, about life's issues, and about the world.

The beggar on the street taught us that God cared so much that He wanted to heal his blindness and make him whole and healthy again. God cares the same way for us. He also taught us the importance of faith.

The woman at the well taught us that we are all sinners and that we shouldn't cast blame on other people's sin unless we're willing to look at ourselves first, at what we've done. In God's eyes, sin is sin. There are no degrees, nothing bigger or lesser; it is all sin. Unless we all admit that we are sinners and atone for it, we will never be right with God.

The widow's offering taught us that in order to receive, you need to give. God loves an honest and joyful giver and honours the person who gives out of whatever they have. She also taught us to trust God with everything we have, not just some of it.

The parable of the sower teaches that if we do His will, He will reward us tenfold and bless us beyond belief. He told us that we will reap what we sow, and if we're willing to sow into His kingdom, our ten percent will become a hundred percent. But if we invest in the world, our hundred percent will only grow by ten percent. His ways are higher than our ways, and we need to tap into His ways in order to be successful.

Jesus taught us through the lepers who were healed that a grateful person is to be honoured. When we receive a blessing, if we aren't grateful for it, we should be ashamed of ourselves. We need to thank Him daily for all that He does for us.

He taught us through the workers in the vineyard that we have our entire lives to figure out how to follow Him and be obedient and work for Him. Once we make that decision, at the end of the day we all get the same gift and the same payment as the one who started early in life, and that gift is eternal life in heaven with Him. He hopes that we will do it at the beginning of our journey so that we can receive His blessings in this life, too, but He will honour us until the end of our journey as long as we get it right in the end.

People affected by poverty and homelessness can teach us that we are so blessed to have what we have. There is always somebody worse off than us, and if we don't learn to appreciate what we have and care for those who have not, we can never receive more from God.

The Bible tells us that the poor will always be with us, and I believe this is because they teach us how to be compassionate and loving. They teach us how to care, how to feel. When we observe their daily trauma, we should all cry—because when we stop crying, we stop feeling. I never want to stop feeling.

50.

LIFELONG LEARNER

*Grace is looking back at your life and seeing
God's hands in everything.*

AS I WORKED AT SILOAM, I LEARNED SOMETHING NEW EVERY DAY. FOR EXAMPLE, I am blessed that I was homeless in Florida where the temperatures never went below freezing. I don't think I would have survived in Winnipeg. I'm also grateful that I get to go home each winter night to a warm house and bed to sleep in. It inspires me to want to work harder for those who do not.

I've learned that there is never a good time to be homeless. Summer, spring, and fall all have their own unique challenges, like battling the heat, rain, dust, wind, mosquitoes, and bugs and not having access to water, pools, lakes, or air conditioning.

Everyone deserves to have food in their bellies. Our foodbanks do a tremendous job. They not only supply food to shelters, but they give hampers to people who live in homes and help these families maintain their housing, which prevents a situation from getting worse than what it is. And it is okay to need help. Life is tough.

I've learned how important it is to have clean underwear when you're homeless. Having one set of clothes is truly a challenge. Imagine living a life where you have no change of underwear and you wear the same clothes every day. It is the most undignified feeling. Having experienced this, I know. When working at a shelter and seeing the women come in looking for new panties, I was reminded of how important it is to have clean clothing—not only for your hygiene, but for your dignity. Clean underwear also provides a protective layer from the cold. And when you add in a woman's monthly cycle, it's a very bad day when you don't have access to clean underwear.

Socks also need to be changed regularly. Once they get dirty, they smell… as my brother Duane's story made clear. People don't want to be around smelly people. Once a pair of socks get wet, they no longer protect you from the elements.

Just walking around causes our feet to sweat, trapping moisture on the bottom of our feet. If it's freezing outside or just below zero, and your socks are wet, the moisture freezes and you risk frostbite. The same is true of gloves. Siloam's healthcare professionals have seen many limbs lost due to the lack of clean and dry outerwear.

We are all lucky to be part of communities that help us succeed, whether it's our work communities, school communities, sport communities, or social communities. We are surrounded by a network of people to help us achieve greatness every day. I'm grateful that homeless shelters are there for our citizens who need it most so they may have a community, too. I am also grateful for charitable organizations like Youth for Christ that find ways to include those who otherwise may not be able to afford activities and programs so many of us take for granted.

I am blessed to have met my husband at the early age of fifteen. Instantly I had two hundred relatives and friends and supporters in my life. If I needed anything, Joe had a connection to help me get it, whether it be a car, a home, or a plumber.

We all need connections to survive, so what makes us think our most vulnerable don't?

I learned about residential schools and how thousands of Indigenous people were taken from their families and culture and forced to live in the white man's world. They were physically, mentally, and sexually abused, and some never got to see their parents again. Many were taken at birth and put into foster care. They are overrepresented on the streets of Winnipeg. We need to be repentant and help them break the chains of oppression they are experiencing.

I learned that merely getting a job isn't always the answer. The first testimony I heard was from a young man in our employment training program who was twenty-six years old. He shared that he had been in seventeen foster homes over eighteen years. As he shared, he wept. He felt unloved, unwanted, uncared for, lost, lonely, and broken. He had no stability and no consistent friends. Yet when people like him eventually end up homeless, society says, "Why don't you just get a job?" Meanwhile, the homeless say, "Why doesn't someone love me and help me find security, dignity, hope, and community?"

We are meant to live in community, and community is what the church provides. I believe that mental health challenges like depression and anxiety are on the rise because spirituality is on the decline. Fewer people are going to church, so they aren't strengthening their spirit man to safeguard against mental attacks.

Back in the day, the church was the focal point of the community. Sunday was a day of rest when gatherings took place to uplift us and encourage us through our struggles. Nowadays, Sunday is just another day, and many people are unchurched and suffering alone. We need to get back to keeping the Sabbath day holy and sharing the good news of the Lord.

I have learned that regardless of religious background or cultural identity, everyone desires to help the less fortunate. Everyone feels good when they can help others, and everyone realizes it will help the world be a better place if we do. It's one thing we all have in common.

So let's start with that. Let's start with what we all agree on: loving one another and caring for our neighbours.

I have learned that our purpose in life is to minister to each other and be a source of strength, hope, and love for those around us to overcome their obstacles and succeed.

I learned that there are many unsung heroes who work behind the scenes, like the cleaning and maintenance staff. They keep their places of business dignified and clean and provide hope. Most people expect shelters and soup kitchens to be dirty, but Siloam has been blessed to have volunteers, staff, and clients who keep it clean in order to inspire volunteers and donors to want to give of their time and resources to provide change for those that need it. These silent workers provide dignity for all of us.

I learned that the worst time of day to be homeless is night. During the day, you can keep busy, eating meals and utilizing programs and services. But at night, as you lay in bed, alone, you realize that this is all you have. This is when the demons come out. Your thoughts tell you that you deserve this fate, that no one loves you, that if you died tomorrow no one would care. You question whether life is worth living. An idle mind is the devil's playground. We shouldn't allow the enemy to pervade our thoughts at 2:00 a.m.

Shelter workers are there to remind these people that, yes, people do care. Our Winnipeg community cares. The staff, volunteers, and donors care. There is a whole city that cares.

And above all, even when no one else is around, God cares. His Word says,

Finally, brothers and sisters, whatever is true, whatever is noble, whatever is right, whatever is pure, whatever is lovely, whatever is admirable—if anything is excellent or praiseworthy—think about such things. (Philippians 4:8)

Shelter staff let their clients know that they're not alone and that they are all children of God with a special purpose. We are there to help them find that purpose.

As 1 Corinthians 12:12–27 tells us, there is one body… but it has many parts. Every part of the mission is important, every person and every program. All of it is needed for people to achieve success. The same is true for any business or ministry; the same is true for this world.

People ask me who the homeless are. Are they "down and outers"? Are they people suffering from addictions or who have mental health issues?

My response is a challenge: try to live on the street for two weeks with no supports, no home, and nobody who cares for you. Eventually you'll turn to some form of self-medication or addiction to take away the pain. You'll start to suffer from mental health issues, and eventually you will spiral into depression. The cure is community and fellowship. People don't care how much you know until they know how much you care.

I also learned a lot about Winnipeg as a city. Winnipeg is made up of pockets of very different ethnic communities, and each one takes care of its members. The Filipinos take care of Filipinos; the Italians, the Italians; the French, the Ukrainians, the Jewish, the Indigenous, etc. Just go to the city's annual cultural festival, Folklorama, and experience the wide range of people who inhabit our city and call it home. We are a multicultural melting pot.

Many people have come here from hardship and adversity, and together we are strong. We need to help each other through hardship, through difficulties, through the cold winters, through floods, and through every other calamity. We each rely on our communities and networks to be the best we can be.

So if we couldn't make it on our own, what makes us think that our most vulnerable could? What makes us think those who have endured so much hardship could do it alone?

I have learned that God has a bigger and better plan for each and every one of us. He wants to help us achieve our best, beyond anything we could imagine. But we need to believe it. We need to press into His grace and into His Word. We need to make choices that will bring us closer to Him so that we can achieve those goals, whatever they may be. And we need to be obedient when He calls us.

God is the super to our natural and the extra to our ordinary. For every career move I took, I felt ill equipped, but His grace gave me the wisdom and work ethic to persevere. If we all were to achieve our absolute best, and we took care of each other the way He intended us to care for each other, then we would indeed have heaven on earth. And if we followed His two simple commands— love your Lord your God with all of your heart, mind, and soul (an internal heart commitment) and love your neighbour as you love yourself (an external heart commitment)— then we would also have heaven on earth. Wouldn't that be a beautiful sight?

I truly believe that if we build strength around our weak and make them stronger, we can have a community of people who are all contributors, not takers, who become economically stronger together. That's what every city and community should strive for in their outreach—neighbour helping neighbour, loving each other to be the best they can be, building the strongest fabric of community we can, achieving the best possible outcome for our community at large. This benefits all of us.

51.

BECAUSE IF NOT US, WHO?

Grace comes through us as we become the hands and feet of Christ.

For it is by grace you have been saved, through faith—and this is not from yourselves, it is the gift of God—not by works, so that no one can boast. (Ephesians 2:8–9)

THE GREATEST COMPLIMENT I EVER RECEIVED AS A LEADER AT THE MISSION WAS from a business that was very hesitant to come in for a tour or volunteer. They gave money and items we needed, but not time. I persuaded them to volunteer. After their volunteer experience, they decided to partner with us. They told me that they were so impressed with their experience that they wanted to make sure every member of their staff had the chance to come in and volunteer to learn the culture of giving. They wanted to build the same kind of work culture in their organization that we had. They wanted their staff to learn to put others first and become servant leaders.

That's a true testament to the staff and volunteers who work so hard at Siloam and other Christian ministries around the world who try to make an impact. They truly are heroes who inspire others to love their neighbours.

Change happens when people step in to help people. We have the ability to feed people and sow good seed into people's lives by being the hands and feet of Christ and helping people along their journeys. This is what God has called us all to do. We can help change lives from the outside in, but only Jesus transforms lives from the inside out.

True transformation happened in the lives of my family members when we decided to follow Christ and be obedient to following Him, when we became willing to press into God and His Word, and use our wisdom and discernment to be obedient to go out and make an impact in other people's lives.

This is what God can do for all of us. My mom said that God had a plan, and He did. But each of us had to be willing to follow that plan. Faith in God allows true spiritual transformation to take place. This is the everlasting change people so desperately need.

In Matthew 4:4, Jesus said, *"It is written: 'Man shall not live on bread alone, but on every word that comes from the mouth of God.'"* He proclaimed this after not eating for forty days. He was tempted by Satan and overcame him by proclaiming the Word.

I'm not special, and my brothers and sisters aren't special. We're just eight people out of millions who go through life like everybody else. We experienced tragedy and triumph. If we could make it after everything we went through, so could everybody else. We all just need a little bit of hope, a hand up, some unconditional love and acceptance, and an opportunity to grow and improve our faith in God. With that, we can achieve all that God has planned for us.

We also need angels. The angels in my life were my godparents, who gave me a rosary that symbolized Jesus and hope to me as a child. Another angel was my schizophrenic mother, who told me God had a plan. Then there were the schoolteachers who told me I was smart in math, the people who operated the foodbanks, churches, and strangers who gave us food hampers and hope. There's also my dad, who brought us to Canada, and my stepmom, who was brave enough to take in four troubled teens. And of course there is my husband and my mother- and father-in-law, who gave me unconditional love at a time when I needed it most. Finally, there are my friends and family who minister to me daily with affection and love and the church family that continually builds me up in faith, love, and encouragement.

You, too, can be an angel. Give to foodbanks, homeless shelters, hospitals, and youth centres. Make donations and volunteer for causes that improve the lifestyles of the people around us and make our communities better places. You can make an impact. You can give hope.

Yes, you are the angels who allow others to be the best they can be. You are the hands and feet of Christ on earth. We need you. Together we can create heaven on earth. Everyone needs to be willing to do their part. If we want a cause to go viral in this world, it should be #loveyourneighbour.

We are the church, the people who inhabit this earth. As Christ's disciples, we are called to invest in the charities and organizations that make a difference in people's lives. Make a pact today to get to know the neighbours on either side of you. Help them. Do something good for them.

Faith without action is dead. If we all took care of our own city block and made sure that our neighbours were stabilized, loved, and cared for, the world would align to God's plan. That's all God asks of us. That's what God is waiting for.

MY FAVOURITE BIBLE VERSE

Is not this the kind of fasting I have chosen: to loose the chains of injustice and untie the cords of the yoke, to set the oppressed free and break every yoke? Is it not to share your food with the hungry and to provide the poor wanderer with shelter—when you see the naked, to clothe them, and not to turn away from your own flesh and blood? Then your light will break forth like the dawn, and your healing will quickly appear; then your righteousness will go before you, and the glory of the Lord will be your rear guard. Then you will call, and the Lord will answer; you will cry for help, and he will say: Here am I. "If you do away with the yoke of oppression, with the pointing finger and malicious talk, and if you spend yourselves in behalf of the hungry and satisfy the needs of the oppressed, then your light will rise in the darkness, and your night will become like the noonday. The Lord will guide you always; he will satisfy your needs in a sun-scorched land and will strengthen your frame. You will be like a well-watered garden, like a spring whose waters never fail. Your people will rebuild the ancient ruins and will raise up the age-old foundations; you will be called Repairer of Broken Walls, Restorer of Streets with Dwellings. (Isaiah 58:1–12)

ISAIAH 58 REMINDS US OF HOW GOD EXPECTS US TO SERVE EACH OTHER, AND HE promises us so much in return. This is such a powerful verse and promise. He promises that your light will break forth, your healing will appear, righteousness will go before you, the glory of the Lord will be your rear-guard, and when you call He will answer!

Meditate on this scripture. It is so rich with promises.

Live a more empathetic and passionate life. Be more compassionate and dig deeper into getting to know the people around you. Get to know them and try to understand their pain, their sorrows, and their decisions. Love unconditionally. Love your neighbour for who they are, not for what you want them to be. Share the love of Christ with everyone you meet.

I also want to challenge all people who have a voice on the world stage: movie stars, professional singers, talk show hosts, professional athletes, politicians—if you believe in God, it is your job to share it with the world. Your job is to spread the gospel. If you have a platform, please use it! It is your chance to change the world. It is gratifying to see musicians like Justin Bieber and Kanye West use their voice for God's glory. That is what He intended. That is why He gave them their gift. But there are so many who don't, so I challenge you to be all that God has called you to be and do as He commands, even if it is uncomfortable.

EPILOGUE

Grace is going through hell in order to see there is a heaven.

OUR FAMILY HAD FEW OPPORTUNITIES TO REUNITE, BUT IN MAY 2014 MY brother Duane had had a good year in business and he and his wife Tina wanted to pay to bring everyone up to Canada to visit our dad, who suffered from vascular dementia. His memory was going quickly, and we wanted to see him while he was still healthy. Each sibling had visited Canada at different times, but never at the same time. Kids, timing, and finances had all played a role in preventing us from getting together in the past.

We had an awesome family reunion outing at Assiniboia Downs, a horse-racing track in Winnipeg, where we wore matching cowboy hats and T-shirts. We knew we looked stupid wearing this, but when you're a large family you do it just for the fun of it.[33] Anyway, printed on the T-shirts was Isaiah 40:31:

> *They that wait upon the Lord shall renew their strength; they shall mount up with wings as eagles; they shall run, and not be weary; and they shall walk, and not faint.*

This scripture marks our journey and God's blessing on our lives. David has it tattooed on his arm. We each have a ton of energy and work in ministry, loving and serving people. God really has been the wind beneath our wings.

Later in the reunion, we went to the lake where we shared our testimonies with each other for the very first time. Remember, when you've gone through

---

[33] We had our picture taken in the winners circle. Ironically, the horse Lovely Sunrise was the winner, beating Rebellious Heart, who came in second. The owner of the winning horse was Let 'er Rip Stable. And the jockey? Christopher (Christ) Husbands. We think Mom was with us, too!

what we'd gone through, you don't necessarily share the details of what happened. It's not something you want to focus on or talk about. You just want to forget about it and move on. You celebrate what's good in your life.

Boy, did we have a good time sharing our stories. Luckily for us, we are each in a good spot and had a tremendous sense of humour about it all.

As we shared our stories, the seed of this book was born, and I was determined to capture our memories into a story to help change lives. Although our stories were tragic, looking back we always managed to find humour in the situation. The blessing is that, with God, we are free and full of joy now. I really don't think you can find a more ridiculous life journey. It almost seems Hollywood-scripted, only it's real.

My son Raffaele stayed with us that week and it would be an understatement to say he was in shock. But it also made his faith that much stronger to hear all the different stories of how we'd narrowly escaped death, whether it was from overdoses, car wrecks, or being in the wrong place at the wrong time. He was amazed to see how far each of us had come.

We prayed together many times that week. We prayed for our families. We prayed for our dad and stepmom to find the Lord. We prayed for each other. But most of all, we thanked God for delivering us through our difficult times and giving us the opportunity to be together. We thanked God for our families and all our blessings. We thanked God for His grace and forgiveness, and for having had the strength to forgive others and each other for everything that has happened. That is true freedom in Christ.

This book is a testament to all that transpired and how the Lord was able to take what the enemy meant for evil and turn it around for His goodness and glory, through forgiveness and belief in Him.

That family reunion truly was a divine appointment, and unfortunately it was the last opportunity we had to be together. Danny died unexpectedly shortly after. He was working on a tile job, pulling up some old carpet, when his respiratory system became infected by mould spores. He immediately got sick and had to go to the hospital where his body started to shut down. His body went into septic shock and within forty-eight hours he died. He was only fifty-seven years old.

It happened on Easter Monday, April 6, 2015, which was another divine appointment. Dan loved and served the Lord with all his heart, and if he could have picked a day to go to heaven, it would've been the day of the resurrection, a day that celebrates the eternal salvation of all mankind. He also had no retirement plan; heaven was it.

As Danny was lying in the hospital and we were praying for him, I believe we were having a tug-of-war with heaven… and I believe he went to heaven.

Actually, I know it. I had a dream where I was standing next to his bed, and he lifted his head, looked at me, and smiled. I bent down, hugged him, and asked him how he was. He said in his usual Danny manner, "I'm all right… I'm great!" Then he laid back down, I hugged him again, and I asked him to come with me. He beamed at me and said, "I didn't realize it was going to be so beautiful." As I walked away, I looked back and saw him with a boyish smile, looking so peaceful.

Then I woke up and realized that he'd been talking about heaven. He was given a glimpse of it and just couldn't leave. Heaven was the one place he'd been waiting for, and once he saw it he had to stay. I'm sure he's there with my mom and the rest of our family who has gone before us. And I fully believe that he went early to prepare a path for my dad, who passed away six months later.

I'm pretty sure Danny and my mom, who prayed for my dad's salvation every day, did everything they could to make sure he made it to heaven. In the end, that was who Danny was. After being saved, he cared more about others than he did about anything else. He is now with my mom, who was our first angel to make it to heaven. Danny is our second.

My dad passed away three days before Canadian Thanksgiving on October 8. I think God realizes that we're such a big family that if he doesn't give us a holiday to pass on, then we won't remember the date of each other's deaths. That's God's sense of humour.

I had the chance to read my dad's memoirs. In them, he shares that his own dad was very abusive, which explains where he learned his behaviours. He also shares that he was born a bastard child out of wedlock. In the 1930s, this was unacceptable and he was shamed because of it. He was constantly bullied and getting into fights. He ended up looking after his mom, who he loved very much.

And in the end, he shares that he accepted Jesus as his personal Saviour. Although we didn't see any fruit from his conversion, for this we are grateful. Behind every person is a story. Praise God we have broken that cycle of abuse.

Despite how harsh my dad was, we are grateful for him in many ways. It couldn't have been easy trying to raise eight children with a wife who suffered from mental health issues. He had OCD and a type-A personality, and he probably shouldn't have had any kids, let alone eight. He worked three jobs in Ohio just to take care of us. When he was with us, he taught us discipline and how to have a good work ethic.

Even though he left us when we were young, we are grateful that he came back and brought us four younger kids up to Canada. He was newly married and could have said no. We probably wouldn't have survived had we stayed in Florida.

He encouraged us to get a good a education. He also loved his grandchildren and taught us all to love God's creation through our experiences at the lake. We each know in our hearts that he loved us as best he could.

My stepmom continues to be a blessing in our lives. She brings joy and laughter and encouragement to family gatherings and we know she loves us. And we love her, too!

I am proud to say that we have all been extremely blessed in our adult years.

Danny, of course, learned the tile trade and taught his brothers everything he knew. He made the choice to be stable while very young so that he could help his mother. In the end, he ended up providing stability for all his brothers and nephews in the business. He spent many years working on Duane's faith so he could teach him to love and serve the Lord. In doing that, as my mother said, Duane was able to teach others to love and serve the Lord. And Duane does this. His faith and knowledge and joy are so full that he cannot contain himself. Dan also reunited with his only son and got to meet his grandchildren before he passed.

My oldest sister, Susie, is doing well and has a beautiful family that cares for her and all of them are successful.

Dave became an X-ray tech and then went to cardiovascular school. He ended up moving to South Dakota where he settled down with his beautiful family and got into the medical field. He currently is a real estate agent and is studying Christianity. He has fostered four children in his home and sponsors several kids in need overseas. He and his wife Donna have four children and seven grandchildren.

Connie took the training to earn her state license and become a medical laboratory technician. By the grace of God, she challenged the state exam on the last day it was an option and was able to pass and get certified.

Connie and Dale were able to provide stability for our family at a time when most of us were unstable. She cared for David and his wife, Danny and his girlfriend, Doug, and our mother. They all stayed with Connie for extended periods of time when they needed a home.

For Connie, marrying young, raising her family, and juggling to help her siblings was no easy feat. She raised her kids to love and serve the Lord and is very active in her church. Having been raised on the street, she has a passion for street ministry and has been actively involved in several churches, leading others in taking the gospel to the street, meeting people where they're at, and showing them the love, compassion, and forgiveness of God the Father. She has two beautiful children and three grandchildren.

Cindy trained to be a dental assistant at Red River College in Winnipeg and received her certification. She recently retired from the University of Manitoba Dental College where she worked for more than twenty years. She went on to marry the boy next door at the lake, Greg Stanley, and now has two beautiful children and one grandchild. They have a cottage that has been a haven for our whole family. She is active in her church and a prayer warrior for her community. She's raising her kids to love and serve the Lord.

Doug took mechanical engineering at Red River College and received his diploma. He then moved to Florida and learned the tile trade and now does contract work. He dabbles in real estate and flips homes. Doug is married with five children. He attends church regularly and is raising his kids to love and serve the Lord.

Duane moved back to Florida after completing high school, where he learned the tile trade from his brother Dan. He has been able to provide a place of employment for many of our family members. He's become very successful in the field and is a multimillionaire today. He and his wife Tina have three beautiful children and two grandchildren. They continue to provide a place for family to visit each other and enjoy the Florida sunshine. He is very passionate about the Lord and is a junior pastor in his church. His children also love and serve the Lord.

Between all eight of us, we have twenty-four children and seventeen grand-children. All of our children are doing amazingly well. Loving and serving the Lord is a choice for them, and a choice for anybody reading this book. It's not something that anyone can force you to do. It's something you choose to do because you know it's the best choice for your life.

We wouldn't be good neighbours if we didn't introduce you to our best friend, the one who helped us through our trials and tribulations, our Lord and Saviour Jesus Christ. It is because of Him and His incredible grace that we are able to share our story today. He offers us an incredible life.

Here's the way I look at it. Who doesn't want eternal life in heaven with Jesus? Who doesn't want all the promises that a relationship with Him can bring? Who doesn't want a special place in heaven prepared for them amongst all the angels?

That really is the question for everyone. We are promised eternal life in glory, free from pain, free from judgment, and free from the negativity we experience here on the earth. We are promised new bodies, and we're promised unconditional love, acceptance, and eternal life in heaven where the streets are made of gold and everything is beautiful.

The other option is hell.

If those are our options, who wouldn't choose heaven?

For God so loved the world that he gave his one and only Son, that whoever believes in him shall not perish but have eternal life. (John 3:16)

But of course God leaves that to us, and encourages us to spread the Word and share it with everyone we know so they all have the opportunity. Whether we take the opportunity is our choice.

If you're reading this book, I hope it's a divine appointment for you to make that choice. And I hope it's a divine appointment for my children to learn more about where they come from and to make that choice. I know that I'll be in heaven and I pray they and each of you will join me there one day.

Please say this prayer and make the choice:

Dear Lord,

I know that I'm a sinner. Please forgive me for my transgressions. I want to be more like You. I believe You died for my sins and rose from the dead. I turn from my sins and invite You to come into my heart and life. I want to trust and follow You as my Lord and Saviour. Help me to become more like You and heed Your voice. Please open my eyes to see You, my ears to hear You, and my heart to love You. And help me to love my neighbour. This I pray in Jesus's name, amen.

As my son Raffaele recently wrote, will you open the door and let God in?

As the world turns and we create more and more avenues to become separated from other people and our relationships, this still holds true today: we were meant for more than our status or our wealth, more than our possessions or our livelihood. We were created to be loved by and to live in relationship with God, and once you find that, all the other things you've been given to create "life" on this planet will be added to you because He has a purpose for each of those things for you.

But before we can truly live, sometimes we need to know why. And above all, sometimes we need to know that we're worth it. The fact that God created us in His image, that He sent His Son Jesus Christ to die on the cross in our place—to be a sacrifice for our sins and the punishment we deserve for our sins, allowing us to live our lives in our own way—is a sign that He loves us and has something greater for us than we can possibly imagine. We are worth everything to Him. You are worth everything to Him and He wants you to know Him and live in relationship with Him.

But love doesn't force other people to love them, and neither does God. If you seek Him each day, you will find Him ingrained in the fabric of your life, walking with you, helping you along, reaching out to you and protecting you.

It's easy to ignore all the blessings we get and focus on the negatives. But God doesn't want us to look to Him only when we're "blessed" or question Him when we're "cursed." He wants us to walk with Him all day, every day, and to understand all the things He sets forth for us: the trials and the pain, the successes and the joys, and the losses. Sometimes we don't get to know all the details, but that's fine, because love never fails. We don't need to know the details if we are assured in God's love for us.

The Bible says that Jesus Christ—God's Son, who came as a man— is standing at the door knocking, waiting for you to let Him in. To let Him in is to accept that He died for you, that He loves you, and that He will change your life as He shows you His Father, God. This concept can be a lot to unpack if you don't know anything about Him.

Sometimes we can be stubborn and not want to answer the door because we want to avoid the conversation. Or maybe we don't know the person on the other side. For many of us, He's been standing there and knocking for quite some time—and He will continue to do so, because He loves us—but we're afraid to let Him in. We're scared of what that will mean, how we might look or be judged, how it might affect us. We're scared of what it might mean in terms of some of the things we've decided to love, the things in our lives that our destroying us.

Sometimes we like the way our pride makes us feel, and we think that it can replace the love that shows us how to heal. We've convinced ourselves that it's less scary to keep love out than to let love in, because letting love in means we need to be vulnerable, trusting that it might change us.

The devil has done a good job convincing us that we, without love, are better than who we were meant to be with love. He's convinced us to love a lie instead of knowing God's perfect love for us. God's love is greater than any form of love we can comprehend. It is so complete, so overwhelming, and so deep that it knows no bounds and permeates all things.

If we choose to spend our lives without knowing God's love, we will always be settling for something less than what we deserve, settling for something that will never satisfy because it wasn't meant for us. When we were created, we were created for perfection. But through our original sin, the nature of which has been passed down through each generation after Adam and Eve, we've been born into lives of destruction.

The good news is that we can choose how our story ends. We don't need to settle for less than the perfection God created for us. We get to choose whether or not we will open the door, let love in, and let ourselves know the God who created us, who loves us more than any other being ever could, who loved us enough to give life to us, who loved us enough to die for us, and who loves us enough to persist for all eternity in His desire for us to know Him and make our own choice to follow Him.

And so now we have arrived at the important question: what choice will you make?

You are not what your circumstance created for you. God sees your struggle, He knows your pain, and He has a greater purpose for you. He doesn't want you to be a slave to your surroundings, feelings, and passions. You are not your pain. You are not the ditch that you feel like you're lying in. You are worth more than your bank account, and you have more value than your looks or what you own. You are meant to be who God has called you to be: His child.

If you hear Him knocking, let Him in. Don't be afraid to allow Him to be Lord of your life; He will make all your paths straight and show you that your true worth comes from trusting in Him and allowing people to know Him through who you are. He sent His Son to die for you so you would have the opportunity to live for Him. He is more than worthy. Don't waste your life and don't settle for less than God's best for you.

We can spend our whole lives questioning our purpose and trying to find meaning… and the reality is that every meaningful thing we have ever considered revolves around a relationship. Without another being, we lack a standard for our interactions.

Whatever you're going through, just know that you aren't trapped in or confined to your house. All you need to do is open the door and let love in. It's what you were created to do. So be who you were created to be: loved.

As Numbers 6:24–26 tells us, *"The Lord bless you and keep you; the Lord make his face shine on you and be gracious to you; the Lord turn his face toward you and give you peace."*

From the mouths of babes. I am blessed to have children who get it. It is only by His grace that we have all succeeded, and what a journey it has been!

I'm now on a new adventure in my career where I hope to continue to make an impact in my community. I finished working at Siloam, took a break to care for my mother-in-law who was recently widowed and suffers from dementia, and wrote this book. I then accepted a job at Youth for Christ, an international organization that inspires youth to love and serve the Lord. I believe we need to invest in our youth and teach discipleship so we can create more helpers for the kingdom. As my story testifies, youth need a place to go where they can be safe, have fun, and be positively mentored by people who care about them. They need a healthy alternative to drugs, prostitution, and gangs.

Youth for Christ is centrally located in Winnipeg, and thousands of cities around the world, to serve all youth, with staff and volunteers who work hard to inspire and love them as God's children. Each location is equipped with a drop-in centre and typically offers pool tables, gaming stations, ping-pong, foosball, air hockey, and snacks and meals as needed. I certainly wish we'd had a YFC to go to. The first pastor of this organization was Billy Graham, the pastor who laid hands on us so many years ago. Coincidence? There are no coincidences. I call them "God-incidences," or divine appointments.

Wherever I go, it will be in service to people and to follow God's will. When you're obedient to His call, He will always take care of you.

Humbly, I'd like to think that I will continue to have some influence in our community by sharing my story and encouraging people to be a part of the solution for change regarding poverty and homelessness, helping youth find their potential, and inspiring people to choose Jesus as their personal Saviour so they become all that He has designed them to be. God has a plan for each of us.

However, I am just one voice of many thousands of volunteers, donors, and staff who work in ministry. I know that this is what God called me to do. This was the plan He had for me, as my mother told me long, long ago. I thought I was going to become an accountant and get a corner office, but that wasn't quite what He had in mind. The job reminded me of where I came from, and where I hoped to inspire people to go. It might not have been the plan I thought I was going to complete, but it was His plan—and it was perfect.

You never retire from God; He just redirects your path.

At a recent Youth for Christ event, celebrating sixty-five years of ministry in Winnipeg, I heard some remarks delivered by Will Graham, the grandson of Billy Graham. He reminded us that at the end of the day we cannot take anything with us when we leave this earth. We cannot take our house, our money, or our stuff. But we can take people—the people we touch for the Lord and encourage to follow Him. We can take them! My family and I love you so much that we want to take you!

At the end of the day, we have to remember that the person experiencing difficulties is somebody's mother, somebody's father, somebody's brother, somebody's sister, aunt, uncle, son, or daughter... and they are doing their best to survive in a world where economics have provided tremendous challenges.

That was me and my family. I look at my brothers and sisters. Each of us has been changed to love and serve the Lord, to make an impact in our community through the hope and love given to us. We have broken the cycle of poverty, homelessness, and brokenness.

I truly believe that when we get to heaven and sit on our Father's knee, we will say, "Father, Father, look what I did! I bought a beautiful home, I went on several trips around the world, I obtained a great education, I married an influential person, and I raised a beautiful family." He will listen quietly and say, "That's wonderful, My child. I wanted you to have all of that and experience My creation, because I wanted to bless you. But what really impressed me was when you did this..."

And then He will show us a small act of kindness that we did for someone else, like buying an item for a food hamper for a needy family, or helping somebody in math, volunteering at a hospital to help the sick, listening to somebody experiencing homelessness, reaching out to youth and listening to their challenges, helping a neighbour or a stranger and showing them love, sharing the gospel and story of His Son, or making a donation to charity. To that, God will say, "That's what really impressed me!"

Then He will show us that person, and the impact our kindness had. He will show us that person's family. We will see their children, and their children's children, and there will be a harvest as far as the eye can see.

"That is what really impressed me," God will say. "Because when you did that small act of kindness for that person, you changed generations of people's lives. And what you did for the least of these, you did for me."

Then He will smile, give us a big fatherly hug, and say, "Well done, my good and faithful servant. Welcome to heaven." What a day that will be!

Surely your goodness and love will follow me all the days of my life, and I will dwell in the house of the Lord forever. (Psalm 23:6)

Will you join me? If we truly and unconditionally love our neighbour, we can change heaven and earth.

POSTSCRIPT: GOD ALWAYS HAS A PLAN
A FINAL MOMENT OF GRACE

AFTER COMPLETING THIS BOOK, AND BEFORE PUBLISHING, THE WHOLE WORLD came to a standstill as we experienced COVID-19. Under quarantine, we all had choices to make about how we would spend our time at home. I was fortunate to be able to work from home and spend a lot of my time praying for people who partner with Youth for Christ. I learned of their hardships and individual situations, and together we sought God for help and support. It was an incredible experience. I also reached out to God and asked for His wisdom and discernment regarding all that was going on in the world. I asked Him to reveal to me His vision and purpose for all that was happening.

The revelation I received was awe-inspiring.

He revealed to me that in the beginning of the pandemic, the world, and in particular Manitoba, shut down for exactly fifty-two days. During that time, we learned in the news that China was able to see blue sky for the first time in decades, that Italy was able to see clean water, that India was able to see the Himalaya Mountains for the first time in decades, that pollution was depleted and that smog disappeared from major cities around the world. We started to see animals come out of their habitats and venture into our cities and into areas people were no longer occupying. In a sense, habitats were being reborn.

We saw people find ways to celebrate even though they were shut in. We found people appreciating the frontline workers, usually considered the least of these. We found people looking for ways to connect with their families and loved ones. Families started eating together and cooking more. Our creativity was reborn as we sought different ways to engage, get along, and build community. We had car rally birthday parties and showers. Suddenly, we were able to do without all the stuff we were used to and focus on the essentials—food, shelter, and family.

God revealed to me that this healing of the earth and healing of people had been in His plan all along. His thoughts are so much higher than our thoughts. It was very simple, and it was in His Word: thou shalt keep the Sabbath day holy.

He revealed that if we were to shut down the world on Sunday and leave the Sabbath day holy, just one day a week, it would equal fifty-two days, the period that we were shut down over quarantine. If we did this, we would see the healing continue. He revealed that if we did this and pressed into a relationship with Him, it would produce healing for our mind, body, and soul and the earth.

This was His plan all along, but we forgot about Him in our greediness to work twenty-four hours a day so we could make more and more money and have more and more stuff.

But when we were in quarantine and couldn't have that stuff, we realized that we didn't really need it. We could go to the store once a week, or once every two weeks, and it was enough. We realized that we could eat at home and enjoy the company of our families. We learned to get away from our cell phones and day-to-day activities, to slow down and just be one with creation. And we craved the outside world, but not for the stuff; we craved the beauty of nature, to be able to walk outside to enjoy the smell of the grass, trees, beaches, and flowers.

I truly believe that this pandemic is a call to make the Sabbath holy again. If we could get back to giving up Sundays, going to church with our families, enjoying the day, and resting from the day-to-day activities of the world, not only could we heal our land but we could heal ourselves and truly be reinvigorated to take on and enjoy the world and live more fully—just as He created.

Then He walked me through the Ten Commandments, one by one, and showed me their importance. These are a set of principles to live by, and we are failing in every one of them.

Thou shalt have no other God before me. He shut down the idols of sports, movies, entertainment, busyness, and business. Even our church structures have become idols. He showed me that we can worship Him anywhere, but we don't because we're too busy doing everything else.

Thou shalt not kill. The death of George Floyd caused a tremendous outpouring of indignation about the mistreatment of black people and revealed how racism exists in our world. The U.S. election showed us that the killing of innocent babies through abortion is also wrong and worth fighting for. In the centre of both platforms is the unjust killing of innocent people, which He has told us not to do.

Thou shalt not steal. The looting and destruction of cities during the Black Lives Matter protests were wrong and shameful, revealing how hateful acts can destroy trust and people's dreams.

Honour thy mother and thy father. The disgrace of our personal care homes during COVID and the loss of our elders' lives show that we are not honouring our parents. We need to stand up and advocate for better care and pay attention to how they are treated. We need to honour those who bore us and gave us life.

Thou shalt not bear false witness. We don't know what to believe in the media anymore. There is slander and accusations everywhere and we have lost the ability to trust. The world is full of deceit slander and false witness. It is destroying us.

Thou shalt not commit adultery. The breakdown of the family unit has put more kids in foster care than ever before. Our children are paying the price of an unstable family structure due to divorce.

How the world will play out is our choice, but once again it boils down to two important commands: love your God with all your heart, mind, and soul and love your neighbour as you love yourself.

Grace is indeed everywhere. You just have to look for it.

#lovegod #loveyourneighbour #bythegraceofgodgowe

ABOUT THE AUTHOR

I WAS BORN THE SEVENTH CHILD IN A FAMILY OF EIGHT CHILDREN. DURING MY lifetime, and especially in my childhood, I faced many challenges. Through it all, I developed a deep relationship with Jesus. Through my faith and His grace, my family and I were able to overcome life's hurdles.

I am an advocate for people experiencing homelessness and suffering from addictions and mental health issues, as well as for the lost, the broken, and all of those in need. I am an advocate for providing dignity and respect to all people in our world—every person, from every cultural background. I didn't choose to become an advocate. I was chosen. God chose me.

I am also a disciple and an evangelist for the gospel of Jesus Christ. While I chose to follow Christ and have a personal relationship with Him, I didn't choose to become an evangelist. I was chosen. God chose me.

Actually, my biggest fear was working with the homeless, public speaking, and becoming an evangelist, yet this is what I do. It is who I am.

Inwardly, I always proclaimed and believed in the Lord. He has always been my rock and my Saviour, but it wasn't something I wanted to proclaim outwardly. Not only was it out of my comfort zone but I didn't want to offend my friends or lose their friendship or their love.

However, as I studied the Bible and everything Jesus has done for us, I asked myself, *Why wouldn't I want to celebrate the incredible man and gift that He was from God?* Jesus came homeless into the world, away from His Father. He was conceived by the power of the Holy Spirit and born into the family of Mary and Joseph in a stable. He was physically homeless.

Jesus came not to take, but to give. He came to love and serve mankind. His message was to heal and help the broken, the lost, and the outcasts, to love unconditionally and serve each other. Indeed, how could I possibly be ashamed of this message?

Then He chose to die on a cross so we could have eternal life in heaven. We should feel so blessed that He cared this much, that He would do this for us.

So no, I am not ashamed. I am very proud to be able to proclaim this message, very proud to be able to be a daughter of someone so great. We should all aspire to be like Him.

Although I didn't set out to advocate for homelessness and those in need, that is who I am. God chose me. He has called me to do this, and I carry my cross proudly for Him.